W9-BJV-229

IN THE HIGH SCHOOL

HARRY ROBERT WILSON

Teachers College, Columbia University

SILVER BURDETT COMPANY

New York San Francisco Chicago

Printed in the United States of America

PREFACE

The primary purpose of this book at this time is to emphasize the part that music can play in democratic living. Someone has said that democracy means "the greatest good for the greatest number." Music has spiritual and aesthetic values that are needed in our democracy. In a machine age beautiful music reminds man that he has a soul, that there is an Infinite with a purpose.

But democracy is not a state or a condition; it is a way of life, and we all must do our part in achieving it. Music, too, must be democratized so that all may share the spiritual food that it has to offer. Shakespeare realized the power of music to reach out above our material wants when he wrote—

> In sweet music is such art,
> Killing care and grief of heart.

And so, we would remind our readers that music is not merely a fair weather activity. It is not a luxury to be enjoyed after the strenuous days of pioneering are past and the nation settles into an abundant plateau of complacency. Music is a vital part of a vigorous culture. Times of emergency and trouble are not the times to curb musical activity. "Everybody Sing" and "Strike up the Band" should be the order of the day in times of stress as well as in times of ease.

There are teachers of music who all too often fail to appreciate the golden opportunity and sacred privilege which is open to them. They fail to rise to the responsibility entrusted to them. In truth, they should realize that they are the guardians of two beautiful jewels, the child and music, both created to bring joy into the world.

As the child grows from youth to maturity, what he becomes is largely a matter of his experiences and the ways in which they affect his inner self and his relations to those about him. The teacher of music shares these experiences. Through his guidance he can bring joy and comfort to the pupil by surrounding him with an environment of beautiful music, by helping him to find occasions to use music in the expression of his inner emotional and spiritual self, and by seeing to it that music contributes to the awakening of social consciousness. These things are peculiarly important and significant in adolescence.

When teachers of music read a professional book like this one they sometimes are looking for some device or trick to "try out on the kids." They are often more concerned with the "what" and the "how" of teaching music than with the "why." If only they would realize it, a little search into the "why" of music education will usually be their best guide in the selection of "what," and will often suggest the "how" that will best fit the situation.

With these thoughts in mind the author of this book has expressed as succinctly as possible the "why" of secondary education. With the adolescent and his needs as a starting point we have endeavored to follow the development of the high school and its curriculum to give the reader a basis upon which to judge and evaluate the music program. After all, why teach music anyway?

After this general picture of the "why" of secondary education we should be able to tell better what educators are trying to do for these young people and how music fits into the total picture. Then our attention may be turned to the "what" of the music program. This phase of the discussion includes the types of activities, the organization and scheduling of these activities, and usable materials for them.

The "how" is not neglected, for now we have a basis for choosing our methods and devices. When we know what education should do for our young people and when we are thrilled with the contribution music can make, our methods will not be heavy-laden and lifeless, but will evolve from sympathetic understanding and an enthusiasm for service.

And so to our readers, whether they be administrator, teacher, or student, the author hopes that this picture of the "why," "what," and "how" of music in the high school will serve their own needs and increase their enthusiasm for young people, education, and music.

ACKNOWLEDGMENTS

In writing this book the author has drawn inspiration and council from many sources. Without doubt the greatest obligation which he has incurred is to Osbourne McConathy, scholar, educator, and musician. Many hours of conferences with him have been of untold value to the author in formulating the underlying philosophy of the book. He is responsible in no small degree for the clarity of expression. And finally, his own contributions, notably the section on "The General Music Class," have brought to the text of the book a lifetime of experience as a teacher and writer in the field of music education.

The author is likewise indebted to Charles H. Lake, Superintendent of Schools, Cleveland, Ohio, and Russell V. Morgan, Directing Supervisor of Music, in the public schools of the same city. Mr. Lake gave many suggestions for the chapter on "Administration and Supervision," and his opinions as a school administrator were extremely valuable. Mr. Morgan made a definite contribution by assisting in formulating the general outline of the book and by kindly permitting many direct quotations from his numerous articles on music education.

Also, the author wishes to thank the many publishers who have permitted quotations of poetry and other material from their copyrighted books. First of all, thanks are due to the Music Educators National Conference for permission to quote freely from the articles in the *Music Educators Journal* and the Conference Yearbooks, as well as permission to draw from its files many photographs of outstanding musical organizations. Likewise, thanks are due to the *Educational Music Magazine* and *The School Musician* for quotations and pictures. Special mention should be made to *Education* for permission to use the material in an article by the author entitled "The Teacher of Music," and published in the May, 1939 issue, as the basis for the content of Chapter XVII. Other publishers to whom the author is indebted for quotations are: D. Appleton-Century Company, publisher of *Supervision* by W. S. Barr, W. H. Burton, and L. J. Bruechner; Minton, Balch & Co., publishers of *Art as Experience* by John Dewey; C. C. Birchard and Company, publishers of *More Than a Pitchpipe* by Ennis Davis, and the *Modern Band Training Series* by Norval L. Church and Peter W. Dykema; The Hillside Press, publishers of *Honors and Awards in American High Schools* by Shu-Kuei Carol Chen; Alfred A. Knopf, publisher of *The Prophet* by Kahil Gibran; The Macmillan Company, publishers of *The Threshold of Music* by William Wallace, and *Secondary Education* by Thomas H. Briggs; National Education Association; W. W. Norton, publisher of the *Psychology of Music* by James L. Mursell; Charles Scribner's Sons, publishers of *Educational Administration as Social Policy* by Jesse W. Newlon, and for extract from Henry Van Dyke's poem, "Music"; University of Pittsburgh Press, publishers of *Home-School-Community Relations* by William A. Yeager.

And finally, the author wishes to express his thanks to his friends and associates who kindly assisted him by answering questionnaires, and by sending to him photographs and practical material without which the book would not be complete. Acknowledgments for such aid are due to: Imogene Boyle, Hempstead, L. I.; Mary Brockwell, Charlotte, N. C.; Norval L. Church, Teachers College, Columbia University; Charles F. Dean, Architect, Sacramento, California; Charles M. Dennis, San Francisco, California; Mary Donovan, Greenwich, Conn.; Marjorie Dwyer, Chickasha, Okla.; Peter W. Dykema, Hastings-on-the-Hudson, N. Y.; Paul Goodman, Frederick, Maryland; C. Paul Herfurth, East Orange, N. J.; P. C. McChesney, Sacramento, California; Lena Milam, Beaumont, Texas; James L. Mursell, Teachers College, Columbia University; Dwight E. Nofziger, Lewiston, Ohio; Lilla Belle Pitts, Teachers College, Columbia University; George H. Putnam, Junction City, Kansas; Alexander Richter, New York, N. Y.; Victor V. Salvo, Katonah, N. Y.; Herman Scholl, Farmingdale, L. I.; Harry Seitz, Detroit, Michigan; Fowler Smith, Detroit, Michigan; Herbert S. Spencer, Springfield, Massachusetts; Carl E. Sutherland, Red Wing, Minnesota; Grace V. Wilson, Wichita, Kansas; Paul L. Young, East Orange, N. J.

It has been impossible to mention everyone from whom suggestions have been received for the ideas in the book. If our records are incomplete and we have failed to mention anyone to whom acknowledgment is due, we ask for indulgence and in the future we will correct the oversight.

Harry R. Wilson

New York, August, 1941.

CONTENTS

New York State School Music Association Clinic Band, Clinic Chorus, Clinic Orchestra. Rochester, November, 1940.

Part One

MODERN TRENDS IN SECONDARY EDUCATION

ODE

We are the music makers,
And we are the dreamers of dreams,
Wandering by lone sea-breakers,
And sitting by desolate streams;—
World-losers and world-forsakers,
On whom the pale moon gleams:
Yet we are the movers and shakers
Of the world for ever, it seems.

With wonderful deathless ditties
We build up the world's great cities,
And out of a fabulous story
We fashion an empire's glory:
One man with a dream, at pleasure,
Shall go forth and conquer a crown;
And three with a new song's measure
Can trample a kingdom down.

We, in the ages lying
In the buried past of the earth,
Built Nineveh with our sighing,
And Babel itself in our mirth;
And o'erthrew them with prophesying
To the old of the new world's worth;
For each age is a dream that is dying,
Or one that is coming to birth.

A. O'Shaughnessy

Chapter 1

THE CHANGING HIGH SCHOOL

The teacher of music must know more than just his own subject. It is a truism that a person who knows only one thing knows not that. The teacher of music, must, first of all, be a teacher of human beings. He must have some understanding of the interests and needs of the boys and girls whom he is teaching.

The school is a social institution. Its greatest function is to help to improve society. In a dynamic society the school must change in response to social needs. If it fails to keep pace with social needs and remains static, it will be superseded by other institutional forms. Many educators today claim that our high schools fail to meet the needs of our rapidly changing society. They persistently call for a reconstruction and reorganization of secondary education in this country. What are they saying? On what educational philosophy do they base their statements? What are their objectives? What are the implications for the curriculum? How will these trends affect music in the schools?

The teacher of music cannot be blind to these issues. For a clearer understanding of these problems, this book includes a summarized discussion of such issues and trends as have developed during the evolution of our present high school.

The Changing Curriculum

Any curriculum should evolve from the needs and interests of the students whom it is designed to serve. The curriculum should be conceived of as the sum total of all the students' experiences under the influence of the school and under the guidance of the teachers. Since experiences become more varied as needs and interests broaden and deepen, the curriculum is constantly growing and changing. The question in secondary education today is not, "Should the high school curriculum be changed?" but rather, "To what extent and in what ways should the high school curriculum be changed in order to meet changing social and individual needs?"

Educational Objectives

If secondary education is to fulfill its functions in our democratic society, there must be fundamental thinking devoted to the defining of educational objectives. Secondary education must be carefully planned. The history of secondary education in this country is a history of the slow revision of traditional practice often with too little consideration for social values. Educators who, at present, are urging a reconstruction of the entire plan of secondary education are making a plea for the study of contemporary life to develop an understanding of the purposes of the educational program.

Education as Preparation

The great tradition in American secondary education centers around the life-preparatory motive. Education as "preparation for life" was the objective around which developed the concepts of (1) education as formal discipline, and (2) education as the acquiring of knowledge and information. These concepts determined a curriculum designed specifically to prepare the student for college, little thought being given to his immediate and practical needs. The validity of these concepts was challenged by the Academy (1751) and by the first English High School (1821), but to little avail; the demands of college requirements took precedence over all others.

A dualism naturally arose in determining the purpose of the high school curriculum. Should it prepare students for college alone or should it also make them ready to meet the practical and more immediate needs of life? The college professors, who still dominated the scene, set forth the proposition: "Whatever prepares for college best prepares for life."[1] This rationalization, as can easily be imagined, failed to satisfy many high school teachers and administrators, as well as an increasing number of parents who were sending their sons and daughters to high school to prepare for the immediate business of living, rather than for college.

Committee of Ten

The growing dissatisfaction with the high school curriculum resulted in the appointment of the Committee of Ten in 1892 and its report in 1894. The Committee was dominated by representatives of colleges and was thoroughly devoted to the doctrine of formal discipline. The Committee recognized that harmony in the field of secondary education depended upon the relaxation to some extent of college requirements. They finally changed their formula to the proposition: "What prepares for life will also prepare for college if it is academic and rightly taught." Four optional curricula were outlined which introduced science, history, and modern foreign language.

[1] *High School Curriculum Reorganization,* The North Central Association of Colleges and Secondary Schools, 1933, p. 7.

Great stress was placed upon the academic and disciplined presentation of these subjects so that students who followed this curriculum would be worthy of college entrance. The Committee of Ten brought the issue to a focus and stimulated discussion. From many sources came the voices of leaders in secondary education offering the proposition: "Whatever is good for the students is good preparation for college." [2]

The Cardinal Principles

With the phenomenal growth of high schools at the turn of the century, the reconciling of life preparation and college preparation continued to be the prevailing issue. Finally the National Education Association appointed a Commission to study and to formulate a statement of the basic principles that would govern the curriculum of the high school. This Commission was not the voice of college administrators and college teachers of the "grand old subjects," but the composite voice of socially minded educational experts, public school administrators, and teachers. The work of the Commission resulted in the formulation, in 1918, of the Cardinal Principles of Secondary Education.[3] They are included here for their historical value in the development of educational objectives for the high school. These cardinal principles are:

1. Health
2. Command of fundamental processes
3. Worthy home membership
4. Vocation
5. Citizenship
6. Worthy use of leisure
7. Ethical character

[2] Ibid., p. 8.
[3] *Cardinal Principles of Secondary Education.* United States Bureau of Education, Bulletin No. 35, 1918.

Early Secondary Schools

The Boston Latin School, established in 1635, was the first permanent institution in America to provide for education on the secondary level. This institution was followed by the Massachusetts Law of 1647, which passed formal legislation providing for Latin-grammar schools. Other colonies soon adopted this law and these schools, designed primarily to prepare boys for college, became scattered throughout New England. The curriculum emphasized religious training, indirectly, for the most part, through extensive study of Greek and Latin. Probably the greatest contribution of these schools was the perpetuation of the tradition of academic education during the infancy of a new country and the establishment of the precedent of public support and control which has become universal in our country.

Through the proposals of Benjamin Franklin the first Academy was established in Philadelphia in 1751. His aim was to make education more functional for immediate life. The academies were popular from the beginning. Although Franklin's proposals were never completely adopted, there was some relaxation from the rigidity of the Latin-grammar schools. New subjects, including music, were introduced. The curriculum was organized with an improved elementary school as a base. This factor introduced the horizontal pattern of American education in contrast to the inherited vertical and parallel patterns. The academies were semi-publicly controlled at the begin-

[7] The horizontal pattern of the United States provides an equal opportunity for all to continue their education on the secondary level in a public high school articulating with an improved grammar school. In contrast, European school systems provide several parallel vertical patterns running from the elementary through the secondary schools, each designed for different selected groups. (See *Secondary Education,* Thomas H. Briggs, Macmillan, 1933, Chapters I-III.)

ning. Later they became private institutions with tuitions that were prohibitive of carrying on a democratic ideal of universal education. Gradually the function of education as conceived by Franklin yielded to traditional forces and the academy became a place for sons of rich men to prepare for college.

Failure to follow the proposals of Benjamin Franklin was the first tragic error in secondary education in this country. Nevertheless, the academy created a universal interest in education beyond the elementary school, opened the doors of secondary education to girls, and prepared the way for the first high school in America.

Early High Schools

As the academy drifted toward becoming an exclusive school which emphasized the old classical curriculum, there was a general demand that public provision be made for higher education for all youth. Consequently, the first high school, called the English High School, was established in Boston in 1821. It had a three-year curriculum intended to prepare for life as well as for advanced studies in college. Only boys of twelve years of age who proved their qualifications through examination in the three "r's" were admitted. In 1824 Worcester, Massachusetts, established a similar High School for Girls.

Massachusetts followed with a law in 1827 which provided for two types of higher schools. Every town or district containing five hundred families was required to establish a school beyond the elementary subjects which taught history of the United States, geometry, algebra, surveying, and bookkeeping by single entry. In addition to these subjects every town containing four thousand inhabitants was required to provide for the teaching of Latin, Greek, history, rhetoric, and logic. The dual preparatory motive is quite obvious in these curricula. Much controversy arose over the right of the State to tax the public for support of such high schools. The Kalamazoo Decision in 1872 settled the question in the courts, and from that date high schools definitely became the responsibility of the State.

The history of the high school from 1821 to 1893 is the story of a struggle between the two preparatory objectives: preparation for life versus preparation for college. Very early in its life, the high school was forced to yield equal place to college preparation as one of its functions. This trend gradually became dominant as the principle was proposed: "What prepares for college best prepares for life." The manner in which the Committee of Ten reversed this proposition and the disappointing results have already been discussed.

Private Secondary Schools

It has been mentioned that the academy gradually drifted toward an exclusive school which emphasized the classical curriculum and the college-preparatory motive. These schools existed side by side with the public high school and there are a number of them, especially in the eastern states, which still provide education on the secondary level. These schools still stress preparation for college but as entrance requirements in many colleges have become less stringent most of them have liberalized their curricula. A wider variety of courses is offered and art and music activities are receiving more and more attention.

Junior High Schools

About 1912 there appeared on the horizon a new type of secondary school, called the Junior High School. Many educators have questioned the wisdom of this choice of name, claiming that it has the tendency to make the junior high school appear to be a sub-secondary school. These schools were designed to bridge the gap between the elementary grades and the high school, and to meet the needs of children in early adolescence. Developing from committees of the National Education Association and its subsidiary organizations, the junior high school was officially recommended in 1918. The functions that this new school hoped to perform included: (1) the continuance of a *common and essential education* as far as it seemed wise and possible; (2) the recognition of *individual differences* in the early adolescent and provision for immediate and assured future needs; (3) an opportunity for each student to *explore his natural interests and sympathetic guidance* in the choice of exploratory courses and activities; (4) the provision of opportunities for the development of *wholesome social relations* among boys and girls of this age; and (5) the *articulation* of the experiences in the elementary grades with those in the high school. These proposals and functions are fully described and expanded in the *Fifth Yearbook* of the Department of Superintendence of the National Education Association.

Junior Colleges

Another organization which is affecting the educational pattern of secondary schools is the Junior College. This movement has had considerable success because it falls in line with the sentiment to extend educational opportunities for all. The economic depression has stimulated an increase in its enrollment because, since no jobs seemed available, graduates from the high school capitalized on the opportunity to continue their education in the local college at practically no additional expense. The curriculum consists of studies similar to those carried on in the high school, but on a more advanced level. Some indication of the extent and importance of this movement is found in the fact that since the first junior college was opened in Joliet, Illinois, over thirty years ago, approximately five hundred and seventy-five junior colleges have been established throughout the country.[8]

Administrative Units

Secondary education has become more extensive and more comprehensive in the United States than in any other country. When we consider that over five million students, or approximately sixty-five per cent of the young people of adolescent age in the country, are attending some type of secondary school, the full import of the necessity for continual research in the education of these students is realized. The secondary school is generally considered to be any institution which provides for the needs of adolescents; namely, junior high schools (grades 7-9), high schools (grades 9-12), cosmopolitan or specialized senior high schools (grades 10-12), junior colleges (grades 13-14), and continuation, technical, and vocational schools.

Several educational plans have been proposed and practised which seem to have their basis, for the most part, in the convenience and ease of administration. Before the advent of the junior high school the plan consisted of eight years of elementary school and four years of high school. The junior high school changed this plan to six years of elementary school, three years of junior high school, and three years of senior high school (6-3-3 plan).

On account of lack of money to finance separate buildings for the junior high school, most smaller towns retained the four-year high school and endeavored to organize a junior high school for the seventh and eighth grades in the

[8] Esther Goetz, "Music in the Junior College Today," Music Educators National Conference, *Yearbook 1939-1940*, p. 392.

elementary school building or in the senior high school building. Other towns developed a plan of six years of elementary school and six years of continuous high school program. This plan often causes overcrowding in the high school buildings. The failure to provide special buildings for the junior high school has, to a large degree, nullified the original purpose of the movement.

With the appearance of the junior college, new experiments of administrative organization were tried, such as six years in elementary school, three years in each of the high schools, and two years in junior college (6-3-3-2 plan). A recent plan of administrative units which is gaining in favor is six years in elementary school, four years in junior high school, and four years in senior high school (6-4-4 plan). This naturally extends the period of general education for the rapidly increasing number of students enrolled in secondary education before they begin a program of specialization in the university. *It also renews faith in the democratic principle that large numbers of individuals are capable of education far beyond the essential necessities of living in a society. And, finally, it adheres to the principle that free opportunity for education on the higher levels will pay dividends to our democratic society.*

Articulation

An education based upon meaningful experience should be consequently a continuous, unified process. This principle does not necessarily mean one building, a single corps of teachers, and an administrative unit continuing from the very beginning to the variable points of completion, as is advocated by some educators. It does mean, however, closer articulation and co-ordination between the various administrative units. It might be well to point out that the break down of the old 8-4 plan of organization was a result of the evident need of a varied type of education for different age levels. The continuous process must be present for effective education, but it must be founded upon a comprehensive program of general education, based upon a philosophy of meeting social needs, with special functions assigned to each administrative unit toward the fulfillment of which it will consistently work.

The Content of the Curriculum

Educational objectives and educational patterns in American secondary education have been reviewed as an aid in forming some opinions as to the general content needed in the curriculum of the high school. The curriculum is the key to education, for it involves all the things that pertain to education, everything, in fact, on which education is based.

If *education is life,* the curriculum must provide the right kind of living, living that will assure a better and richer future life. If *education is growth,* the curriculum must provide experiences that will assure a continuous expanding and transforming of individual interests, abilities, and attitudes. If *education is the development of desirable functional abilities, interests, and attitudes,* the curriculum must provide experiences that will foster and enrich these qualities. If *education is to preserve democratic ideals and contribute in any way to the re-shaping of society,* then the curriculum must insist upon democratic procedures, encourage discussion of controversial issues and lively criticism of all its activities, and develop an attitude of inquiry into all social conditions and problems.

The curriculum exists only for the purpose of developing the inherent potentialities and capacities of students. *Growth is determined by and through meaningful experiences.* Such experiences bring about desirable changes in

Cleveland Heights (Ohio) A Cappella Chorus Cleveland Art Museum. Collinsville Township High School Band.

the personality, character, and conduct of students. These desirable changes may be stated in such aims as the following:

1. Development of an awareness of the problems of living.
2. Development of careful and critical thinking.
3. Development of emotional control and stability.
4. Development of attitudes of responsibility, tolerance, cooperation, and service.
5. Development of group consciousness.
6. Development of desirable changes in overt behavior.
7. Development of creative expression.
8. Development of appreciation in art forms.
9. Development of a workable philosophy and religion for modern living.

Acquisition of knowledge, facts, and skills is valuable only to the extent that it contributes to these desirable changes. *They should be means to growth, not ends in themselves.* Such desirable changes in students can best be brought about through a curriculum based upon the problems with which students are confronted. These problems should serve as a core for the curriculum. They should determine the content of course syllabi.

Everybody is concerned with such fundamentals as: How to maintain physical health, how to get along with other people, how to make a living and attain economic security, how to adjust to the natural and social environment, how to enjoy various forms of beauty, how to acquire a knowledge of the cultural heritage in order to better understand our own civilization, how to raise the standard of living, and how to develop a workable philosophy or religion for everyday living.[9] All students are con-

[9] New College Catalogue, 1938-1939. Teachers College Bulletin, Teachers College, Columbia University.

fronted with such problems to a varying degree. In gaining an understanding of them, students move gradually from a consideration of personal and immediate problems to the larger social implications of these issues.

An educational program based upon the principles given above postulates a curriculum designed to develop an awareness of such problems of human existence and a broad, intelligent view of the major fields of knowledge which are used in the solution of these problems. The areas of experience will include activities and courses in the broad fields of the social sciences, natural sciences, music and the arts, language arts, physical activities, and socializing experiences. "They will also emphasize the spiritual aspects of experience, insisting that knowledge, art, morality and religion are the aspects of life of supreme moment." [10] These suggested areas of experience mean that subjects will not be compartmentalized but will be integrated in such ways as to lead the student to more unified purposes. They mean that activities will not be confined to the four walls of the classroom but that all available resources in the community will be utilized to bring about those changes in students necessary to meet life's problems. Finally, they mean that the students will be brought in contact with the substantial body of knowledge which acts as a stabilizing basis in a changing civilization.

Organization with the foregoing principles as a basis will undoubtedly produce a number of changes in the usual conventional curriculum.[11] Distinction between curricular and extra-curricular activities will probably be abandoned. In fact, more and greater emphasis will be placed upon student-initiated activities. To make integration effective,

[10] Robert R. Rusk, *Philosophical Basis of Education*, Boston: Houghton Mifflin, 1929, p. 109.

[11] William L. Wrinkle and others, *The New High School in the Making*, New York: American Book Company, 1938, Chapter III.

the various broad fields will be planned in relation to each other. Approximately an equal amount of time during the day's activities will be devoted to each broad field.

Another problem is that of *grade placement,* in which more research is needed, for it is a problem that is still unanswered. It is very difficult to determine the grade placement of various subjects and courses. Undoubtedly one criterion is the interest of the student with careful consideration of his breadth of experience in the field. Educational science has shown us that many subjects can be postponed for several years to good advantage. Since the ability to succeed in an abstract type of experience increases with mental maturity, it seems feasible that certain courses, for example, some in mathematics, could be postponed to later years in high school to good advantage. It will probably be best not to offer vocational courses and specific college preparatory courses until the final years.

The principle of *individual differences* in education is well established, but we still think in terms of time-units in placing students in grades, regardless of the wide variation of individuals in the same grade. This traditional practice will be hard to overcome because it is so firmly established that there will be parental and professional objection to abolishing it. There are trends, however, toward regrouping students according to social maturity rather than by chronological age or length of school attendance. Some educators think that the solution can be found by organizing the experiences in the broad fields in sequential units throughout the secondary schools. Whatever organization is adopted to meet these problems will probably involve a high degree of individualization within courses so that students in the same course will be working on problems and materials which at present would be placed in different grade levels.

Conventional *marking and grading practices* have been inadequate. They give little indication of students' actual achievement; they give the parents very limited information regarding a student's success in school activities; and they have too often served as a protection for uninteresting and ineffectual teaching. Students have become more interested in getting good marks than in getting an education. The two are not synonymous. Various kinds of measurement will always be needed in education, but they should be used to improve learning rather than to determine grade or school marks, promotion or graduation.

There is a general trend toward placing graduation from the high school on the basis of qualitative rather than quantitative standards. It will take more than polite attention on the part of the student for a number of years before he can be graduated. When he is best fitted for what he is to do next in the continuous process of education will be the time to give him final recognition for achievement by graduation.

There are many obstacles to the organization of the high school curriculum in the direction that this summary of present trends has tried to point out. Among these are the college entrance requirements, legislative restraints, influence of pressure groups, and the attitude of parents and of the students themselves. Moreover, a serious obstacle is to be found in the complacency of certain high school teachers and administrators. Greater respect for subject matter than for children, vested interests, lack of purpose, fear of nonconformity, complacency engendered by tenure of office, unwillingness to make concerted efforts, and inertia—these are some of the obstacles which impede the reorganization that is imperative in the secondary schools today.

CONCLUSION

We have traced in this chapter the path which secondary education has followed for the past three hundred years in arriving at its present status. Progressive changes have always come slowly. Reconstruction in education is necessarily a slow process. The teacher is the key to the situation. Enlightened education depends upon enlightened teachers. It is the duty of music teachers in high schools to acquaint themselves with the various issues in secondary education and to study carefully the contribution which music can make in developing a curriculum that will consist of meaningful and enriching experiences.

TOPICS FOR GENERAL DISCUSSION

1. What is meant by the statement "The school is a social institution"? To what degree should the school be expected to improve society?

2. How can the curriculum evolve from the needs and interests of the students it is designed to serve?

3. Enlarge on the statement that "education is preparation for life." What are the implications for the high school curriculum?

4. What was the doctrine of formal discipline? Why was it discredited? What did President Elliot of Harvard mean by his statement, "Music, if rightly taught, is the best mind-trainer of the lot"?

5. Under what pattern of administrative units were you educated? What were the advantages and disadvantages?

6. Compare the content of the curriculum in your high school with growing trends as indicated in this chapter.

MUSIC

Music—There is something very wonderful in music. Words are wonderful enough: but music is even more wonderful. It speaks not to our thoughts as words do: it speaks straight to our hearts and spirits, to the very core and root of our souls. Music soothes us, stirs us up; it puts noble feelings in us; it melts us to tears, we know not how:—it is a language by itself, just as perfect, in its way, as speech, as words; just as divine, just as blessed.

Music has been called the speech of angels; I will go further, and call it the speech of God Himself.

CHARLES KINGSLEY

Chapter 2

MUSIC AND THE ADOLESCENT

THE HIGH SCHOOL STUDENT

As stated in the first chapter, the content of any curriculum should evolve from the needs and interests of the students it is designed to serve. The starting point is the student. An understanding of his physical, mental, and emotional qualities is a prerequisite to the selection and organization of subject matter. Consequently, the curriculum of the high school should be organized in the light of the nature of the high school student.

The curricula of secondary schools must be designed to meet the needs and interests of pupils in their adolescent years. Adolescence may be regarded as that significant period in life extending from puberty to adulthood. Adolescence, however, in order to be understood, must not be studied as a phenomenon separated from pre-adolescence and maturity. Much of the basis for adolescent phenomena is found in childhood, and many of the results manifest themselves in adulthood. Most psychologists agree that adolescence is not a saltatory change in the life span, but a gradual growth in physical, mental, and emotional maturity.

Although changes during adolescence are generally considered to be gradual rather than cataclysmic, nevertheless there are certain characteristics that are evident during this period of life which call for sympathy and understanding and which have important implications for education and curricula.

By far the most important factor in this difficult period of life, because it so deeply affects all other characteristics, is the growth to physical maturity. The one greatest single factor in this physical growth is puberty, the earliest age at which one may beget or bear a child. Although puberty marks the beginning of physiological maturity, developmental changes are not complete for several years thereafter. These developmental changes include continued growth in size and shape of the heart, growth in size of the larynx and length of vocal chords with the resulting change in the boy's voice, increase in blood pressure, rapid increase in lung capacity, continued cellular development of the brain, growth of the uterus, marked changes in the glandular system, and the initial functioning of the sex glands. Some glands that functioned in childhood decrease in their activity. These glandular changes give a general condition of instability which, however, is often accompanied by greater energy and activity.

A singular phenomenon of adolescence is the fact that, on the average, girls reach the stage of puberty and the resulting physical and mental maturity at least one year earlier than boys do. This condition presents a peculiar adjustment problem in co-education because adolescent girls are in the same classes with pre-adolescent boys.

Although the brain ceases to grow in size at approximately the age of fourteen, cellular development on which mental growth depends continues for several years. Moreover, the effect of puberty, growth to physical maturity, and changes in the endocrine system have far-reaching effects on mental adjustments and attitudes of living.

These biological changes have their most profound consequences in the emotional life of the adolescent. The opposite sex is seen through different eyes. Approaching adulthood brings feelings of power and independence. The world takes on a different hue. All phases of life have more meaning and significance. New vistas are opened toward art and beauty. Religious fervor is often heightened. Disillusionment in accepted ideals is likely to bring skepticism. Environmental conditions which fail to nurture wholesome individual and social adjustments often cause extreme and detrimental emotional behavior.

In general, adolescence marks a period of progress toward greater independence and responsibility, greater interest in the opposite sex, a greater degree of socialization in general, and a deeper awakening of emotional life with more coordinated aims and purposeful activity. These characteristics of adolescence indicate that interests in general will be broadened to include to a greater degree many phases of life that were only passing or incidental interests in childhood. Several problems are created which center around the basic needs of this crucial period. These needs may be described as:

1. Gradual freeing of self from childish dependence so as to become an individual personality within the family group.
2. Association and wholesome relationships with members of the opposite sex.
3. Gradual assumption of responsibility for self-support.
4. A point of view upon the world that will unify life and give it meaning.
5. An awareness and understanding of the meaning of a democratic society and its implications for contemporary life.

This broadening and deepening of interests and basic

needs of the adolescent are a challenge to secondary education. The high school must not only continue the valuable educational experiences of the elementary school, but must provide unique experiences which will fulfill the special functions of the secondary school as determined by these interests and needs. The remaining chapters of this book are devoted to the implications which this challenge has for the teacher of music.

Music in the Curriculum

To justify its existence in the high school curriculum, music, like other experiences in the curriculum, must meet the interests and the individual and social needs of students. There is no lack of evidence of the interest that these young people have in music. When free from academic restraint, they are usually singing or listening to the radio. It is often desultory singing and aimless listening. Have you ever noticed how spontaneously high school students sing when on picnics, parties, or excursions? One may question the quality of the experience, but the quantity and intensity of the interest in music must be recognized.

Thomas H. Briggs of Columbia University has two guiding principles of education which are especially cogent at this point. On one occasion he stated them in this manner: "The first one is that the primary duty of the school is to teach people to do better the desirable things that they are likely to do anyway. Another duty is to reveal higher activities and to make them both desired and maximally possible." [1] If these common-sense principles are followed, the duty of the teacher of music is clear. He must guide and lead this innate interest in music into the higher realms of rich and purposeful musical experiences.

[1] "Music in Secondary Schools"—Music Educators National Conference, *Yearbook 1936*, p. 42.

Music as a Need

John Ruskin said, "The four necessities of life are food, shelter, raiment, and music." He saw undoubtedly the wholesome effect of music on the emotional life and the many ways that it serves the needs of both individuals and societies.

In these days of materialism music has been portrayed at times as "the useless art." Since immediate practical values were not always obvious, exponents of this indictment did not question the non-utility of music. The inability to define the utility of music is no proof that it does not exist. As William Wallace says, "No one has a right to quarrel with Nature and say roughly, 'This is useless'; its existence proclaims its utility." [2] And no one can doubt the omnipresence of music today with the advent of the radio. The radio reaches two hundred million listeners, and sixty-seven per cent of its output is music. It is probably safe to say that more music is being made today than at any time in the history of the world. But herein lies a danger, the danger that the amateur spirit in music will be superseded by the work of a few highly skilled professionals who will make our music for us. Instead of being real partakers of musical experiences we might become just a nation of onlookers and casual listeners.

Music may lack the practical value of food, shelter, and raiment, but its history and development belie its lack of utility and prove its value not only as an enrichment of life, but, in truth, as a basic need. Any effort to catalogue this value will probably weaken its significance. However, a discussion of music as a physical, an aesthetic, and a social need may be helpful.

[2] *The Threshold of Music; an Inquiry into the Development of the Musical Sense.* London: The Macmillan Company, 1908, p. 13.

Physical Need of Music

The effect that the tonal experience has upon the quality of our emotions in turn generates a feeling of well-being through the entire physical organism. The aural experience has always been the intimate sense of man as well as of animals. There is obvious import for primitive living in the fact that the connections of the cerebral tissues with the ear constitute a larger part of the brain than those of any other sense. For the savage, the ear gives the warning signal of approaching danger. The resultant emotional state is caused by the uncertainty of the impending experience.

Sound stimulates directly, as if the commotion were stirred by the organism itself. It does not need the interpretation of allied ideas which are associated with the indirect emotion of sight. Consequently, the physiological organism responds to the tonal experience of music in somewhat the same way as a resonator does. Psychology has shown that the whole organism responds, involving the central and peripheral nervous system, all the muscles and internal organism, and especially the autonomic system with its endocrines which furnishes a physical basis of emotion. Carl E. Seashore states that "musical sounds affect nervous control, circulation, digestion, metabolism, body temperature, posture and balance, hunger and thirst, erotic drives and pain, and indeed reverberate in both voluntary and involuntary action."[3] Experimental psychology substantiates this sweeping statement in varying degrees. The important factor is that, in the musical experience, the emotional state resulting from these physical changes is beneficial, whereas emotional discharge in uncontrolled experience is often

[3] "Why Do We Love Music?" *Music Educators Journal*, Music Educators National Conference, September, 1938, p. 28.

High School of Music and Art, New York. Senior Symphony Orchestra, Alexander Richter, Conductor.
Senior Choral Ensemble, Helen Clarke Moore, Conductor.

harmful. *In the musical experience the emotion is controlled and disciplined by and through the media and form of the art expression which, in turn, clarifies the emotional reaction and safeguards any tendency toward emotional outburst.* The resultant feeling is one of well-being and bodily glow which, with some individuals, approaches the ecstatic.

These physiological reactions to music and the resultant condition of good feeling and happy state of mind have long been associated with the curative effect of music. Modern medicine recognizes the therapeutic value of music in the treatment of many forms of diseases, especially those of a mental and psychiatric nature. There is no brief that music should be included in the curriculum for its therapeutic value, but it is acknowledged that the data of abnormal psychology help to solve many of the problems of normal psychology. The beliefs, clinical evidence, and semi-experimental studies of the exponents of musical therapy give striking instances of the influence of music upon the organism.[4] Also, the physical and muscular coordination developed by exercising the rhythmic sense through musical experiences is another contribution to the general state of well-being throughout the body. Teachers in physical education are becoming aware of this value of music and are using it extensively in their work. Music teachers also are becoming increasingly conscious of their responsibility in utilizing this value.

And so music as a salutary emotional experience, a pleasurable experience, and a satisfying experience is literally a tonic for the whole organism. It can serve, in turn, as a stimulation to various forms of activities and a relaxation from the tensions and strains of daily living. It can be

[4] Willem Van de Wall, *Music in Institutions.* New York: Russell Sage Foundation, 1936.

a "soothing balm" in times of stress and again can fire the ambition to worthy purpose. For the adolescent of high school age who is in a period of emotional uncertainty, music serves as a healthful physical and emotional release in a world filled with personal and social conflicts.

Aesthetic Need of Music

The rich heritage of art and music is ample proof that there is a need for forms of beauty in our individual and social lives. It is the monument of man's need of food for the spirit as well as food for the body. Since primitive times man has endeavoured to express and objectify his emotional experiences in some beautiful form. Edward Howard Griggs summarizes it by saying, "Beauty is the most useful thing man knows, for it is the chief instrument in deepening the spirit. The ideal is a little more real than anything else on earth, because it is the dynamic energy behind all conduct." [5]

Santayana, in *The Sense of Beauty,* points out that a thing, to be beautiful, must be beautiful in its materials, in its form, and in its expression. Music is woven out of beautiful sounds. We have already noticed the satisfying emotional effect of the tonal experience. The sounds of our tonal world are beautiful to us because through this beneficent physiological response, we have come to recognize the elements that make them beautiful. When these beautiful sounds are woven into beautiful rhythmic-tonal patterns, we have music. Musical forms embody melody, rhythm, harmony, balance, symmetry, and contrast. Through the purity of form it satisfies our need for artistic creation. John Dewey describes this quality of music as follows: "It is the peculiarity of music, and indeed its glory, that it can

[5] "Music in the Cultural Life of America." Music Educators National Conference, *Yearbook 1938,* p. 11.

take the quality of sense that is the most immediately and intensely practical of all the bodily organs since it incites most strongly to impulsive action, and by the use of formal relationships transforms the material into an art that is most remote from practical preoccupations."[6] By "practical preoccupations" he apparently excludes the expression of our loves, our sympathies, our fears, our cares, our aspirations, our feelings for fellowship, and our communion with the Divine. For these things and more are expressed for us in music, although musical feelings are broader and more pervasive than the poignant and disturbed feeling-reactions that arise from worldly circumstances. And so, in this day of increased tension, music, as one embodiment of beauty, is needed to enrich life by enlarging emotional and spiritual expression. It is needed because it affords opportunity for growth through a satisfying self-expression in beautiful form.

Social Need of Music

Whatever else music may be, it is a language. It has been called the language of the emotions. It is frequently referred to as the universal language. Any language functions only in terms of human relations.

When the various types of musical activities are examined, it becomes quite obvious that music is normally a social act. The adequate performance of music involves a listener. It is true that the performer and listener at times are one, but still the performer is endeavoring to interpret the message that the composer is trying to convey to human ears and understanding. Moreover, in another sense, history will testify to the fact that the most characteristic musical performance is by groups of people, small and large, who are sharing an enjoyable experience. Likewise,

[6] *Art as Experience*. New York: Minton, Balch and Company, 1934, p. 239.

listening not only involves the aural experience of hearing a tonal language, but also is most satisfactory in an informal situation which is shared by others. Even in the creating of music the composer has a message for human ears. He seldom has a specific audience in mind. *However, what he has to say is meant for the minds and hearts of men.*[7]

Now man is a social being. He is what he is because he exists in a social environment. As a result he has social needs. He needs affection from others; he needs to develop some means for living harmoniously with others; and he needs a feeling of belonging to, contributing to, and being accepted by, various social groups.

Music has long been used as a medium by which men can gratify their needs for social satisfaction and unity. Through the magic of rhythm in song, the primitive man made work seem lighter. This same rhythm, with heightened emotional quality, has united and inspired marching feet to victory in battle. Also, spiritual leaders have been quick to see the inspirational and unifying effect of music in religious worship. Moreover, music has been a friend of man as he loves and as he plays. The mere quantity of music as an expression of love that is extant is some manifestation of the emotional need that music fills for man in his relations with the opposite sex. Then, too, as man plays, he joins with others in singing and in dancing. The teacher has some clue to the value of the musical activities in the school by the songs that students sing in informal groups. *If school songs are never sung, then something is the matter with the songs or the way they are being taught.*

Music educators are beginning to place great emphasis upon the social values of music. This is as it should be. Practically no other subject in the curriculum develops a

[7] Mursell, James L., *Human Values in Music Education*, Silver Burdett Company, 1934, p. 66.

sense of personal and group responsibility to the extent that participation in musical ensemble does. In these groups students learn that worthy results depend upon the best contribution that each individual can make, plus that individual's ability to participate actively with others in the group. Is not this the ideal training for citizens of a democracy—individual responsibility plus effective group participation?

In the article referred to on page 31, Griggs expresses this idea so beautifully that it is well worth quoting here:

"Music is at once the most personal and the most social of the fine arts; it searches down the heart of the individual being and calls out emotions far too deep for words to embody. Music is an art we enjoy together, the more persons present, the greater joy for each one. It is a social art. Music sweeps, fuses, and unites. When we express our common states of feeling together—all of us feeling the same mood, the same emotion, and giving the expression in music—social solidarity is created, a unity of spirit, a community of spirit that makes much for civic activity and civic service. Therefore, when we are singing a hymn that has high aspiration for the whole people, when we sing it together, we are expressing certain common moods and emotions together, we are uniting in a spirit of patriotism that is not the blatant, ugly attitude called by that name, but is that hunger for human brotherhood, for the larger unity of all in one whole of humanity—that is the hope of mankind. We seldom think of music in this aspect, we do not think of it as the great instrument for training citizens that it is." [8]

Music and Experience

The reader has probably noticed the continuous use of the word "experience" in this book. Through constant repetition it may lose some of its effectiveness, but there is no word to take its place. The points of view expressed

[8] "Music in the Cultural Life of America." Music Educators National Conference, *Yearbook 1938*, p. 16.

Combined Glee Clubs, East Orange (New Jersey) High School and Clifford J. Scott High School Performance of Horatio Parker's Hora Novissima.

New Jersey All-State High School Chorus and Orchestra, Atlantic City, 1940.

in this book are based upon the philosophy that education is the result of significant experiences.

John Dewey points out that there are two aspects to experience. First of all, it is the "interacting" of man with his environment, and second, it is continuous and ever expanding.[9] Consequently, if education is the result of significant experiences, then the curriculum must consist of activities that are meaningful in the present life of the student. The greater the significance of these activities and experiences, the greater the extent to which they will affect the individual and his expanding environment as he moves in the continuous stream of life experience. This environment, both general and musical, not only produces musical impressions upon the student, but also leads to and draws out spontaneous musical expressions.

Therefore, if music is to contribute to this process of education, the curriculum must consist of significant and varied experiences in music. A musical environment must permeate the school. Music must not be relegated to a corner in the basement or housed in a special sound-proof cell. It must find its way into the assembly; it must be heard in classrooms, at social functions, on trips and excursions, throughout the community and in the home. These musical experiences must be so *vital* that music will continue to be a part of the life-experience of all students. They must be so *significant* that all students will continuously be led into an ever enriching experience with music. They must be so *varied* that all students will have the opportunity to experience music in all the media and forms that can be called musical experiences. Music educators must ever bear in mind the many types of musical experiences in planning a curriculum for high school.

[9] *Education and Experience*. New York: The Macmillan Company, 1938, p. 42.

Music and Integration

The word integration has appeared on the educational horizon during the past few years and has claimed increasing attention at all educational conferences. It is constantly being given more space in educational literature. There is nothing new about integration. On the contrary, it is as old as life itself, for it is the fundamental factor in all organic growth.

Webster's dictionary defines integration as "the act or process of integrating." This definition has more significance than it seems to indicate on first thought. It implies that integration is a process. It is not a static term. It is a dynamic and moving term. The dictionary adds that specifically it is the "process of making whole or entire; formulation of a whole from constituent parts." Thus by thinking in terms of verbs instead of nouns one clarifies the meaning in the educational process of such words as integration.

The unifying of constituent parts in experience is taking place as best it can in all living and learning. To the extent that the individual can thus integrate or bring together in a whole the various phases of experience as he adapts and adjusts to a changing environment, to that extent is he living and learning. To the degree that the inner volitional self is coordinated with overt action, to that degree is the individual in a stabilized or integrated condition, ready for purposeful activity.[10]

This concept of integration has caused educators to reconstruct their point of view regarding the learning process. It is fraught with significance in all that it implies for curriculum change. Curricula must consist of experiences that provide the environment in which this integrating process can take place. It means planning courses in the

[10] Pitts, Lilla Belle, "Music Education, Isolated or Integrated," Music Educators National Conference, *Yearbook 1937*, pp. 112-116.

various fields of human knowledge—social sciences, natural sciences, the arts, philosophy and religion—with insight and imagination which will fuse and integrate all the elements of these fields as they relate to man living in a past and present universe. Courses in special fields, such as skill subjects, do not necessarily need to be isolated, but should point to the same fundamental aim as the general courses do.

A curriculum organized to bring about the realization of this aim will include more than an incidental correlation of relationships. Integration of the curriculum means more than just correlation; it is the unifying of the work and experiences in several fields or the various phases of one field in such a way as to achieve some fundamental aim. It has been indicated that this fundamental aim is the development of integrated individuals in tune with life.

Music must do its share to contribute to this aim. As a subject it adapts itself effectively to a curriculum organized for this purpose. Music has long been a companion to man in all his experiences. It is natural to give it a vital place in the study of man's relationship to his environment. Music will contribute to all general courses which attempt to develop an appreciation and understanding of man's experiences.

Some music educators fear that in integrating music with other subjects it will lose its own identity and become a handmaiden to those subjects. Since music has a unique value for man, he will cherish this value and will keep it for what it is. This unique value is especially evident in many of the more active phases of the music program, such as singing, playing, and creating music. These activities themselves must be better integrated so that they will not become an isolated part of the student's environment. As long as these activities are made a vital and enriching experience in the life of the student, there will always be a place for them in the high school curriculum.

Singing as a Musical Experience

The most natural and at the same time the most universal medium for experiencing music is that of singing. For purely economic reasons it will always be a major musical activity in the schools. However, there are also psychological reasons for making the singing of beautiful songs the core of the music program.

The physical mechanism of the vocal action consists of the breathing organs, vibratory muscles of the larynx, and the resonators and articulators which include head and nasal cavities, soft and hard palate, tongue, teeth, lips, cheeks, and jaw. The complete vocal mechanism includes neural connections between the larynx and facial muscles, the ear, and the diaphragm, as well as the cortex of the brain, the organ of our highest and most refined controls. [11] The singing act involves the complete coordinated action of this total structure.

As a result, singing affects the entire body more directly and more intimately than any other musical experience does. Through training, the playing of instruments may become as satisfying as the experience of singing; but for psycho-biological reasons, singing should continue to be the initial and universal means of musical expression. Noteworthy are the reasons for studying singing which are given by the American Academy of Teachers of Singing. This group of specialists claim that "singing fortifies health, widens culture, refines the intelligence, enriches the imagination, makes for happiness and endows life with an added zest." William Byrd probably had such benefits in mind when he wrote in 1588:

[11] Mursell, James L., *The Psychology of Music*. New York: W. W. Norton and Company, 1937, p. 226.

"Since Singing is so good a thing
I wish all men would learn to sing."

5 1-2

Playing as a Musical Experience

Although singing may be the most intimate, the most universal, and the most economical means of musical expression, the playing of instruments is, for many people, by far the more satisfactory. Several factors enter into this conclusion. For instance, many people have vocal equipment that is too limited for the fullest expression through the medium of music. For others, the technical manipulation of the instrument is a delight in itself. And finally, the modern composers from the time of Haydn have devoted most of their energies and expressed their deepest and most significant musical ideas through the medium of instruments. Even the great modern masterpieces of choral literature have elaborate instrumental accompaniments.

This tendency of composers can be easily understood when we examine the musical possibilities in the striking development of instruments within the past two centuries. In the first place, instruments greatly increase the resources of the composer. Then, again, range of pitch is greatly extended, harmonic resources are enriched, varied melodic styles are made possible, dynamic contrasts are increased, rhythmic patterns can be made more intricate, and the variations of timbre are greatly expanded. The opening of such avenues of almost unlimited means has naturally inspired the masters to greater musical expression. The player of instruments has the rich opportunity to experience directly some of the more profound masterpieces of musical thought.

Listening as a Musical Experience

Although the performance of music gives greater satisfaction, the listening to music should probably be the first musical experience to consider. Music is a tonal art and involves listening. The efforts of both the composer and the performer are directed toward the listener. He is indispensable. The host of listeners will always be by far the largest group of musical consumers, and the high school curriculum should provide for the needs of this group.

Today many music educators are apprehensive lest we become a nation of passive listeners. The influence of the radio, phonograph, and cinema undoubtedly is leading us in that direction. Music education can counteract this tendency by giving larger numbers of students the greater satisfaction of playing and singing, in addition to experiences in listening. It can greatly enhance the appreciation of the nation by making the listening more discriminating. Rudolph Ganz, the well-known pianist, once said that there are three kinds of listeners: those who listen with their heels, those who listen with their hearts, and those who listen with their heads. The implication is quite obvious. *Listening to music in any sense is more than a passive experience; it is more than a warm bath. Listening that is worthy of the name leads to a consciousness of the inherent social qualities of music and an appreciation of its transcendent beauty.*

Composing as a Musical Experience

We have deliberately used the word "composing" instead of the word "creating" in order to avoid much of the confusion attending the word "creative" in educational circles today. As emphasis has been placed upon the creative process, all phases of music teaching have had a tendency to become "creative." The making of instruments by children has been labeled "creative music," appreciation has become "creative listening," and playing and singing have become "creative performance." It seems only a matter of time before mastery of the score will become "creative note-reading."

It is not to be denied that an element of the creative, in varying degrees, is in all these activities. In fact, anything is creative which brings old material together into new relationships. If new meaning is given to a work of art through perception and interpretation, then the creative process is undoubtedly involved. However, the most elevated type of creative musical expression, and probably the most satisfying, is composition. There is no doubt that some performance, and even some listening, is more creative than some composition. Nevertheless, if the quality of these musical acts is of comparative standard, the objectification of one's own experiences expressed in tonal-rhythmic patterns, is one of the keenest delights in music.

Music education has made some advancement in extending the idea that the performance of music is not limited to a few talented people. *The mystery surrounding musical composition should be dispelled.* Small children show a natural aptitude for singing their own tunes in order to give musical meaning to their daily experiences. The school must nurture this natural aptitude and make it a normal means of expression. It has been killed all too often by the time the pupil has reached the senior high school. A definite effort must be made to arouse again the desire to express one's experiences in musical design. *We expect creative expression* in literature and in the visual arts of high school students. *Why not in music?* It is granted that the technical difficulties are not exactly comparable. But are they insurmountable? If composition is taught directly and not through a maze of harmonic and contrapuntal rules, we will nurture the creative process which is stressed in modern educational thought and provide opportunity for many students to develop natural aptitudes.

Conclusion

This chapter has been devoted to setting forth the principle that teachers of music have access to a priceless heritage through which it is their privilege to lead others to richer living. They hold the key to a store of resources through which young people can discover delightful and colorful experiences. The remaining chapters will concern themselves with opening this treasure-house and exploring its contents.

Topics for General Discussion

1. Music is often called a highly emotional art. In light of the need for emotional stability during adolescence should there be more or less music in the curriculum of the secondary school?

2. There are two procedures in handling the boy's changing voice: (1) holding the boy on high treble voice parts until the change is complete, (2) encourage the dropping of the voice by assigning the boy gradually to lower voice parts. Which procedure would you advise and why?

3. In the event of an imaginary curtailing of the school budget, organize a short talk to be delivered before the local board of education defending the continuation of music in the high school curriculum.

4. Read the complete article, "Music in the Cultural Life of America," by Edward Howard Griggs in the Music Educator's National Conference Yearbook 1938, page 16. What are the implications for the high school curriculum?

National High School Symphonic Band, Music Educators National Conference, 1940. Central High School Music Festival, Detroit, Michigan, 1939. Harry Seitz, Director, Victor Kolar, Guest Conductor.

Part Two

MUSICAL EXPERIENCES

I HEAR AMERICA SINGING

I hear America singing, the varied carols I hear,
Those of mechanics, each one singing his as it should be blithe and strong,
The carpenter singing his as he measures his plank or beam,
The mason singing his as he makes ready for work, or leaves off work,
The boatman singing what belongs to him in his boat, the deckhand singing on the steamboat deck,
The shoemaker singing as he sits on his bench, the hatter singing as he stands,
The wood-cutter's song, the ploughboy's on his way in the morning, or at noon intermission or at sundown,
The delicious singing of the mother, or of the young wife at work, or of the girl sewing or washing,
Each singing what belongs to him or her and to none else,
The day what belongs to the day—at night the party of young fellows, robust, friendly,
Singing with open mouths their strong melodious songs.

WALT WHITMAN

Chapter 3

INTEGRATING MUSIC IN THE CURRICULUM

In the preceding chapter a discussion of integration discussed the meaning of this term as it is used in present day educational literature. It was pointed out that there were opportunities for integrating music with other subjects in the curriculum of the high school and also for integrating various phases of musical activity into a more meaningful whole. Let us now examine more thoroughly the application of integration as it relates to music in the high school curriculum.

Integrating Music in the Core Curriculum

As educators have realized the necessity of basing the curriculum upon vital experience, many types of curricula have been introduced in various administrative units of the school. The older "subject" curriculum is being replaced by a more flexible program based upon pupil interests and needs and often labeled the "experience" curriculum. The change in this direction is especially apparent in the elementary school. The high school has been reluctant to make many changes. The aversion to experiment at this level has been due to conflicting philosophies of the purpose of the high school; the difficulty of administering an "experience" curriculum for students of this age; and most important of all, the need for more teachers who are qualified to carry on an integrated program of work and study.

However, some high schools have endeavored to make subject matter more unified and meaningful by introducing and adopting the "core" curriculum. In this curriculum plan, a certain amount of time—approximately from two to three periods each day—is devoted to the study of a unified core of subject matter. The core of this type of curriculum is usually the social sciences.

In the development of the core curriculum many hitherto unsuspected relationships between the general academic subjects and music have come to light. This important revelation has increased the importance of music in the eyes of the general educator, and reaffirmed the music specialist's faith in the value of music to contribute to the life situations that the school attempts to parallel. Educators have been quick to see that music can bring an emotional and expressive quality to many learning experiences that vitalizes and vivifies all elements of the experience. In the development of the social sciences it early became evident that the music and art of a nation must be studied if one would gain a clear understanding of the culture of that nation and a feeling for the best things in its life. Moreover, the character of an historical epoch cannot be completely sensed and adequately revealed without an acquaintance with the manner in which the people of the period expressed themselves in music.

Since music has many valuable contributions to make to the curriculum that attempts to unify the student's learning experience and insure the integral wholeness in the situation that is demanding his attention, let us examine some of the problems involved in the relationship of music with the core studies.[1]

[1] Louis Woodson Curtis, "Music and the Core Curriculum," Music Educators National Conference *Yearbook 1938*, pp. 347–351.

First of all, it is necessary to determine whether it is *appropriate* and *valid* to include music in the unit of interest being studied. Although it is true that music can enhance many learning experiences, it is equally true that music has no place in some units of study. An understanding of the Elizabethan era, for instance, will not be complete without some acquaintance with the English madrigal. At the same time, it is difficult to see the validity of including music in a unit of mathematics even though the musical scale is said to be a table of logarithms. Not every unit of work needs a musical interpretation. It stands to reason that it is unwise to force music into any unit where there are no plausible or valid relationships.

A second problem in integrating music with units of study arises from the *scarcity of material* that is authentic and at the same time appropriate. Music materials for the study of ancient cultures that are extant are very limited, but much music is available for making a rich contribution to the study of life in the Elizabethan Age. It is ludicrous to play the "Turkish March" of Beethoven for the purpose of acquiring a better feeling for Byzantine culture. At the same time, one will hardly deny that Frenchmen such as Bizet and Ravel have written some of the best and most colorful Spanish music.

As far as possible music materials should be drawn directly from the people around whose culture the unit of study is organized. It must be authentic in mood, scales and modes, harmonic structure, melodic style, and rhythmic characteristics. To the extent that modern composers have used the national idiom of a culture, their music may be used to enrich the integrated study of that culture. For instance, the music of Grieg and Sibelius reveals the spirit of Norway and Finland.

Likewise, in the study of historical epochs, authentic

music material is most desirable. Let the students feel the mysticism of the early Christian church through singing and listening to some of the old modal chants. Let them march with the Crusaders to the ancient tune, "Fairest Lord Jesus." Let them sense the refinement of the Rococo period in art by dancing the minuet and listening to the music of Mozart! Let them discover the essence of man's struggle for freedom of expression in the symphonies of Beethoven.

A third consideration is the validity of the *types of musical activity* included in the integrating program. There is great danger that the contribution of the music teacher will be limited to explanations and discussions about music. He must be on constant guard against this danger. Of course there must be time for discussion, but the emphasis must be upon musical activity.

Singing, naturally, will take a leading place in the integrating program. Moreover, it must be good singing if it is to be effective. If the teacher inherits students from elementary and junior high schools who have an adequate command of musical skills, good singing is possible at the first reading. If not, it is entirely legitimate to rehearse the material which is being used, although formal drill on skills in this situation is taboo. The same statement can be made for the playing of instruments by students who are qualified. Likewise, listening to music is a major activity in integrating music with all units of study. The extensive material made available by the recording companies is a godsend to the teacher of music in the integrated core curriculum.

On the other hand, teachers of music in the high school often fail to take full advantage of the possibilities of creating music in an integrated activity. The elementary school discovered very early the rich value of the creative element in a truly integrated learning experience. There is no reason to doubt that such experience will be equally rewarding in the high schools if the teachers are prepared to carry the creative activity forward. Composition of music has always been surrounded by an aura of mystery. If given an opportunity and some guidance, many students will be discovered who can write effective chants in the modes, oriental melodies in the pentatonic scale, simple rounds, and characteristic dance tunes of various countries. These can be harmonized by music students or by the teacher. How they like to try their hand at writing a jazz tune! Such creative experiences can be rich in aesthetic value for students. It also stimulates them to relate new meanings and information about various peoples to their own cultural life.

These three problems which arise in trying to integrate music with the core subject depend upon the relation between the general teacher and the special music teacher. Unless there is sympathetic understanding between these two leaders, all attempts at integration are futile. As was indicated in the previous discussion, there must be a common goal and an ultimate aim. This statement implies that there will be cooperative planning among the teachers organizing the units of study and frequent conferences between the general teacher and the music specialist.

To be successful the direction of the music experiences described above must be assigned to the music specialist, not left to the inexpert guidance of the general teacher. It naturally follows that the work with the integrating program should not impose an added burden on the music teacher, but should be included in his teaching schedule as part of his assigned duties. When his schedule is arranged, adequate time should be allotted in planning the integrated program to make the contribution of music a valuable part of the whole experience. In addition to having this regular time allotment for music study in connection with the unit, the general teacher should be free to call in the music specialist as the need arises.

One of the primary functions of music in the core curriculum is to stimulate interest in art in general and music in particular. To do this the teacher of music must have at his disposal superior equipment and adequate materials. This includes pianos that are in tune, good phonographs, books, radio, music, and records. Too often the attitude is taken that makeshift equipment and material will suffice, since the core of the learning experience is not music. Where this is the case, it is far better to omit music participation entirely. Such an attitude will be conveyed to the students and will result in a desultory interest in the arts instead of an interest that is highly stimulative and active.

INTEGRATING MUSIC IN THE BROAD FIELDS CURRICULUM

The reorganization of the high school curriculum has emerged in some schools into a type called the "broad fields" curriculum. Like the core curriculum, it is an attempt to integrate learning experience by unifying subject matter. Instead of one field serving as a core of emphasis, the various fields of human knowledge and experience are given equal emphasis. These broad fields are usually designated as the social sciences, natural sciences, humanities or the arts, philosophy and religion. Some subjects which it is difficult to include in these broad fields, such as languages, vocational subjects, and skill subjects, are taught in separate courses.

Many good things can be said about the broad fields curriculum, especially for the senior high school. It is easier to administer than the core curriculum for students of this level, with their many diversified interests. It provides opportunity for the integration of much subject matter that has been separated in the past. And yet it makes ample provision for differentiation to meet the needs of these students, who are rapidly approaching adulthood. It stresses a general education based upon appreciations, understandings, insight, and general power, as opposed to an early specialization that is overdone. A very important consideration is the fact that the high school teachers of today can see value in unifying the subject matter in their own broad fields and are willing to plan syllabi which will make this subject matter more meaningful to the students. This in-service training of teachers is an extremely important administrative duty. The success of an integrated curriculum of any type is contingent upon developing these teachers into a real educational corps.

Finally, the form in which any integrated curriculum will emerge is determined by the maturity of the students and their ability to transform their continuous interaction with an ever increasing and varied environment into purposeful activity. Integrative action may take place in a limited subject-matter area, but as environments expand it is more difficult to bring a series of activities into a meaningful whole. Consequently, in the elementary school, where the environment of young pupils is expanding more rapidly than their ability to grasp relationships, it seems best to organize a curriculum around daily experiences and centers of interest which induces thinking and acting in integrated units.

On the other hand, the high school student is more capable of seeing the relationships between varied experiences as they fit into a total pattern of living. He is at the stage of living where broad fields of knowledge relate closely to his interests and activities. However, isolation of various phases of these broad fields into limited subject areas still leaves him confused in his ability to relate the innumerable elements into meaningful wholes that are useful for purposeful activity.

The Arts in the Broad Fields Curriculum

The aims of the teaching of arts in the high school should be to develop: (1) an awareness of the social value of the various arts, (2) an understanding of their functional value, and (3) an appreciation of their inherent beauty.

To achieve these aims the organization of experiences in the arts involves several considerations which may be stated as follows:

1. Art forms are a reflection of the social milieu that produced them.
2. Psychological elements of the creative process in various media are similar.
3. All art forms have common qualities and related elements.
4. Participation in any art enhances appreciation of that art.
5. Knowledge of any art enhances appreciation of that art.

It is not within the scope of this book to discuss thoroughly the implications of these considerations for the curriculum. It seems necessary, however, to touch upon them briefly.

Since art is the expression of how some individual or group feels about an experience, it must reflect to some degree the social milieu. To express, a person must experience. To experience, a person must react to some environment. An artist may live in a limited or isolated environment. However, to the extent that his environment is a part of the large social environment, his art works will reflect the philosophy and mores of that total environment as well as his immediate surroundings. A better understanding of the social milieu which produced a work of art will give a student a clearer conception of its expressive qualities.

The psychological basis for all artistic creative expression is the same. It is the media that varies. Individual expressions proceed from a felt need. This felt need or impulsion arises from the "strains and stresses" which the organism encounters as it reacts to environment. As this impulsion follows its course through the environment the organism is forced to make choices. In this way it becomes aware of itself and develops emotional reactions. When the experience is significant and strongly emotional, the self often wishes to give permanency to the experience and communicate it to others. This desire culminates in the production of a work of art. Expressing this significant emotional experience in the design of an art form is the creative process of the artist. It involves selection, clarification, assimilation, insight, and technical skill. This creative expression includes both the giving of form to new experiences and the giving of new life to old forms. Inherently or through experience the creator is sensitive to various media. The choice of media, which is part of the process, depends upon this sensitivity and suitability. An understanding of the creative process as it relates to art forms enables the student to better reconstruct for himself the artistic expression that goes into a work of art. Greater discrimination and deeper appreciation will result.

There are common qualities or elements in all art forms which unite and integrate the work of art with the action that produced it. The emotional quality of the experience which produced an art object permeates and pervades the whole work. This quality is expressed in organized form.

This form is dependent upon all the aesthetic elements of design, rhythm, symmetry, balance, dominance, and unity in variety. These elements may have different meanings for various individuals sensitive to different media. To deny their existence in a work of art is to deny form. To deny form is to deny artistic expression. The student should at least be aware of these common elements in order to appreciate the basic qualities of all art forms.[2]

Every work of art, depending upon the medium, has individual and unique qualities and characteristics. An appreciation of these qualities is best nurtured by a growing sensitivity to the medium. Participation in any art is probably the best means to develop this appreciation. In music it means discriminative listening, active performance, and at least some attempt at composition. In the visual arts it means an attempt to use a brush, "getting your hands in clay," or at least having some close contact with the materials of the medium. In literature it means reading poetry aloud and "trying your hand at composing a sonnet." To achieve its aims the art program must provide experiences in all art forms through active participation. For the course in the arts this means laboratory periods, adequate equipment for individual work, and rooms equipped for experimenting, practicing, and listening.

Genuine appreciation is dependent upon perception and is based upon evaluation. Evaluation involves more than pure impressionism. It includes an element of honest criticism based upon knowledge. One is always skeptical of people who say, "Oh, I just love music but I don't know a thing about it." *If this love is genuine, they will learn something about music.* To develop appreciation in all the arts, there must be provision for study of the technical and

[2] For a direct application of these ideas, see Unit II, "The Interrelation of the Arts" by Alfred Howell in *Music, The Universal Language,* McConathy, Morgan, Lindsay, Silver Burdett Company, 1941.

historical facts which have affected the production of art forms.

And so in organizing the experiences with art in the broad fields curriculum, attention should be given to the social milieu that affects art forms, the factors in the creative process that produce art forms, and the qualities that pervade all art forms. To the extent that students acquire a knowledge of art forms and a sensitivity to various media through participation, appreciation will be enhanced and an understanding of the need for art expression in individual and social living will be realized.

Music in the Subject-Matter Curriculum

In the preceding paragraphs the relation of music to some of the newer trends in high school curricula is discussed. The established curriculum, called "subject matter" for lack of a better name, is still the practice in most high schools. In this curriculum, how can music be more effectively integrated with the life in the school, with the life in the community, and, finally, with itself?

The general assembly is undoubtedly one of the most advantageous means of achieving this integration. Chapter IV will be devoted to the place of music in the assembly. Likewise, Chapter V will be devoted to the use of public performance for this purpose. Let us now turn our attention to courses in music, such as theory, harmony, appreciation, and history which at present are usually taught as unrelated experiences.

Too often the content of music courses in the subject-matter curriculum has been determined by college entrance requirements and state syllabi. At present there seems to be some relaxation and reconsideration of these requirements and demands so that individual schools will have more freedom in determining the kinds of music courses and the content of syllabi which they will use.

In considering the integration of these music courses, two points should be borne in mind. In many high schools, orchestras, bands, and choruses are scheduled and graded similarly to other school subjects. Many of these schools also offer courses in theory, harmony, appreciation, and history which students in the performing groups are required to attend up to a certain minimum. The integration of these courses to a point where students in the performing groups will get a well-rounded viewpoint of music should be given thoughtful consideration in curriculum building. Unquestionably, it would be desirable that all students in performing groups should have a minimum of such background experience even though the school might wish to offer further elective courses.

The second point is that in every school there are many students who are interested in music as a general culture, but who are not concerned with musical performance. Music courses open to such students have often been given under the title "music appreciation." Such courses too frequently depend only on listening to phonograph records. Educators are in agreement as to the desirability of a general music course which will meet equally the needs of students interested in performance and students concerned with music as a broad culture.

General Music Course

To meet the foregoing needs, the high school may well consider inclusion of an integrated music course, scheduled for one period each day, and, if practicable, covering at least two years of study. In this general course, music will not be approached through the segregation of its component parts, such as theory, history, listening, and performing, but through the fusing of these parts as they contribute to the appreciation and understanding of music as an art form. The primary aim of this general music course is to acquaint students with the wide and rich heritage of music literature. If we are going to use music as the means for affecting the lives of young people, then their familiarity with a wide variety of typical examples of the best in music is paramount. On account of the limited technique of high school students, it is not always possible to do this in the performing organizations. Moreover, not all students who are interested in music are members of these groups, but practically every student who loves music can sing to at least a certain point of effectiveness. He can sing well enough to make many of the fine melodies of music literature a part of his own active experience. Today, also, through mechanical means, a splendid library of the finest music has been brought within the reach of all. The entire course should be enriched by introducing the related arts as an expression of man in his search for beauty.

There are several approaches to achieving this aim of the general music course. Among these approaches we should consider singing many typical examples of beautiful music of various styles and epochs; listening to music through mechanical reproduction and in school and community concerts; studying the important phases of music history with an acquaintance of actual music representative of various eras; and studying the theory of music especially as it applies to the compositions at hand. All the foregoing activities and experiences should be brought to bear upon the study of well-selected examples of music literature.

Every music teacher will have his own preference in the relative emphasis upon these different approaches. This natural attitude is wholly commendable and desirable providing that he does not "ride his hobbies" to the exclusion of the other approaches.

The students also will be found to have individual preferences which they would like to follow. This, too, is equally desirable and should be encouraged. Some students will like to approach their music through further singing and playing and they, naturally, will be the members of the school performing organizations. They can well lend their performing skill to the advantage of their classmates in the general music course. Some students will be interested in composing and should be encouraged to go further in the study of music theory and compose in as many forms as practicable. It is not uncommon also to find students that enjoy arranging music for orchestras, bands, or for choral groups. Some students find pleasure in writing criticisms of concerts or in doing special research work along the lines of music in which they are interested. The teacher should endeavor to discover each student's talents or predilections and help the student develop accordingly. All the foregoing, however, should mean that these special interests should be carried on by individual students beyond the activities followed by every student.

Naturally, the difficulty of this approach will be found in the fact that relatively few teachers have a background that makes them capable of encouraging and carrying on these varied activities in a single setting.

Singing Approach

The singing approach through a course in general music such as is here discussed is quite a different thing from the singing of an a cappella group or the singing of a general assembly. Excellence of performance as such is less important than the joy of gaining familiarity with the beauty of the music under consideration. To be sure, the performance must be at least sufficiently carefully and beautifully done to reveal the qualities of the music. A slipshod performance will not do this. On the other hand, the careful attention and long and repeated rehearsing of a composition necessary for performing by an a cappella choir, would nullify the purposes of the general music course in several ways, particularly because it would limit the amount and variety of music with which the class might become familiar. Students whose voices are not particularly good would be too self-conscious if their participation were criticised on the basis of fine choral singing. Yet they might find great joy and aesthetic satisfaction in becoming familiar with beautiful music through singing it.

Music Theory Approach

Perhaps the most important point for the music teacher of the general music course to bear in mind in the "theory approach" is keeping the theory studies directly associated with actual musical works. Theory as an isolated subject of study has its values to the advanced student. For the beginning student, especially of high school age, an harmonic progression, or a structural organization, has no virtue or value as an isolated fact and is of little worth unless it is a familiar and friendly landmark as one meets it in a musical composition.

This course should include the writing of simple compositions. The teacher must forget harmonic excellence for its own sake. Parallel fifths must cease to be considered catastrophic crimes. It is not beyond the scope of this class to present simple chord connections especially as they are found in the music which students are performing or to which they are listening. If some freedom is given to the use of I, IV, and V_7 chords in several keys, we may be surprised at the musical ideas of individual students which this approach to composition encourages. New chords should be pointed out in the singing of songs, the playing of instruments, and the analysis of great masterpieces. There is no set sequence for the introduction of new chords. When students find striking progressions in the music they are hearing and performing, they should try to use such progressions in their own compositions. The writing of rounds, hymns, chorales, dances, piano pieces, and simple songs will naturally follow. Studies of these smaller forms should lead to writing in the styles of various historical periods and composers. Studies of the composers will lead to elementary analysis of the larger forms.

Listening Approach

Much listening to music is desirable. The phonograph is an invaluable adjunct but it is only one means of bringing music to the listening ear. The radio, attendance at concerts, and listening to performances by groups within the schools, such as orchestras, bands, and choruses, should all be a part of the general music course. The general music course should naturally involve the consideration of music in units of study. Haphazard and unorganized selection of compositions in unrelated sequences will naturally fail in the purposes of such a class. In such units of study as may be chosen, every possible variety of experience should be sought. Singing of choruses by the class; listening to music in all of its different possibilities; composing music that will carry out the idea of the unit; reading about composers, historical matters, both of music and of general history and about sources of inspiration from which compositions may have sprung—all contribute to a larger appreciation. The listening program should offer a rich and closely related group of compositions and it is in this connection that the use of phonograph records is essential.

Music History Approach

In planning this course, music must be selected which will illustrate various epochs and styles. Students need not pursue their studies in chronological order beginning with the music of the Greeks or with the cacophony of today. Instead, their progress may follow any order in which the class shows an interest. The important first thing is to find that the study of a piece of music from its historical perspective and background can enhance the interest in the composition and our enjoyment in listening to it.

An excellent beginning may be through folk and popular music as an expression of the people. This is the music which the pupils are ready to understand and the forms in which they can create. An amazing amount of history of music can be taught through the folk song. Think of the composers that have used folk tunes as the source of their inspiration. The history of music is tied closely to its geography. True understanding, appreciation, and enjoyment of a musical composition is possible only when one is able to sense it as an outcome of a period and place.

Organization of the Course

The two-year sequence of an integrated course of this nature might be organized by semesters. These semester courses need not be in any particular sequence. Each might include many examples of music literature and many units of study which would be stimulating and enjoyable to the students and would be available to them in such semesters as their general schedule of studies would make practicable. The following topics might be used for semester outlines for such a general music course, or for units of study within the course.

1. Folk and popular music
2. Program music
3. "Pure" or absolute music
4. Functional music
5. Rhythm in music
6. Melody in music
7. Harmony in music
8. Design in music
9. The modern spirit in music
10. The romantic spirit in music
11. The classic spirit in music
12. The religious spirit in music
13. Music and the related arts
14. Music associated with historical events
15. Racial and national characteristics in music
16. Choral and instrumental styles and forms
17. Environmental influences in the work of great composers
18. Vocal and instrumental timbre in music

A true love for music is acquired along such winding paths as this integrated course presents. The teacher grows with the student in sensitivity, musicianship, and creative ability. Such musicianship includes not only ability to evaluate music, and, to some extent, the ability to make and write music, but most important of all, the ability to find through music a greater awareness of our own inner aesthetic and emotional satisfactions.

Teachers may fear this approach to music study because of its lack of conventional sequence. The sequence is really determined by the need for growth in musical expression by listening, performing, and creating. The teacher must plan carefully the materials he selects in order that relation-

Greenwich (Connecticut) High School, Class in General Music, Miss Mary McElligott, Instructor.

Girls' Choral Group, H. P. Harding High School, Charlotte, North Carolina, Miss Mary Brockwell, Instructor.

ships between different phases of music can be understood and easily grasped. Students must have suitable textbooks that offer the finest typical examples of the rich literature of music as well as books in the theory and history of music. Supplementary reading material must be available in biography and general appreciation. An ample supply of choral literature representing various periods in music history which can be sung by this group must be on hand. The record library must be adequate; rooms for listening and practice must be available. All students who are actively performing in one or another of the musical organizations of the school should be members of this class, but the class should also enroll any other students who are desirous of enriching their lives through a finer cultural background. If the teachers are prepared through a broad musicianship that is cultural, if they complement this preparation with careful planning, such an integrated course in music study affords a delightful and rewarding experience for both the student and the instructor.

Conclusion

And so, if the theory of integration is accepted as a sound educational principle, the music teacher must be continually on the alert for ways in which music can serve as an enrichment of the experience of living. He must be ever aware of the place of the musical experience in the total compass of culture. And he must continue to seek for relationships which will unify musical experience into a more meaningful and purposive pattern of living.

Topics for General Discussion

1. Have you had any contact with the experience, core, or broad fields types of curricula? What were the advantages and limitations of each type? In what ways do they differ from the subject matter curriculum?

2. It is often said that correlation is that which one does to subject-matter while integration is that which happens to the student. What is meant by these points of view? What are the essential differences between correlation and integration?

3. If you were participating in an integrated course in which the units of study were organized around various cultures, in which units would you introduce the following compositions?

1. Bolero—Ravel
2. Die Meistersinger—Wagner
3. The Magic Flute Overture—Mozart
4. Aïda—Verdi
5. The Swan of Tuonela—Sibelius
6. Le Sacre du Printemps—Stravinsky

4. Discuss the common elements that are attributed to various arts. Are such things as rhythm, harmony, color, form and design the same in both the tonal and visual arts?

5. Have a round table discussion of your favorite approach to the appreciation of music. Have you ever been forced to participate in a musical activity which you did not enjoy? How did it affect your attitude toward music?

6. If you were teaching a general music class in a high school, which approach to the study of music literature would you wish to emphasize? What are the chief reasons for your choice?

FROM "KING RICHARD II"

Act V, Scene V

"Music, do I hear?
Ha, ha! keep time. How sour sweet music is
When time is broke and no proportion kept!
So it is in the music of men's lives."

WILLIAM SHAKESPEARE

Chapter 4

THE GENERAL ASSEMBLY

To many principals of high schools and directors of music the general assembly is a nightmare; to very few is it a joy and a significant opportunity. This attitude is usually the result of a lack of planning; it is due to a lack of purpose and of educational objectives in administration and teaching. The music instructor frequently regards the assembly as a chore instead of a challenge.

PURPOSES OF THE ASSEMBLY

Educators have presented many purposes and objectives for the school assembly, all of them valid in varying degrees. To make these objectives more effective, it is best to limit them in number and in scope. It may be helpful to suggest a few of them as presented by educators who have devoted much attention to the general assembly.[1]

To Unify the School

The high school of today is a very heterogeneous group. So often students move from one classroom to another, giving little thought to the relationship of subjects or personal relations with their fellow students, teachers, school, or community. These students and their teachers need to be brought together in a common activity at regular intervals.

[1] Elbert K. Fretwell, *Extra-Curricular Activities in Secondary Schools*. New York: Houghton Mifflin Co., 1931, Chapter IX.

The general assembly is the one activity that can bring together the members of the school-community. Students become better acquainted with one another and with their teachers by seeing them in a different rôle. They view their principal in a different light from that of a mere disciplinary officer.[2]

The assembly can engender that mysterious and valuable quality called "school spirit." The morale of the school is built upon loyalties and devotion. Group spirit or consciousness is built upon the students' recognition of relationships with one another and the resulting pride in the group activities and accomplishments of which they are a part. The students themselves are the body through which the soul of the school finds expression. The general assembly provides the best opportunity for fostering a unified and dynamic school personality.

To Integrate Activities and Experiences

The many seemingly disconnected and unrelated departments of the school can be brought together in the assembly through concerted effort in a common cause, such as advertising an athletic event, presenting an operetta or pageant, rewarding merited achievement, inaugurating the school officers, or observing some special patriotic or festival day. The assembly may be a veritable clearing house for all school activities and it can serve as a means to show the relationships between departments in these activities.

To Integrate Classroom Teaching

The integration of classroom teaching can be encouraged through the assembly by showing the relationships between the various fields of human knowledge, such as the social sciences, natural sciences, the arts, philosophy, and religion.

[2] Harry C. McKown, *Extra-Curricular Activities*. New York: The Macmillan Company, 1937, Chapter V.

The social and economic problems of today can be interpreted in the light of technological advancement. International relations can be studied in the light of scientific development. Art forms can be appreciated as a product of the social milieu. Through programs for special days, original dramatizations of classroom activities, motion pictures, and interesting talks, these relationships can be made to seem more natural and lifelike in the assembly than in a formal classroom presentation.

To Develop Student Participation

Lest the programs become a series of announcements and a parade of dry lectures, opportunity for student participation should be definitely one of the purposes of the high school assembly. This means participation in planning the program as well as directing it. Students should be included on the central committee that plans the program. They can often give the principal and teachers suggestions that will greatly increase interest in the assembly.

Participation does not mean individual performance only. It may also mean group performance. Students vary in their ability to speak, act, sing, or play before the assembly. It will be impossible to give every student an opportunity for individual expression. However, every opportunity should be used to make the assembly a place for developing student leaders. Moreover, every student during the year can have the opportunity to contribute his individuality in some group effort, such as, in singing, in dramatic activities, in preparation of committee reports, in school yells, or in the Salute to the Flag.

To Broaden and Deepen Student Interests

Educators are beginning to recognize in the assembly an unworked educational "gold mine" with which to achieve their objectives. They are beginning to realize that the old routine assembly program of a hymn, announcements, and a talk was a waste of valuable time. More attention and planning are now being devoted to regular assembly programs in order to make them inspirational as well as educational.

The experiences of the average high school student are limited, and consequently his interests are few in number. The program of the assembly is an ideal medium through which to explore the wide variety of possibilities in the whole expanse of man's activities. For this reason it offers a beautiful opportunity for extending the range of the interests of the student by bringing him into contact with these activities and experiences.

Through the assembly, the student becomes increasingly aware of valuable ways to use his leisure time. As he sees the variety of activities in which the other students participate and find enjoyment, he has a desire to investigate and try them himself. Through the assembly the student comes in contact with the allied arts as they are related to life and to one another. He may never be an ardent producer of music and art, but he may be brought in contact with them as a consumer for the rest of his life. The true aesthetic sense of the student is often awakened for the first time in the school auditorium. Through the assembly the parallel interests of the school and the community can be correlated and integrated. The student becomes aware of the needs of his community and the practical value of his education. The assembly offers a place for showing the relationship between school activities and adult activities and life itself in the community.

To Create Wholesome Attitudes

The virtues and ideals which the school seeks to instill in all students can best be promoted through demonstration in the assembly rather than by moralizing or memorization of platitudes. When a student participates in a presentation or demonstration which embodies such virtues as courtesy, service, promptness, industry, and honesty, he will more readily become interested in these ideals of conduct. The best way to learn something is to teach it to someone else. By participating in the assembly program the student is actually teaching his fellow students. As a result, his own ideas become more clarified and he discovers their value in his effort to convince his friends of the truth of those things that he believes in and does.

Through preparing, organizing, and presenting assembly programs a great opportunity is realized in the development of self-expression. In the new education, great stress is laid upon the power of self-expression to produce individuals who can think clearly and critically. By emphasizing student expression the school assembly can contribute immeasurably toward graduating students with poise, initiative, a spirit of cooperation, enthusiasm, and self-confidence.

In the line with these attitudes, correct audience habits should be emphasized in the assembly. It is as necessary for future citizens to be as courteous in audience situations as in individual relations. Consequently, students should not be forced to march in regimental fashion from the homeroom to the auditorium. They should be permitted to go to the assembly and take their seats in an individual and natural manner as if they were attending the theatre or church. Attendance at the assembly should be required and seats assigned, but any kind of strict regimentation suppresses the voluntary character of the meeting. These procedures are part of the educational value of the assembly itself and patience must be exercised until the students realize the privileges that they possess and the necessity for orderly conduct.

Someone has said that a democracy consists of the privilege and opportunity of doing the thing that one is most capable of doing; and secondly, recognition for doing it. By recognizing publicly worthwhile achievement of whatever nature, students not only acquire this democratic spirit of recognizing merit, but they, themselves, are stimulated to greater achievement. When these experiences are related to the privileges, opportunities, and recognition for achievements in our own democracy, an intelligent patriotism and responsibility toward their own country can be instilled in these future citizens.

Music in the Assembly

Music has a most important contribution to make to the assembly program. Not only should there be some good music in every assembly but several programs each year should also be devoted entirely to music. Music in the assembly means more than the solitary chapel hymn. The program often stands or falls on the success of the music.

This fact places a great responsibility upon the director of music. He must work in close harmony with the principal. By all means the director must be on the central committee which plans and organizes the program. His own planning for musical programs in the assembly must cover at least an entire semester. It is very easy to place the brunt of the responsibility of the assembly program upon the music director; but he should insist upon the cooperation of the principal, the teachers, and the students in stating objectives and planning programs.

Group Singing

Dull programs and dry lectures are often saved by lively music. This does not mean that there will be no serious songs in the assembly, but all the singing must be very much alive and must provide a joyful experience for the students. Enthusiasm must prevail during the general group singing. Most music directors do not realize that this activity can be the most significant offering in the music curriculum. Make your school a singing school!

Many music educators feel that only peppy unison songs should be sung in the assembly. They fear that they will antagonize some students by including songs that are unpalatable. They will give no place to anything that suggests a resemblance to instruction in music. If this attitude directs the activity, there is danger that assembly group singing will become trivial and superficial.

Perhaps the assembly is the most natural situation in which to obtain effective instruction in group singing. This instruction, however, certainly must not be formal drill. It must be incidental and interspersed at frequent intervals. It must not be overdone. Greater joy in singing for all will result in a feeling of more power in expression through song.

Let us have some tuneful legato songs, as well as songs with strong rhythms! Let us not confine the singing to unison songs, but by all means include some part-songs in the repertoire. The extreme range of many melodies makes part-singing easier for changed voices in some songs than unison singing does. Part-singing in the assembly will be more successful if some time is devoted to its preparation in the general music class or the general chorus. A little time spent on the music with these groups will familiarize them with the various parts and they will serve as a nucleus of leaders during the singing by the entire assembly.

Seating Plan

Good part-singing brings up the problem of seating arrangements. Good part-singing is almost impossible unless the students are seated by voice parts. It is up to the music director to convince the principal that such a seating arrangement is not only feasible but necessary for the success of the singing in the assembly. There is no difficulty unless the students are forced to march to the assembly from the home-rooms and sit as a class under the eagle eye of the teacher. It has already been advocated in this chapter that students be permitted to take their seats in the assembly in an informal and individual manner. These seats, however, should be assigned according to the voice part.

At the beginning of the year the music director should announce certain hours during which he will be available in his office to assign seats for assembly. Students who heed this announcement should receive the choice seats in their respective sections. If a person is doubtful of his singing voice, a one-minute test will give enough information to place the student for assembly singing. At the second assembly all students who do not have an assigned seat should be asked to sit in the section of the part they wish to sing. Their names and seat numbers will be checked and added to the seating chart. Several teachers should have charts of various sections of the auditorium and should check attendance. In many schools, teachers also have assigned seats and participate in the singing with the students. No auditorium should be considered too large for such a seating arrangement. If class feeling is rather strong in the school, each class may sit together. Members of glee clubs and choirs who may be called upon occasionally to perform upon the stage should be assigned seats near the aisle, if possible. The following seating plan is suggested for consideration.[3]

[3] Note: This seating plan was adapted from one suggested by M. Emmett Wilson, *Educational Music Magazine,* November-December, 1937, p. 21.

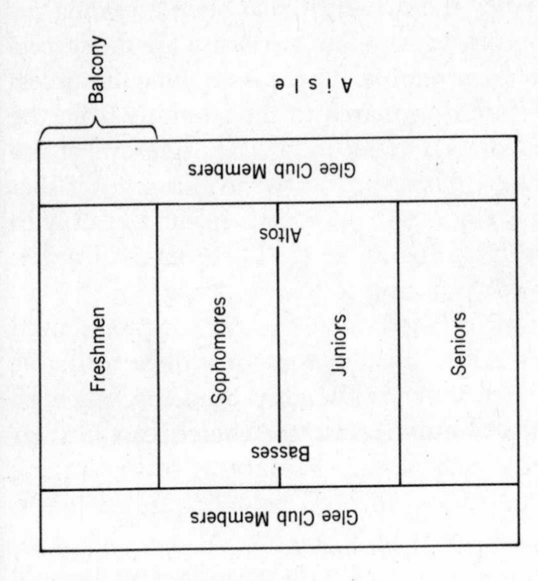
Balcony
Aisle
Glee Club Members
Altos
Freshmen
Sophomores
Juniors
Seniors
Basses
Glee Club Members
Aisle

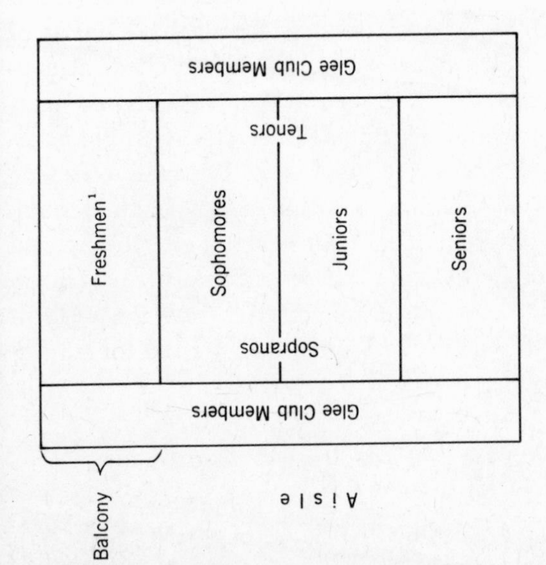
Glee Club Members
Tenors
Freshmen[1]
Sophomores
Juniors
Seniors
Sopranos
Glee Club Members
Aisle
Balcony

Orchestra

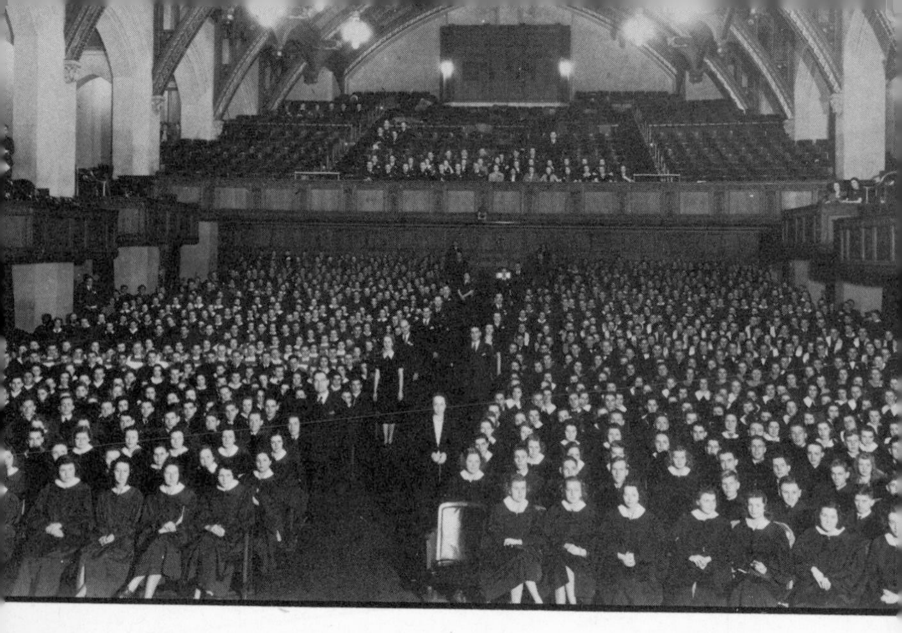

Michigan Choral Festival, North Central Conference. Choirs listened to each other and also sang together.

Pupils of Catholic Elementary and Secondary Schools of St. Louis (Mo.) present a sacred cycle in song and tableau for Music Educators National Conference, 1938.

Selection of Material

The success of assembly singing depends largely upon the type of material available for the teacher to use. Too many schools have limited the choice of songs to those found in the average community song book. Naturally, there is a place for this type of song as well as the better grade of popular songs, but a great opportunity is missed if only these kinds of songs constitute the musical diet of the assembly.

Song books should contain a variety of song material. There should be popular songs, folk songs, community songs, and songs universally accepted as great literature which challenge these young people to increasing musical effort and assure them of increasing musical power. Books should be attractive and durable. Too many schools are content to use "left-over" books for assembly singing when, in truth, the greatest care should be taken to select song books for this activity.

Some schools have used song slides to advantage in assembly singing when the purchase of suitable books has not been possible. However, the practice of some schools in making their own song slides from published books is decidedly unprofessional and, in many cases, it is an actual infringement of the copyright law. At best, song slides have certain musical limitations, the darkened auditorium creates problems for the leader, and the failure to insert the proper slide in the projector at the proper time often causes confusion. Song slides may be used occasionally for certain events but they should never supplant appropriate song books as the most satisfactory material for assembly singing.

The Song Leader

General group singing in the assembly calls for inspirational leadership. It is successful only if the leader is an efficient conductor. The leader may be a man or a woman, but there must be charm of personality combined with enthusiasm and musicianship, or group singing will fall flat. Enthusiasm must not be confused with an unrestrained "rah-rah" spirit. The conductor is a song leader not a "cheer" leader. The leader who devotes all of his efforts to "pepping up" the assembly may find that he has lost all touch with beauty. A certain amount of frivolity and good humor is desirable but, if it is overdone, he will defeat his own purpose. Under inspired and experienced leadership, group singing can be one of the most joyful experiences in the life of the student. Let us remember, however, that interest in group singing does not develop overnight; it must be carefully fostered and developed over a period of years.

Performance by Musical Organizations

Let the orchestra or band play a swinging march as the students enter the auditorium! Use the orchestra as much as possible to accompany the group singing of the entire assembly.

Use the assembly as a place for all musical organizations to perform. An assembly performance is a stimulation to these organizations to do better work. It is a natural motivation for more efficient rehearsals. Moreover, students enjoy hearing these school organizations if they are good. The director must see to it that they are good. Musical organizations need this preliminary experience before performing for the general public.

The various musical organizatons—the orchestra, band, choir, glee clubs, and small ensembles—can make the program more varied and interesting. They can even be called upon to "pinch hit" for a delayed speaker or to help meet unforeseen difficulties in a planned program. Such organizations should carry the burden of the special music assemblies. There is no better way to foster the appreciation of music by the general student than through performance by the school musical organizations.

Radio and Phonograph

There may be many small schools where the radio and phonograph have value for the assembly program. In general this value is limited. If the music instructor cannot play a march on the piano, then a phonograph record may be used. If there are no school musical organizations to give adequate performance for programs on special days, it is permissible to use the phonograph and the radio.

As a rule, however, the phonograph and the radio are not very effective in school assemblies. In the classroom they are of untold value, but a large audience, such as the assembly, becomes restless. The visual aid of seeing the performer is absent. It is more difficult to listen to music without this visual aid. The phonograph might be used to prepare the entire student body for an important school or radio concert. It might be of advantage to call an assembly for a radio program of international significance or an outstanding musical event. But the assembly should be of, for, and by the students.

Outside Groups

Both local and professional artists should be asked to contribute to the success of the assembly program. Such artists are often delighted to perform for school children and enjoy this contact with the school. Also, local choral and instrumental organizations are usually glad to take the time to appear before the high school assembly. Performance by these artists and groups brings the students in closer contact with the musical life of the community, and the organizations in turn become more aware of the musical life of the school. Another interesting feature for musical programs is to work out an exchange with other schools. The choir or band of the visiting school performs for your assembly and you then pay them a return visit with your musical organizations. Keen interest is aroused in comparing organizations from various schools, and the exchange often serves as a stimulation to your own group to do better work.

When inviting artists and groups from the outside to perform for the assembly, the music director should not hesitate to suggest the type and length of numbers to be performed. Few artists realize the musical interests and needs of these young people. Left to their own choice, they may select numbers which vary from a long and difficult sonata to a poor quality of jazz. Singers select technical arias to show off their voice and, sadly enough, succeed only too well. Students like to hear a few remarks by the artist concerning the selection to be performed, but the remarks should be very brief. A few tactful suggestions to the visiting artist or group can make their performances more interesting and a valuable contribution to the assembly program.

Whenever possible, the music director should prepare students for the music that they are to hear by visiting artists. This will be difficult unless the senior high school has a general music course as found in the junior high school. Nevertheless, in the general chorus, glee clubs, instrumental organizations, and even in the assembly, some preparation can be made for intelligent listening. Let the groups sing and listen to some of the songs and pieces that the visiting artist will sing and play. Do not hesitate to take time from regular rehearsals for this purpose, for here you have a chance to teach a discriminating appreciation of music.

Special Musical Programs

Just how many special musical programs there should be in the assembly during the year is a debatable question. The answer will probably depend upon the effectiveness of the general programs and the quality of the musical programs. They should not become a needless burden on the shoulders of the music director. They should occur often enough to hold the interest of students in the assembly programs and to relate music to their other school and life experiences. In addition to the music planned for each assembly, six special assembly programs consisting almost entirely of music do not seem to be too many for one school year. These six programs may cover special days such as Christmas and various patriotic days.

For these programs an occasional miscellaneous concert by the school organizations is in order, but for the most part, the musical programs should have a definite theme as a basis for selecting the numbers and arranging them. A few typical programs, each based on one topic, may be suggestive and helpful.

One very obvious approach is to take the music of one composer and build an interesting program from it.

SCHUBERT

Marche Militaire . . . . Orchestra
Who Is Sylvia? . . . . Assembly
Brief Talk on Schubert's Life and Work. Student
Group of Lieder . . . . . Visiting Artist
Ave Maria (Violin Solo) . . . . . Student
Ballet Music from Rosamunde. . . . . .
Orchestra (with Dancer)
Impromptu in A-flat (Piano Solo) . . Student
Serenade . . . . Assembly
Unfinished Symphony (First Movement) . Orchestra

An excellent approach to music programs for the assembly is to show the relationships between music and other art forms. This type of program stresses cooperation with other departments.

Music and the Dance

Farandole (L'Arlesienne Suite)—Bizet. . Orchestra
Estudiantina (Lacomb) . . . .
General Chorus or Assembly
A Short Talk on the Relation of Music to the Dance . . . . Student

Older Dance Forms:

French Suite (Bach). . . . . . Piano Solo,
(Sarabande, Courante, Gigue). . Dance Group
Minuet in G (Beethoven) . . . Violin Solo,
Danced by Six Couples
Amaryllis (in the style of a Gavotte) . . . .
Girls' Glee Club
Country Dance (Beethoven). . . . Orchestra

Music and the Ballet:

A Short Talk on the History of the Ballet . .
Student
"Pizzicati" from Sylvia Ballet (Delibes) . Orchestra
A Modern Dance Group . . Original Music

Popular Dance Forms:

The Arkansas Traveller. . . . . *Assembly*
(Square Dance)
A Tap Dance (popular song) . . . . .
Piano Accompaniment
The Fox Trot . . . .
Popular Orchestra with Demonstration
The Emperor Waltz (Strauss) . . . . .
Orchestra (Chorus)

Holidays and festival days are ideal for interesting assembly programs. We have used the following program for Christmas with excellent results.

Christmas Music

A Medley of Christmas Carols. . . . Orchestra
O Come, All Ye Faithful . . . . . Assembly
Silent Night . . . . Hummed by the Choir
Reading of the Christmas Story from the Bible. . Student

(This reading is interrupted at appropriate places to insert the following numbers:)

The Shepherd's Song (Bohemian Carol) . . Choir
Pastoral Symphony from *The Messiah* (Handel). Orchestra
The Holy Child (Wilson) . . . . . Choir
Ave Maria (Bach-Gounod) . . . . Soprano Solo with Humming Choir
We Three Kings of Orient Are (Carol) . . . . . Assembly with Incidental Solos
Joyful Noel (Gavaert). . . . . Choir
Joy to the World . . . . Assembly

In these programs more material is included than is probably needed for the usual assembly period. The few representative examples by no means exhaust the many possibilities for interesting programs in the assembly. A suggested additional list of topics would include the following:

Thanksgiving Day (or any other festival day)
The Music of Italy (or any other country)
Beethoven and His Music (or any other composer)
Songs of Many Lands
National Hymns
Music and Literature
Music and the Church
Music and Nature
Music and the Seasons
Music of the Plains
Music of the Plantation
Music of the American Indian

A series of six programs for the year could be based on:

The Message of Music
Rhythm in Music

Instrumental and Vocal Timbre	Melody in Music
Form in Music	Harmony in Music

Many music instructors may doubt the wisdom of these types of suggested programs for assemblies. They will declare that there is not sufficient time to prepare such ambitious programs. Where will they find the talent and how can they include this preparation in their program even if time and talent are available? First of all, the music teacher must realize the educational and musical possibilities of the assembly. Secondly, his musical inheritance must be of such calibre that he has the ability to get musical results with limited rehearsal time. Then, too, such programs are possible only in a school situation where the students have had fine musical training in both the elementary and junior high schools. As you can see, preparation for the high school assembly programs literally begins in the first grade. Such programs must be adapted and adjusted to the technical and musical powers of the organizations in each individual situation. Finally, such programs depend upon the closest cooperation of both the vocal and the instrumental teachers and their ability to make friends with the teachers of other departments.

Conclusion

A word of caution or advice should be given regarding music in the general assembly. Issues have been discussed largely from the point of view of the music educator. Suggested organization and activities for the assemblies have also implied that the music instructor is free to act as he desires in planning the music. This is not always the case. The assembly is legally an administrative unit. Often the principal has very definite ideas about the purpose of the assemblies, the type of programs, and the place of music in them. Most administrators today have a very sympathetic attitude toward the place of high grade music in the assembly. Occasionally, a principal may differ with the teacher of music on the kind of music that should be used. Naturally, the music teacher must be a loyal supporter of the policies of the administration. However, the principal is not usually so adamant that he fails to accept suggestions that will improve assembly programs. By persuasion, by tact, by having definite educational objectives, and by demonstration the music director can convince the principal of the rightful place of music in the assembly and the contribution it will make to life in the school.

Topics for General Discussion

1. Of the objectives of the general assembly suggested in this chapter which one do you consider to be the most important? Give reasons for your choice.
2. Was part-singing a regular feature in the assembly of the high school you attended? From your personal experience do you think that part-singing in the high school assembly is feasible?
3. Have you ever attended a high school assembly during the presentation of a radio music appreciation program? What was the reaction of the students?
4. Formulate several assembly programs around the topics suggested in this chapter as well as some programs based upon original topics of your own.
5. Evaluate at least five song books which seem suitable for high school assembly singing. Select ten songs from these books and present them to a group of students to obtain their reactions.
6. Discuss the advantages and disadvantages of song slides in assembly singing.

THE SYMPHONY

From the poem, MUSIC

Music, they do thee wrong who say thine art
  Is only to enchant the sense.
For every mind motion of the heart,
  And every passion too intense
To bear the chain of the imperfect word,
  And every tremulous longing, stirred
By spirit winds that come we know not whence
  And go we know not where
  And every inarticulate prayer
Beating about the depths of pain or bliss,
  Like some bewildered bird
That seeks its nest but knows not where it is,
And every dream that haunts, with dim delight,
The drowsy hour between the day and night,
The wakeful hour between the night and day,—
  Imprisoned, waits for thee,
  Impatient, yearns for thee,
The queen who comes to set the captive free!
Thou lendest wings to grief to fly away,
And wings to joy to reach a heavenly height;
And every dumb desire that storms within the breast
Thou leadest forth to sob or sing itself to rest.

HENRY VAN DYKE

Chapter 5

PUBLIC PERFORMANCE

In addition to the appearance of the musical organizations in the assembly programs throughout the whole of school life, there should be opportunities for these organizations to appear before the general public. Reasons for these performances must be well founded in definite educational purposes and objectives or they may become a burden which will lessen their value.

Values in Public Performance

Integration

The public performance tends to unify the various phases of the music department as well as to enlist the cooperation of the entire school. In presenting their groups to the general public the choral and the instrumental instructors must resolve their differences and combine all forces for a successful performance. This attitude is reflected in the work of the students who discover more fully for themselves the effectiveness of the different media for making music. A public concert combines and includes solo and group performance in playing instruments and singing. The composition classes can make contributions. Discriminative listening can be encouraged through the performance itself, through the preparation of numbers, and through the use of the same materials in general music classes. All these musical activities not only foster a deeper appreciation but also make music a more meaningful part of life.

Motivation

Students in the musical organizations should be introduced to a wide variety of compositions. Lest acquaintance with all these compositions become superficial and develop a careless attitude on the part of students, a few numbers should be practised with care for detail until they can be performed in as perfect a style as the ability of the group permits. Such performance calls for long, sustained practice on individual compositions. Students grow restless during such rehearsals unless there is a concert, a contest, or an operetta in the offing. Only then will they understand the teacher's careful attention to detail and insistence upon perfection. During such preparations the students are more willing to strive for exact rhythm, phrase nuance, uniform bowing, tone quality, dynamic shadings, and clear diction.

After the performance many students will return to careless habits and attitudes toward musical study. However, some students will be made aware of the patience and care necessary in artistic effort. All of them will retain at least some of the things that they learned about music in the preparation for the concert. A number of these preparations will develop to varying degrees a desirable attitude of careful artistic effort in individual as well as group study, and students will become dissatisfied with slovenly performance for an audience of their immediate friends, or even for themselves. Standards in performance will gradually be raised for the school and for the individuals. In this way the public performance engenders careful discrimination in listening and contributes to the goal of deeper appreciation.

Social Values

The sociological significance of music in the schools is made apparent through the public performance. First of all, provision is made for the social act that accompanies all performances of music; namely, the expression of individuals or groups to other individuals or groups through the medium of tone. There must be the performer, even though mechanical, and the audience, even though it is the performer himself, or there is no music. In other words, *music must be performed to exist.* There is usually a friendly audience for the high school performance and music serves as a means of bringing the performers and the audience into closer relationships. In this way the public performance fosters a closer affinity between the school and the community.

In the second place, most of the performing at school musical functions is done by small and large groups of students. Preparation for these performances requires the wholehearted cooperation of all the participants. Although individual artistic effort is encouraged and rewarded, the perfect musical ensemble is the result of collective effort. *Education toward a democratic spirit brings forth fruit in the music ensemble as it prepares for public performance.*

Advertising and Finance

It is not possible to discuss public performance in the high school merely in terms of the preceding educational values. The practical values of advertising the school or teacher and raising money are so often the prime objectives that they must be given some consideration.

It is perfectly legitimate and commendable to acquaint the public with the work of the music department. The public should have a chance to hear the orchestra, the band, the chorus, the choir, and small ensembles on special occasions. Opportunity should also be provided for the public to observe the general class work and regular rehearsals as well as demonstration classes and rehearsals for parents' nights. On the other hand, advertising the music department can become a harmful practice if the students are exploited solely for the personal aggrandizement of the teacher, or if such demands are made upon their time and energy that practically all educational values are impaired.

During economic depressions and budget cuts the board of education often turns its thoughts toward reducing the expenses of specialized activities, including music. It is the duty of the music director to make music such a vital part of school and community life that it becomes an indispensable part of the curriculum, as it rightly deserves to be. Judicious presentation of the music department will bring this realization to the board of education, the administration, and the public.

By getting results and bringing evidence of these results to the public eye and to the attention of the administration, the music director is enabled to secure money for better materials and equipment for his department. Yet, when all these things are done, money is often not available to purchase new music, that new instrument, or those new uniforms. Theoretically, all equipment should be purchased through appropriation from the regular school funds. However, when an appropriation is impossible, a concert or an operetta to raise money for a worthy purpose is often a challenge and a salutary project for the students in the music department. As a rule all school concerts should be free, but digression from this rule may be valid on such special occasions.

Types of Public Performance

General Concerts

The largest number of public performances in the high school should be concerts which demonstrate the quality of work being done by musical organizations. All the purposes of public performances which have been discusssed are embodied in this type of concert. Preparation for such a concert is synonymous with the work done in most musical classes and activities.

The general concert should be a diversified program and should utilize more than one organization. However, it is not necessary for every organization to perform at every concert. We have seen school concerts that resembled track meets rather than musical programs, so intent was the instructor upon providing a variety of entertainment. Feature one organization at each concert and support this group with one other large group, small ensembles, and solos. This plan avoids too many delays in the shifting of groups of performers and paraphernalia, and eliminates programs of undue length. One hour of music, including the necessary pauses between numbers, with added allowance for changing the stage, is usually ample time for a school concert. *Plan the time of your program and stick to it!*

Preparation for these concerts requires definite planning. It is not sufficient to "throw a few numbers together." If they are successful, nearly all the techniques described in this book will be involved. *It is crucial that the standards of performance in these concerts be high.* The higher calibre of school concerts in the past twenty years has been a strong impetus for the growth of school music in this country.

The program should be planned to blend both cultural

and entertainment values. The director must provide for contrast between numbers in mood, style, and key. However, the aesthetic principle of unity in variety functions in the building of artistic programs. It may be interesting to study several programs that have been used in high schools. The first one is a varied program featuring the music of two composers, Mozart and Brahms. Interesting program notes were written by students.

PROGRAM

MUSIC OF WOLFGANG MOZART (1756-1791)

Eine Kleine Nacht Musik . . . String Orchestra
  Allegro
  Romanzi
  Menuetto
  Rondo
Sonata in D Major . . . . . . Two Pianos
  Allegro con spirito
  Andante
  Allegro molto
Quartet in D Minor . . . . . String Quartet
  Allegro Moderato

Intermission

MUSIC OF JOHANNES BRAHMS (1833-1897)

Song from Shakespeare's Twelfth Night
Song from Ossian's Fingal — Girls' Glee Club, Accompaniment Harp and two French Horns
Intermezzo, opus 118 #1
Intermezzo, opus 118 #2 — Piano Solo
Liebeslieder, opus 52 . . . . . School Choir
(Waltz songs with two piano accompaniment)

The following program of American Choral Music features one outstanding organization and uses incidental

The Bohemian Girl, *East Orange, New Jersey.*
H.M.S. Pinafore, *Greenwich, Connecticut.*

solos to add interest and variety. It is a panoramic view showing the historical development of the choral music of this country. The music falls naturally into five groups:

1. Music of the Colonial Period which includes two numbers popular during the Revolutionary War as well as a song by Francis Hopkinson, usually considered the first American Composer.

2. Music of the Civil War Period which includes two war songs of the North and South as well as two typical love songs of the day.

3. The group of folk songs does not represent an historical development but it is an important phase of our choral music.

4. A group of popular songs is necessary to make this type of program complete. This one introduced an old song of the nineties, a barber-shop quartet, and a current dance song of merit.

5. The last group is representative of the work written by one of our contemporary American composers.

A PROGRAM
OF
AMERICAN CHORAL MUSIC
BY THE
A CAPPELLA CHOIR

I. Music of the Colonial Period

Chester Hymn . . . William Billings
My Love Is Gone to Sea (Treble Voices) . Francis Hopkinson
Yankee Doodle (Incidental Solos) . . . . . . Traditional

II. Music of the Civil War Period

Battle Hymn of the Republic (Incidental Solos) . . . Traditional
Lilly Dale (Choir with Tenor Solo) . . . . . H. S. Thompson

Come Where My Love Lies Dreaming
(Small Ensemble) . . Stephen Foster
Dixie (Choir with Incidental Solos, Audience)

III. Folk Songs

Were You There . Negro Spiritual, Arranged by Burleigh

I Couldn't Hear Nobody Pray . . . . . Negro Spiritual

Red River Valley
Pretty Little Miss (Small Ensembles) . . . . Mountain Tunes, Arranged by Horton

Ten Miles Away from Home
(Choir with Baritone Solo) . . . Old Oklahoma Song, Arranged by Harper

IV. Popular Songs

Frankie and Johnnie . American Ballad, Arranged by Clokey

Medley of Old Songs (Barbershop Male Quartet) . .Improvisation

Star Dust (Choir with Soprano Solo) . . . . . H. Carmichael

V. Americana (for mixed chorus) . . . . Randall Thompson

1. May Every Tongue
2. The Staff Necromancer
3. The Sublime Process of Law Enforcement
4. Loveli-Lines

Very often the school is asked to give a concert in the church. The music director must be careful not to show partiality among the churches, regardless of his own affiliation. If he permits his groups to appear in one church, he must be willing for them to perform for another. The following program was used in one church service.

A Service of Music

Prelude
  Trio in G (First Movement) . . . Haydn
    (String Trio)
Hymn
  Day Is Dying in the West . . . Lathbury
Prayer
Choir
  Cherubic Hymn . . . . . . Bortniansky
  Hospodi Pomilui . . . . . . Lvovsky
Offertory Solo
  Romance . . . . Wieniawski
    (Violin Solo)
Treble Chorus
  Lift Thine Eyes (from "Elijah") . Mendelssohn
String Quartet
  Andante Cantabile . . . Tschaikowsky
Short Talk: Music and Worship
School Choir
  Gallia (Cantata with soprano soloist) . Gounod
Benediction

The following program features the instrumental organizations. The a cappella choir, which supported the band and orchestra, performed on risers in front of the platform so that no time was lost in setting the stage.

The program is an ambitious one which only highly developed ensembles should attempt.[1] Taking into consideration this fact it is gratifying to see high schools giving creditable performances of such musical masterpieces.

Program
by the
High School Symphony Orchestra and Band
supported by the
High School A Cappella Choir

[1] Note: This program was presented by the Hempstead High School, Hempstead, L. I.

PART I—HIGH SCHOOL SYMPHONY ORCHESTRA

The Star-Spangled Banner
Symphony No. 4 . . . Peter I. Tschaikowsky
Andante sostenuto: moderato con anima in movimento di valse
Scherzo (Pizzicato ostinato) .
Finale; Allegro con fuoco
Concerto for Oboe and String Orchestra (On themes of Pergolesi) . . . John Barbirolli
Oboe Soloist (Professional)

PART II—HIGH SCHOOL A CAPPELLA CHOIR

Alleluia . . . . . . Randall Thompson
Out of the Silence . . . . . Cyril Jenkins
The Lord's Prayer (Organ Accompaniment) . . . . . . Mallotte-Deis

PART III—HIGH SCHOOL SYMPHONIC BAND

Pictures At An Exhibition . Modeste Moussorgsky
A Hut on Fowl's Legs
The Great Gate of Kiev
Concerto for Solo Clarinet and Band . . . . Carl Maria von Weber
Clarinet Soloist (Student)
The Flight of the Bumble Bee . . . . . Nicholas Rimsky-Korsakov

PART IV— HIGH SCHOOL A CAPPELLA CHOIR AND SYMPHONIC BAND

Tone Poem: America . . Ernest W. Williams

Very often schools are requested to give programs for civic clubs. In order for these programs to be suitable for the occasion they are usually more flexible and in a lighter vein. They offer an opportunity for the teacher to feature the small ensembles. The following program of approximately thirty minutes' duration was interspersed throughout a special luncheon of a civic club.

PROGRAM

1. In Festive Mood . . . . . Carl Busch
   Small Brass Ensemble
2. Beautiful Dreamer . . . . Stephen Foster
   Madam, I Have Come A-Courtin' . . . . .
   Kentucky Mountain Song
   Small Choral Ensemble
3. Adoration . . . . . . Felix Borowski
   Violin Solo
4. The Erie Canal . . . . American Folk Song
   Good-bye Ol' Paint . . . . Cowboy Song
   The Band . . . . Fishburn
   Boys' Glee Club

Musicales

In addition to the general evening concerts which feature the large musical organizations with occasional soloists, many schools are introducing afternoon musicales which stress solo performance. These musicales serve as an outlet for talented students in the voice and instrumental classes as well as for those students who are studying privately with outside teachers. Such recitals are usually very popular wherever they have been introduced, because students like to see their friends and fellow-students perform as soloists. The musicales provide opportunity for young soloists to develop poise and artistry. The small choral and instrumental ensembles are especially suited for this more intimate type of concert. Finally, an appreciative audience is being created which can listen to recital music in different fields with more intelligence and discrimination. Every teacher should carefully consider the possibilities of afternoon musicales to enrich the music program.

The Operetta and Musical Play

Recently there has been much agitation against the school operetta, especially in high schools. Too often the music instructor has been asked to produce a school operetta for the purpose of raising money to purchase musical equipment and even suits for the football team. Too often the operetta has sapped the energy of the music instructor until little vitality remained for more constructive duties and obligations. Too often the operetta has disrupted all other musical activities far beyond its prerogative as an educational and musical experience.

It is time to re-evaluate the use of the operetta in the school in the light of these caustic criticisms. It has been pointed out that teachers of music are continually being called upon to provide entertainment for the school and the public. The operetta provides an ideal vehicle for these entertainments. People love a good show. They will even pay money for such entertainment, and the music and physical education departments always need more money. To please the townspeople operettas are often selected for their amusement value with little thought for the literary and musical content.

Lack of superior material is the prime argument used by music educators who disparage the use of operettas in the school. The only answer to this argument is to create a demand for operettas which have educational as well as entertainment value. All music educators as well as the public endorse the Gilbert and Sullivan operettas. Some excellent abridged editions have been published which are especially suited for small high schools. Larger schools should produce the originals. However, Gilbert and Sullivan operettas cannot go on forever. Even these operettas vary in their effectiveness.

One way to cope with this limited supply of superior operettas is to write your own. Attractive musical plays have been created by students in high schools as well as in elementary schools. These musical plays are often constructed around some central theme with music selected from various sources. They are often built around the music and life of one composer. At times the libretto is adapted from some dramatic story or poem, and music is selected and composed which will create an attractive operetta. Occasionally both the libretto and the music are original. Such musical plays are often superior to certain operettas on the market. They afford a double motivation since they include all the educational and social values found in the presentation of an operetta, plus the joy of creating something original.[2]

Another factor to be considered in the production of operettas is the amount of time and energy that this activity demands from the music department. Undoubtedly, this factor is the latent reason for much adverse criticism of the operetta by the music instructor. This evil can be reduced through better organization. The operetta should not be the project of one department; it should have the participation of many departments. In many schools throughout the country, the teachers of dramatics, household, industrial, and fine arts, the dance, and English cooperate and contribute an equal share to the success of the production. On the program the name of the music director should not stand out in bold relief over the names of the other teachers. *The operetta is for the students, not for the glorification of the teachers.* The production should be organized to utilize student initiative and participation

[2] Note: The writing of musical plays will be more fully discussed in the section on experiences in composing music.

in all the details. These include costumes, properties, scenery, staging, advertising, and criticism. Thought and attention to this preliminary planning will lighten the labors of the music teacher to the degree that even he may share in the satisfaction that the students enjoy in the production of the operetta.

Many music educators decry the operetta for its effect upon the balance of the music program. One or two weeks are used for preliminary preparation, six or seven weeks for rehearsals, and one or two weeks for recovery. However, should we not capitalize on, rather than disparage, an activity in which there is the possibility of vitalizing the entire musical program, of motivating the cooperation and interest of the entire school, and of serving as a basis to integrate and show the relationship in allied arts?

First of all, the entire production of an operetta need not cover a period of more than five or six weeks, an appropriate time allotment for a valuable unit of work. Efficient organization and direction eliminates tedious rehearsals. In the second place, the operetta can be made an educational adventure. If the libretto has literary value, it should be used in the English classes. The music should be of such quality that it will serve as a musical treat in chorus and choir rehearsals and in the voice class. Let many people learn the solos! Sing them in unison with various groups. The dramatic situations should challenge the histrionic ability of the students. The staging should afford the various departments a chance to study and experiment in the art of the theatre. Unless the operetta or musical play has the qualities to sanction this participation and integration of effort, it should be replaced by other activities.

Opera

On account of the limited material of good quality in the field of operetta, many music teachers have turned to the opera. With superior translations and carefully abridged editions that do not destroy the musical value of the work, the field of the opera may be seriously considered by the music educator who has under his direction the resources for adequate production of standard works. The same criticisms exist in the use of the opera as in the production of the operetta except for the musical value. In this field, however, we are confronted with a dearth of suitable material. The average opera makes too great a demand upon the resources and talents of high school students. Translations, for the most part, are atrocious. Moreover, the opera libretto is not always a significant literary work. Then, too, in the production of the opera, high school students suffer in comparison with professionals. We question the advisability of using adult soloists for the production of standard operas in high schools. Too much outside rehearsal time is required of the students. It ceases to be their production and they lose their initial interest. We repeat that as soon as we have abridged editions of standard operas that retain their musical value and possess superior translations, the opera as a project in the high school is feasible and commendable. Such projects would stimulate the introduction of local opera companies throughout the country.

Pageant

The musical play in an expanded form becomes a pageant. Even more than the operetta, the pageant enlists the cooperative effort of the entire school. It lends itself to the creative expression of large numbers of individuals.

It can often serve as a demonstration and culmination of the musical work of an entire year.

Very often the pageant may present historical events which have local significance and the entire community becomes keenly interested and cooperates with the school in every way possible to make the production successful. Teachers should be ever alert for pageant material which possesses local flavor.

Since the pageants usually develop around themes of historical, religious, and social significance, they offer superb opportunities for creative work and integration with other subjects. The social science department may assist in selecting various tableaux, the art department may plan the scenic effects, the home economics department may design and make the costumes, students in the English department may write original dialogues, and the students in the music department gain invaluable experience through research to find significant music appropriate to the theme. Furthermore the pageant often offers opportunities for composing original music. The pageant imposes puzzling problems of organization upon the music teacher. Outdoor pageants present their own peculiar musical difficulties. The problem of timing itself is no simple matter. The entire production must "click." Under the guidance of a teacher who has the ability to organize and execute a pageant, it may become a genuine educational and musical experience for school and community.

Cantata

The cantata has many of the attractive features of the operetta without its drawbacks. There is a wider range of selections in the field of the cantata which are based upon texts that are interesting and have high literary merit. The music is often superior to the music of the operetta. The cantata also provides opportunities for solos, which, however, may be sung to good advantage in unison by members of the group. Preparation for the cantata may take more of the music instructor's time, but this preparation may easily be included in the regular musical activities. Unless the cantata develops into some form of pageantry, the organization necessary for its production is much simpler than that needed for the production of an operetta. Responsibility for the success of the cantata rests largely upon the music department, while the operetta involves several departments, and even the entire school. Moreover, there is suitable material in the field of the cantata for special days and various seasons which will relate to any group of activities integrated around unified interests in some special occasion.

However, the superior virtues of the cantata embrace its limitations. It fails to enlist the cooperation of other departments of the school and does not involve participation and integration of the entire school in a common project to the same degree that the operetta does. It does not utilize the arts allied to music or bring to light the relationships between them. It fails to capitalize on the high school student's love for dramatic situations and the values accruing from participation in these situations. The cantata is not as exciting to the student as the operetta is. It fails to arouse the same initial interest in the project.

To offset these remarks it can be pointed out that the interest in the cantata does not wane as quickly as the interest in the operetta does. The initial interest in the cantata may not be as intense, but it is more steadfast. Since the music of the cantata is usually superior to that of the operetta, the singing of the cantata is more often a lasting musical experience. Advocates of the operetta can easily cite the Gilbert and Sullivan operettas to refute this statement, but we must remember that there are only a few Gilbert and Sullivan operettas.

Oratorio

The use of the oratorio in the high school maintains the same relationship to the opera as the cantata does to the operetta. Many of the master composers have devoted their most serious efforts to the oratorio as a means of musical expression. It is true that most of the standard oratorios are beyond the vocal resources of the average high school. However, by judicious cutting and abridging, many of these oratorios can be made available and can still be most effective when sung by a high school chorus. The same criticism as indicated in the discussion of the opera against using adult soloists does not apply to the oratorio. Special soloists for the oratorio is traditional procedure. Long and tedious rehearsals are not required of the chorus for the sake of the soloists. Chorus and soloists can rehearse separately. As a result, through the singing of expert soloists the performance is often as keen a musical experience for the chorus as for the audience.[3]

Students like the challenge of singing some of the choruses from the great oratorios. They like to "dig in" to something solid. However, do not push these young voices beyond their capacity. Do not produce oratorios just to test the power of high school students. They have proved their ability to give adequate performance of them under direction. *If you do not thoroughly understand young voices and choral singing, curb your ambitions and select less pretentious material.* If you do understand the limitations of the voices of these young singers and you

[3] Note: The use of the oratorio in the high school will be further discussed under the General Chorus in Chapter VI.

have the resources at your command, gently lead them to experience some of the glories of choral literature found in the oratorio.

Broadcasting

With the advent of the Music and American Youth programs sponsored by the Music Educators National Conference, the field of radio performance for high school organizations has rapidly expanded. It affords an excellent opportunity for acquainting the public with the standard of work being done in the school. Where the school concert reaches a few hundred people, the broadcast may reach thousands or even millions. However, if the public is to be properly impressed, it was found from the beginning that these broadcasts must be of very high calibre.

The same observation is true for all school broadcasts of music organizations. The school concert audience is quite different from the radio audience. The former usually has a personal interest in the performers which colors judgment. The radio audience listens primarily to be entertained and the personal interest is often lacking. Also, the enjoyment by a member of the school audience is not confined to what he hears alone. He is affected by the "bright and shining" faces of the eager students trying to please. The radio listener does not have this visual aid and judges a performance by what he hears, and compares it to the work of professionals. Finally, the school audience is sympathetic and, if the performer and conductor are enthusiastic, the listeners are often impervious to poor intonation, uneven attacks, and inadequate interpretation. On the other hand, the microphone is merciless. It is an ultrasensitive ear which records what it hears accurately and objectively. Poor intonation, thin and colorless tone quality, "muddy" and unrhythmical performance seem actually to be intensified. Undoubtedly, there should be radio continuity which prepares the listener with a description of high school broadcasts but it should not be used as an apology for poor performance. We repeat that these broadcasts must be of very high standard if they are to be accepted by the public.

Preparation

Several of the problems attached to broadcasting can be eliminated if they are considered during the period of preparation. First of all, if the rehearsal room is treated acoustically and reverberation is eliminated, sounds will resemble more closely those heard in a broadcast studio. Secondly, the conductor must learn to listen as objectively as possible. Since the microphone is only one ear instead of two, more accurate judgment may be obtained if he will shut his eyes and listen to the rehearsal occasionally with one ear stopped tightly. Another device to eliminate visual aid in hearing is to turn the back to the performing group and cup the hands behind the ears. If conductors do this they will hear more accurately the effects as they will sound over the air.

A third consideration in preparing for a successful radio appearance is deliberately emphasizing those performance factors which are vital to good broadcasting. The most marked of these is pitch discrepancy. The good teacher will ever be on the alert for poor intonation, but he must be doubly so for broadcasts. Likewise, extra care must be devoted to precision in attacks and releases of tone, for they contribute to rhythmical clarity which is so essential in radio performance. Also, crescendos and dimuendos should not be too sudden, and dynamic extremes should

[4] J. Leon Ruddick, "Microphone Technique for Instrumental Groups," Music Educators Nat'l Conference, *Yearbook 1939-40*. Chicago, Illinois, pp. 294-297.

be limited. If the volume of tone exceeds a certain point, it will be necessary for the radio engineer to turn the volume control down to avoid "microphone rush," and vice-versa, if it becomes too soft, he will turn the control up or otherwise the music may not be heard at all. When the engineer is forced to do this, the performance is uneven and rough. To obtain a smooth performance the dynamics must be retained within the limits where the engineer can "let it ride," or in other words not interfere with the dynamics through the manipulation of volume controls. The newer and improved microphones of today provide for a sufficiently wide range of dynamics to assure artistic interpretation. Many of these factors of musical performance can be checked through the use of recording equipment and sound mirrors as discussed in Chapter XI.

On the Air

For the broadcast itself, the music teacher must assume certain responsibilities and, in turn, be willing to trust the radio engineer and producer with certain details. "One of the most essential functions in the preparation of a musical broadcast is the clearance of musical numbers by the copyright staff of the network. Music in the public domain may be broadcast freely, but it often takes an expert to determine whether a given composition is or is not in public domain. Music published more than fifty-six years ago is unprotected by copyright in the United States, but a later arrangement of it may be protected, and that arrangement may not be broadcast except by agreement with the copyright owner. The broadcaster is interested, therefore, not only in the compositions to be presented in any program, but also in the editions to be used. The National Broadcasting Company pays hundreds of thousands of dollars each year for the privilege of broadcasting copyrighted music. If its copyright staff were not eternally vigilant, it might pay millions in damages for infringement of rights. The copyright division works in close cooperation with the legal department, and the two together take every precaution to prevent the broadcasting of a single measure of protected music for which no license has been granted."[5]

We have included this quotation to indicate the importance for the teacher to send in plenty of time the information necessary for the clearance of all numbers to be broadcasted. This information includes name of composition, composer, arranger, and publisher. If a number is being performed from manuscript, a written statement must be secured from the composer granting permission for broadcasting. If it is an arrangement, proof must be provided that the words and melody are in public domain. Much delay and misunderstanding can be avoided if the teacher will cooperate with the broadcasters in this matter.

The musical numbers of the program must be *carefully timed* by the teacher, saving an adequate amount of time for the announcements. The teacher should provide ample information from which the broadcaster can write suitable continuity. This serves as another reason for submitting programs early, for no continuity can be written until the program has been received at the station and approved. In addition to continuity writers, radio stations employ engineers, who take care of the technical phases of the broadcast, and also, production managers who supervise the presentation of performances before the microphone, adjust the balance of voices and instruments, work with the engineer in the placement of the microphone, and in general, do everything in their power to assure a smooth

[5] Ernest La Prade, "The Broadcaster and Music Education," Music Educators Nat'l Conference, *Yearbook 1938*. Chicago, Illinois, p. 212.

Joplin (Mo.) High School Orchestra. John Adams High School Orchestra (Cleveland) rehearsing in Studio of WHK for national radio network through "Music and American Youth" broadcasts.

performance. Ordinarily radio engineers and directors are competent and they can be relied upon to put the program on the air to its best advantage, but they cannot be expected to make it better than it is. The teacher's safest procedure is to adhere carefully to the instructions of the director.

One of the most intricate problems in broadcasting large music groups is the placement of the microphone.[6] This is really a function of the radio engineer and program director and the teacher must naturally accept their suggestions. A few observations may be appropriate here which will give some basic reasons for the accepted practices. First of all, radio is monaural—the microphone is like one ear—not binaural and therefore, it does not have aural perspective. The microphone reports what a very sensitive ear would hear at a given spot in the studio or auditorium. It might appear that a number of microphones would improve reception, but engineers are almost unanimous in saying that under most conditions one microphone is better. The microphone must be placed at a distance and height where it will receive the composite tone most favorably without admitting room reverberation. This statement is true regardless of the type of microphone. Too much shifting of orchestra players often confuses them more than it aids in securing better broadcasting. However, it is usually advisable to move the brass from directly in front of the microphone. As a rule, a large choir will sound better if they stand in the following arrangement. Do not have the piano directly between the singers and the microphone. Small groups of singers and players will blend and balance better if they do not sing or play full voice. Large choirs should sing full voice but as suggested previously, they should be careful of dynamic extremes.

[6] Ernest La Prade, "Problems in Microphone Placement," Music Educators Nat'l Conference, *Yearbook 1938*. Chicago, Illinois, pp. 226-231.

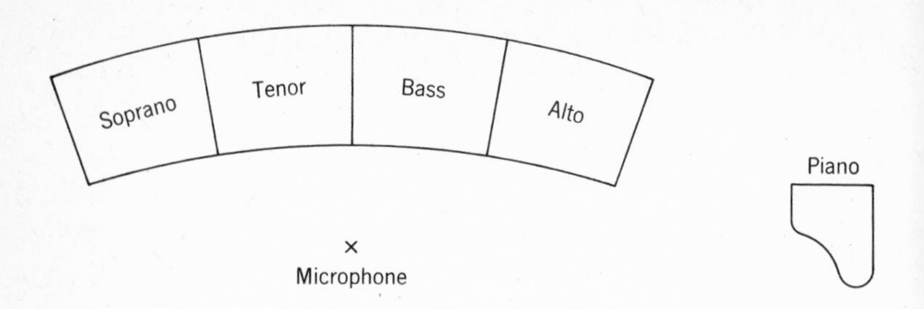

These few remarks are only suggestions and the advisable procedure is for the teacher to have high school performing groups in the studio one hour before broadcasting time to work out with the engineer and director problems which will assure the most favorable reception.

Value

Broadcasts may serve as a real educational force if they help to fulfill the aims of the music curriculum as a whole.[7] They serve as a motivation for students to extend their efforts toward superior performance. They reach out into the community and bring the activities of the school into the home. Radio programs should be truly representative of school life and activity, and they should include a large per cent of the student body as well as a few selected soloists. Preparation for these broadcasts should be a part of the regular activities and not impair other work in music.

Contests and Festivals

Much time and many words have been devoted to the discussion of competition in education. The proponents of contests in general point out the fact that this is a competitive world and that contests prepare students for re-

[7] Will Earhart, "Preparation for a Broadcast an Educational Force," Music Educators National Conference, *Yearbook 1938*. Chicago, Illinois, pp. 217-220.

ality. Competition is one of the strongest human drives and it stimulates activity and progress in any field of endeavor. Competition makes one aware of his own weakness and strength in comparison with the weaknesses and strengths of others. It is desirable as long as the object is a worthy one.

Opponents refute these arguments by pointing out that the world needs cooperation, not competition. Cooperation will not be fostered through contests. Contests overstimulate students until there is a serious mental and nervous strain which offsets the impetus to do better work. Competition leads a student to regard his own interests as opposed to group interests and it teaches him to regard ability to excel over another as success and the aim of life.

The reader undoubtedly has quite definite opinions about the relative value of these arguments. The opinions of most instructors grow out of practical experience. Since both harm and good can result from contests, the nature of the experience determines the basis of opinion.

Let us examine the music contests in this country and endeavor to evaluate them. There is no doubt that the impetus of the contest has been an important factor in the phenomenal growth of music in our schools. It has had a decided effect upon raising the standards of music for the high school. A better quality of performance has resulted from the incentive for intense and sustained preparation. In addition, the use of a better type of material selected by a special committee, has resulted in the wide adoption of contest material for regular class work. Moreover, contests have encouraged an interest in music by promoting concerts in which representatives in many high schools may join and where large numbers of students have the opportunity to hear other organizations perform music of outstanding worth which they have studied. As a vital factor in musical progress surely these values offset the false delusions, the nervous strains, and the emphasis on the competitive spirit. However, as long as these evils exist, the positive values of the contest are questionable. Has anything been done to lessen the attendant evils? To answer this question let us examine the music contest of the past with the more modern type of competitive music festival.

To picture the early contests we must imagine a school orchestra or glee club introduced in the early fall to the required numbers that must be performed at the contest to be held late in the following spring. Rehearsal after rehearsal, hour after hour is spent on perfecting this one number. There is perhaps a little respite at Christmas time and then a return to the contest music. The number is finally prepared—but at what costs to a rich and varied experience in music, to an attitude of deep devotion for music. The long awaited day approaches. Our school is sent to the contest with instructions to "bring home the bacon."

The day of the contest is spent in an occasional "brushing up" rehearsal. Individual school groups remain huddled together. They observe each other with challenging eyes. Few friends are made with members of other groups; few discussions are heard about the music in other schools.

The auspicious moment arrives. After a last minute "pep" talk our glee club marches on, sings, waits for a rippling applause from a scattered audience, and marches off. After several hours of suspense our group hears the fatal message: we lost to Abbeyville by .2 of a point. Scoring by the judges was on a grading scale of 100 points, and groups were rated one, two, or three on this scale. There was often only one judge, and it is not far from the truth to say that every organization except the winning one agreed that he was not qualified. Such grading and rating were sure to cause unfair judgment and intense dissatisfaction. Little or no constructive criticisms were given to teachers and their groups. Students had some opportunity to hear the work of other groups, but there was no event to climax the entire contest, such as a joint concert to give the contestants one real musical experience.

The auspicious moment has become a disastrous event. Dejected groups and their teacher return home with a suitcase full of excuses. "We had to sing too early in the morning." "We had no time to tune up." "We had to stand and wait two hours before our turn to sing because the contest was poorly organized." Occasionally the teacher was bitterly criticized; sometimes he even lost his job; more often the matter was passed over with a "better luck next time." But after all, was the musical value in adequately preparing one or two numbers after long, arduous practice, and the educational value in the contest itself worth this bitter disappointment? Are such keen disappointments necessary to prepare one for life?

How about the winners? Did the winning group of Abbeyville gain a true evaluation of themselves? Did not this kind of winning give the student a false conception of his true musical power? Did the winners become more deeply interested in music as a result of the contest, or were they primarily concerned with just defeating their opponents? Answers to these questions would cover as wide a scale of varied opinion as there were contests and individual schools participating in them.

From this black picture which exaggerates an extreme position for the sake of contrast, let us turn to the more recent development of the music contest—the competitive festival. A list of contest music is selected by an expert committee from various fields of competition. These lists include a choice of several compositions for a required number, a longer list of compositions from which an optional number may be selected. These lists are usually not released until late in the first semester. Organized choral and instrumental clinics give the teachers an opportunity to study these compositions with outstanding conductors in their respective fields. Even with this late release teachers are encouraged to postpone intensive rehearsals on the required numbers until a few weeks before the festival in order that the other phases of the musical program may not be disrupted.

The various groups depart for the competition festival, determined to do their best. But it has ceased to be a determination to defeat an opponent. Music education in this country will always be indebted to the late Frank A. Beach for his introduction of a new rating system. This rating plan definitely classifies each competitor as highly superior, superior, excellent, good, average, or below average in terms of individual performance without comparative judgment with other competitors. This decidedly superior rating system has done much to stimulate the ambition for higher artistic standards year after year. Each group is now competing with itself and it can evaluate itself in terms of artistic standards rather than in terms of comparative standards. As a result of painful experience the competitive festival has an organization superior to the older contest and schedules are more closely observed. Competent adjudicators are the rule rather than the exception. They are nearly always three in number. They have had an opportunity to study diligently the numbers to be performed and they are supplied with adjudicator comment sheets which encourage detailed constructive criticisms. These same adjudicators conduct clinics for the teachers which offer valuable opportunity for discussion and criticism of various phases of performance, such as tone, technical aspects, and interpretation of the music. These clinics can be of untold value to the young instructors who participate in them.

As a climax to the festival, members of groups from different high schools join forces to give a final concert for the general public. These combined groups sing and play masterpieces of music literature under the direction of well-known conductors. These numbers are included in the contest lists sent out by the committee and they have been prepared in advance by individual groups. The outstanding soloists of the week have a chance to display their powers at this general concert. During the rehearsals of numbers for this concert, competition is submerged in a cooperative artistic project. New friends are made. The joy of making music on this memorable occasion deeply affects many students' attitude toward the need for music in their lives. Many students and teachers return home disappointed with their ratings, but resolved to increase their standing the next year. The festival has given them a beautiful experience with music and an incentive toward reaching higher artistic standards.

Surely the competition festival is superior to the old music contest of the past. The motivation has partially shifted from an extrinsic one based on competition to an intrinsic one based on interest in music itself. Are music teachers and students of high schools in this country ready to make this shift complete? In 1936 a resolution was passed in a meeting of the Music Educators National Conference to eliminate the word "contest" and substitute the term "competition-festival." Let us make the complete step and eliminate the word "competition." *The emphasis then will be placed upon making and listening to music together.* The competitive feature will continue as long as there is a sufficient number interested to justify its continuance. Gradually the festival will contribute to integrating music with valuable educational and social experiences.

Conclusion

As an outgrowth of the early contest idea there has been an amazing development of district, state, and regional music contests during the past few years. They serve as a means for preparing and selecting groups to participate in the national contest. There is grave danger that this highly organized system of contests will defeat our true aim as educators. The entire set-up is susceptible of emphasizing the competitive spirit, and in actual practice appears to be doing so. However, these pitfalls can be avoided. These events should be made to serve the goals of music education; they should foster the festival spirit; they should emphasize the making of beautiful music together.

A new and interesting plan has been devised in New York State for the classification of ensembles participating in competition-festivals. Instead of classification being based upon size of enrollment in a school, it is based upon the *ability to perform*. For each of the five major organizations (Band, Orchestra, Mixed Choir, Girls' Choir, Boys' Choir), six grades of music will be outlined. The director of any of these organizations shall determine in which grade he cares to enter his group. In place of one required number, there will be six. Each band, orchestra, and choir will enter the stage prepared to play or sing six numbers from any one grade. The adjudicator will select any one of the six as the audition number. In order to assure progress, any organization receiving a I rating should automatically enter the next grade higher the following year, unless, due to the graduation of students or some other reason, the director desires to remain in the same grade. Organizations receiving a II or a III rating should remain in the same grade. Organizations receiving a IV or a V rating should drop to an easier grade of music. This plan seems to be a step forward in the classifying of organizations and the selection of material for contests.

One final word should be said about the operetta and cantata. There are so many good things that can be said in their behalf that a place should be found for them in the musical program of the high school. The number of operettas produced in this country each year is some proof of the interest of students in this type of activity. It all depends upon the teacher. If he can utilize the values of the operetta and cantata by giving the students a genuine educational and musical experience, then he will enhance the program by including them in the curriculum.

Topics for General Discussion

1. Have you been associated with any high schools in which public performance was emphasized to the detriment of educational values? What type of music course of study was the result of this policy?

2. Plan several programs which could be performed by high school organizations of average ability. The list of materials in the appendix of this book will offer many suggestions.

3. Examine six operettas suggested in the appendix and evaluate their general suitability for use in your high school.

4. Select an opera, such as *Carmen,* for study. Consider such changes as are necessary in length, vocal demands, transposition, translation, and orchestration in order to make it adaptable for use in your high school.

5. The football team needs new uniforms but there is no money in the school budget for their purchase. Should the music department be asked to give an operetta to raise money for the purchase of these uniforms? Give reasons for your answer.

6. Should there be an admission fee for school concerts? For cantatas? For operettas? For spring festivals?

7. What has been your experience with music contests? Do you believe that their virtues offset their vices? What are the essential differences between the contest, the competition-festival, and the festival?

THE SINGERS

God sent his singers upon earth
With songs of sadness and of mirth,
That they might touch the hearts of men,
And bring them back to heaven again.

The first, a youth with soul of fire,
Held in his hand a golden lyre;
Through groves he wandered, and by streams,
Playing the music of our dreams.

The second, with a bearded face,
Stood singing in the market-place,
And stirred with accents deep and loud
The hearts of all the listening crowd.

A gray old man, the third and last,
Sang in cathedrals dim and vast,
While the majestic organ rolled
Contrition from its mouths of gold.

And those who heard the Singers three
Disputed which the best might be;
For still their music seemed to start
Discordant echoes in each heart.

But the great Master said, "I see
No best in kind, but in degree;
I gave a various gift to each,
To charm, to strengthen, and to teach.

"These are the three great chords of might,
And he whose ear is tuned aright
Will hear no discord in the three,
But the most perfect harmony."

HENRY WADSWORTH LONGFELLOW

Chapter 6

SINGING ACTIVITIES: GENERAL CHORUS

The sensitivity to the beautiful in music which we desire for all students has a golden opportunity for fruition through the singing activities. Singing has been discussed as the most natural, the most immediate, and the most intimate experience in music. *It is through singing that the student will learn to accept and love the song.*

Is it not, then, a misfortune that many students fail to continue their interest in singing after the junior high school? Can this be due to the failure of the high school to offer adequate opportunities? The boys' voices are beginning to settle into tenor and bass classifications. A few contralto voices are in evidence. Soprano voices are fuller and more mature. A large and varied field of choral literature is available. Music that represents the genius of the greatest masters is ready to lead these young people to even greater heights of aesthetic enjoyment. A rich offering of opportunities for singing must be presented in the senior high school in order to make these boys and girls aware of the joy of singing with their more developed voices. They must again realize the naturalness of expressing themselves through singing beautiful music.

General Chorus

The singing activities in the assembly were stressed in Chapter IV. We are now concerned with the general chorus, which is just exactly what the name implies—a chorus for everybody. Every student who indicates a vigorous or even a feeble desire to sing should be encouraged to elect this course. There are some high schools that make provision for every student to sing in one big chorus once a week. The chorus will vary in size, according to the enrollment in the high school. In a large school the chorus may enroll several hundred students, there may be a beginning and an advanced chorus, or there may be a chorus for each grade. In a small high school the general chorus may become the mixed glee club or the cappella choir. In the latter case some degree of selectivity may be necessary. If this arrangement is followed, more emphasis should be placed upon part-singing in the assemblies.

Scheduling the General Chorus

Scheduling the general chorus often presents difficulties. Two periods of forty-five or fifty minutes each is the normal amount of time to be devoted to this activity. The music teacher must arrange with the principal a time which has the minimum of class conflicts in order that all students may have the opportunity of this experience. Several plans are possible. A large membership in the chorus may make it possible to clear one or two periods each week in most academic classes. The activity period presents another possibility. Scheduling difficulties can usually be overcome if the principal is convinced of the value of the activity and asks the music teacher to sit down with him and plan together. Strange as it may seem in some quarters, many schools begin by scheduling the music classes. Most educators readily see the social and aesthetic values of the general chorus and its wholesome effects on the entire school.

Arranging the Voices

A large chorus of mixed voices, where eight-part music is sometimes used, presents several possibilities for seating plans. To say definitely which is the best plan is difficult. There is considerable variance of opinion and practice among choral conductors. In deciding upon a seating plan the conductor must take into consideration the number of voices, the balance of parts, and the appearance of the chorus.

The following diagrams suggest several arrangements which are being used with apparent success by various choral directors.

CHART NO. 1

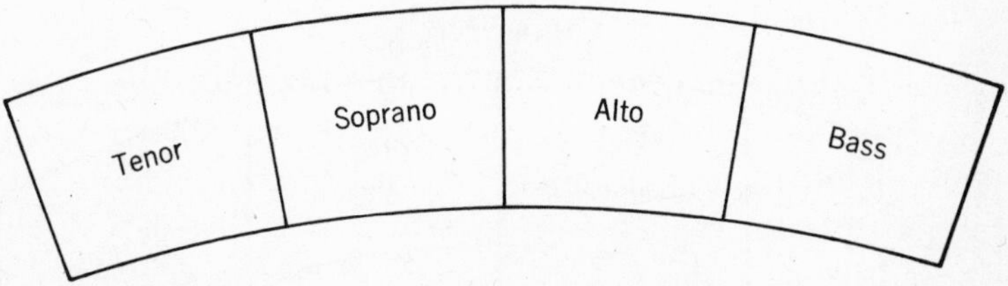

Tenor
Soprano
Alto
Bass

This arrangement has long been a standard for four-part singing. It is still often used by small choruses, especially

CHART NO. 2

1st Tenor	2nd Tenor	1st Bass	2nd Bass
1st Soprano	2nd Soprano	1st Alto	2nd Alto

when there is no raised platform for rehearsal or performance. It seems inadequate for a very large chorus. The tenors and basses are too far apart for effective performance of sections in choral works for male voices.

Diagram No. 2 illustrates another well-known standard arrangement which is especially popular with church choirs, but it is a doubtful arrangement for school choruses. Much of the flatting in these organizations is caused by placing the boys behind the girls. Even for the selected school choir or the professional choir such an arrangement has marked disadvantages. This lies in the fact that the first and second choirs do not have contact on the stage and it is often necessary for members to shift position on the stage for different numbers. Such contact is very necessary for compositions using double choirs.

CHART NO. 3

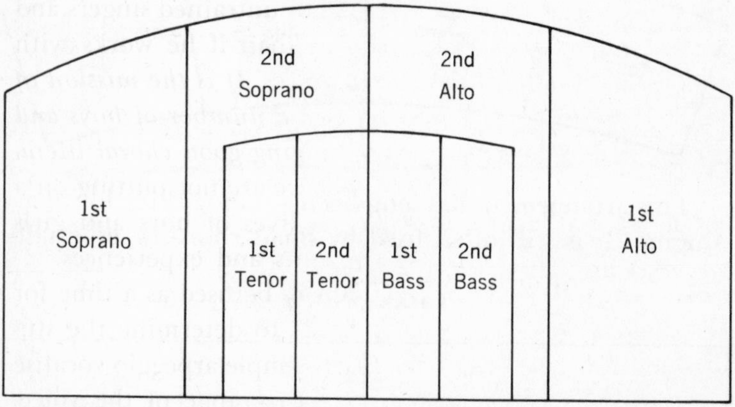

2nd Soprano
2nd Alto
1st Soprano
1st Tenor
2nd Tenor
1st Bass
2nd Bass
1st Alto

This arrangement of voices has several advantages, especially if the chorus is standing or sitting on a level while singing. When the male sections are encircled by the higher voices of the girls, less flatting will occur and there will be a better chance for true intonation. The men are in quartet formation and have access to the front line center facing the audience. In rehearsal the young tenors and basses are near the conductor and he can quickly assist them in difficult passages. This arrangement seems to facilitate sectional practice during rehearsal for large choirs of one or two hundred singers. If any of the altos are used to strengthen the first tenor section, they should sit directly behind the boys to give them added courage. As schools are engaging more competent vocal instructors, the tenor sections are improving and the support by alto voices is not necessary. This move in the right direction not only protects the girls' voices but also achieves better vocal balance and contrast.

Testing the Voices

In the general chorus, voices are tested not for selection but for classification. It is a much finer tribute to a conductor if he can take a large group of untrained singers and weld them into an artistic chorus than if he works with only a smaller group of selected voices. *It is the mission of the music educator to lead as large a number of boys and girls as possible into the joy of singing good choral literature.* It must be remembered that we are not putting on a show; we are trying to make the lives of boys and girls richer and fuller with fine thoughts and experiences.

One or two rehearsal periods may be used as a time for testing voices. Play unrelated tones to determine the student's ability to match tones. Use a simple arpeggio vocalise on the vowel "ah" to determine the range of the voice. Sing some easy song to determine the quality of the voice and the ability of the student to sing a tune. *Remember, a voice is classified by the quality as well as by the range.* This principle should always be followed.

Do not give a test in sight-singing. It will only be embarrassing to the student and discouraging to the teacher.

Sufficient reading power will be developed through singing. True, many compositions will be learned by ear. But why not? Isn't music for the ear? This method may perhaps develop a myriad of discriminating listeners.

A simple test, such as that described above, is always interesting to the student and establishes a personal rapport with the conductor. The conductor makes the following discoveries about the chorus:

1. The outstanding voices and the voices that are especially weak and need individual attention.
2. Voices of limited and of extensive range.
3. Potential leaders and soloists in various sections.
4. Boys' voices that are still changing and need careful watching.
5. Classification of voices into eight parts, first and second sopranos, first and second altos, first and second tenors, and first and second basses.

Know this!

Balancing the Parts

The voice test will probably disclose a shortage of tenors. There can be more serious difficulties than this, however. The penetrating and higher voices of a few tenors will balance many times their number of basses. Careful attention should be given to the voice of the boy which is still changing. It is probably best to place him on the tenor part. He is less liable to mistreat his voice singing first tenor than alto. When his voice has settled he will sing tenor or bass. On the tenor part he will become acquainted with the idiom of this part. If he becomes a bass he will have had some contact with the bass clef. In addition to serving as a protection to the voice, singing the tenor part will have a tendency to quicken the descent of the voice and to help it settle into its permanent quality.

Divide the chorus into eight parts at the very beginning,

even though only four-part compositions are sung at first. The seating plan should be made to provide opportunity for division in each section. This allows the use of optional notes to avoid voice strain. Eight-part music should be a goal for all ambitious choruses.

Rehearsing the Chorus

Many books have been written on how to rehearse a chorus. Only a point of view, however, and a few suggestions will be presented here. In each rehearsal let everyone have at least one satisfying musical experience. What is meant by a musical experience in a chorus? Simply this! It is the joy of singing some beautiful piece of music with abandon. It is the sheer joy of singing that causes faces and eyes to light up and imagination to awaken. It should be repeated that each rehearsal period must provide these experiences. Imagination is awakened through an understanding of the meaning of the text and the message of the music. "With abandon" implies the opposite of self-consciousness. It means giving one's self unreservedly to the music at hand. It is apparent in the vital *pianissimo* as well as in the unrestrained *fortissimo*. It is through such experiences as these that a genuine appreciation of beautiful singing in the chorus body will develop. From this growth the teacher will derive his greatest source of satisfaction.

Do not spend so much time on detail that opportunities for such experiences are lost. Do not spend too much time getting ready to sing. *Singing is the best way to get ready to sing*. This does not mean that beautiful tone will evolve solely from the emotional content of the text and music. (We have heard this doctrine preached.) There are times when only specific suggestions and demonstration will get the desired tone quality. It does mean, however, that the best way for "warming up" is to "warm up" on a song in-

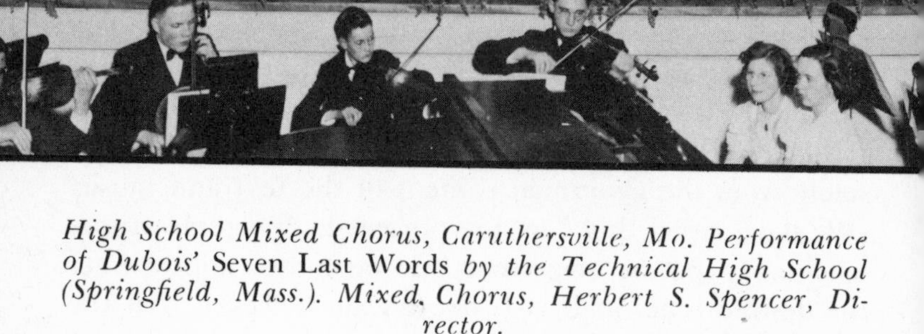

High School Mixed Chorus, Caruthersville, Mo. Performance of Dubois' Seven Last Words *by the Technical High School (Springfield, Mass.). Mixed Chorus, Herbert S. Spencer, Director.*

stead of a vocalise. Develop vocal exercises from the words, the phrases, the chords, the figurations, and the rhythmic patterns of the song.

Don't belittle the importance of planning and organization of the rehearsal. Let every student be aware of the fact that attendance is checked. He must be assured that his presence is needed. Don't use chairs that encourage students to slump in them. The right kind of chair begets good sitting posture for singing. Insist upon good lighting and plenty of fresh air. Attention to these details often prevents drooping spirits and sagging pitch.

If the difficulties were only vocal and musical, the life of the choral conductor in the high school would be a peaceful existence. But he is dealing with young individuals, full of red blood and energy, who through his leadership are led to a greater understanding of music and a deeper love for its beauty. The path has many turns and obstructions. Many times this enthusiastic energy, for which we are truly thankful, causes dissension in the ranks when misdirected, and our old friend discipline arises. The development of the spirit of cooperation is the problem of the individual conductor, and depends largely upon his teaching ability, leadership, enthusiasm, knowledge of his subject, and tact. The secret of solving most disciplinary problems is to be found in the creating of interest by keeping the singers busy. Do not spend needless time with one part while another part has nothing to do but get into mischief. If a singing-part needs individual attention, be sure to employ the entire chorus at brief interims. If corrective measures are necessary, don't threaten and then do nothing about it. Insist upon order and cooperation so that the rehearsal will run smoothly and efficiently. *A sense of humor helps!*

But a more dangerous enemy than discipline, encased in

the word "inertia," is waiting to frustrate the hopes and ideals of the teacher. Inertia is in evidence in every department of choral work.[1] It is evident in the irregular manner of going on and off the platform at a concert, the listless rising and sitting of the chorus, the attack and release of notes, and the lack of responsiveness to the beat of the conductor. These defects can be corrected, but they will persist unless the conductor is blessed with unlimited patience and unrelenting perseverance.

In such instances as those mentioned above, inertia can be detected and tactfully corrected; but there is one place where it is a more deadly weapon because it is not obvious and its presence is not suspected by the singers. This place is in the articulation of words. All singers seem to succumb to this evil unless it is forcibly thrown off. When any of our muscles have acquired certain habits for several years, they rebel against the slightest disturbance of those habits. Articulation of vowels and consonants will become natural only after continued perserverance and exaggerated movement of muscular action. The singers must realize that without the words, only part of the meaning of the song is conveyed to the listeners. In truth, they themselves are only partly aware of its significance. And so, when the teacher can instill in the chorus a spirit of cooperative effort and awaken a desire for efficient habits, inertia and discipline will be banished.

Selecting the Music

Probably the greatest single factor in the success of musical organizations is in the choice of material. The efficient conductor will devote much time and thought to it. The music and texts should be of a superior type, well adapted to fit the character and capacity of a chorus. *In the study*

[1] Henry Coward, *Choral Technique and Interpretation*. London: Novello and Company, p. 73.

of music, the music itself is the greatest educator. Consequently, choose music that is worthy both musically and poetically; music whose tone and words are welded into an artistic whole.

Do not underestimate your chorus. These young people like a real challenge. They like to feel that they are accomplishing something; that they are "going places." The singing of music that is too easy and trivial becomes a chore. Singing some of the choruses from Handel's *Messiah* or an eight-part chorus by Bach is a real challenge.

This suggestion naturally leads to the question of the use of opera and oratorio for high school students. These young singers can give adequate performance of the chorus parts of standard operas and oratorios. This fact has been demonstrated by various energetic and ambitious conductors throughout the country. The danger lies in making the performance of such standard works a means for "showing off" before parents and community.

There is no doubt that oratorios and operas make great demand upon young voices. We do not believe in pampering voices, but we recognize the fact that if young or old voices are continually pushed to the limit of their capacity, they will become hard and unpleasant and the vocal habits of the singers will become so fixed that beautiful singing in the future may be greatly endangered. However, if the teacher is aware of these dangers and is careful not to demand too much from young voices in the high school, one big work each year should be possible. When mature soloists are imported, the performance of such a work can be the crowning musical experience of the year. This performance need not always be a big show. Invite the parents to an informal singing of some big masterpiece united with soloists for the occasion. Let the chorus remain in their rehearsal seats. In this manner they can become personally acquainted with a large number of beautiful masterpieces of choral literature without the strain of preparation necessary for critical performance.

If an opera or oratorio is used during the year, it should be supplemented by easier choral material with emphasis on a cappella numbers. In these compositions the conductor can center attention upon singing as a tonal art. Care of the voice should be stressed and the love of sustained legato singing developed. As a warning, it is suggested to all teachers that they should not hesitate to select numbers which seem to have been written for adults. These young men and women like to be thought of as young adults. They need music which will nurture mature emotional development, as well as music which seems to present only the emotional qualities of immediate interest.

Conclusion

Formerly the general chorus in the high school was the core of the music program. Today it is rare. In some places it has been entirely replaced by the a cappella choir.

The trend toward selective choral organizations is probably due to the fact that the general chorus has confined its efforts to community singing and the repertoire has never passed the "Over the Bounding Main" stage. Is not this a reflection upon the musical ability of the teachers rather than upon that of the students?

Selective musical organizations will not bring about Walt Whitman's dream of "I hear America singing." With the limited possibilities for developed part-singing in the general assemblies, we should like to make a plea for the return of the general chorus. We would even go so far as to say that it should be required for the first year in the senior high school. If it is a four-year high school, we should expect students to participate during the first two years.

The students might substitute some other form of musical activity, such as orchestra or band, a special choral organization, or one of the music classes. *In fact, we believe that all high school students should participate in some organized musical activity or study throughout their attendance in a secondary school.* A well-organized assembly with emphasis upon music might constitute this activity. Such a program naturally calls for more music teachers who are fully equipped for their responsibility.

Topics for General Discussion

1. Refer to "The History of Public School Music in the United States" by Edward B. Birge and other sources for reports of the types of choral programs given in the high schools during the first decade of this century. Contrast them with the programs of today. What are the striking differences?

2. Can you think of any reasons other than those suggested in this chapter why the general chorus has been displaced by smaller and more selected choral ensembles?

3. Examine at least three cantatas or oratorios listed in the appendix of this book and discuss their adaptability for use by a high school chorus.

4. Some educators have developed a more informal plan of performing oratorios. Rehearsals are held until the chorus and orchestra are familiar with the music. At the performance the soloists are seated on the stage and the orchestra in the pit while the chorus members remain in their usual seats in the auditorium. Friends and parents are invited to attend and sit in the back of the auditorium and in the balcony. What are the advantages and disadvantages of this plan in comparison with the usual type of public performance?

THAT MUSIC ALWAYS ROUND ME

That music always round me, unceasing, unbeginning,
  yet long untaught I did not hear,
But now the chorus I hear and am elated,
A tenor, strong, ascending with power and health,
  with glad notes of daybreak I hear,
A soprano at intervals sailing buoyantly over the tops
  of immense waves,
A transparent bass shuddering lusciously under and
  through the universe,
The triumphant tutti, the funeral wailings with sweet
  flutes and violins, all these I fill myself with,
I hear not the volumes of sound merely, I am moved
  by the exquisite meanings,
I listen to the different voices winding in and out,
  striving, contending with fiery vehemence to excel each other in emotion;
I do not think the performers know themselves—but
  now I think I begin to know them.

WALT WHITMAN

Chapter 7

SINGING ACTIVITIES; SELECTED GROUPS

There are students in the high school who are eager to participate in choral ensembles which challenge their individual musical ability and enable them to devote more time to singing the wealth of choral literature than is possible in the general chorus. While it is the first job of the high school to provide singing experiences for the entire student body, it should also provide special musical opportunities for talented students. The general chorus serves as a training period for members of the selective organizations. It must be remembered, however, that the primary function of the chorus is not to train singers for the a cappella choir, the glee clubs, and the small singing ensembles. Rather, it is to be found in the thrill of studying some of the larger musical masterpieces by joining a much larger group of singers. A great deal of the material available to the small selective groups calls for exacting performance. The enthusiasm with which gifted high school students accept and master this challenge is often one of the greatest delights of the music teacher.

The A Cappella Choir

Along with the development of an instrumental program, the growth of a cappella singing is a most hopeful light in the musical activities of our high schools. The choral renaissance of recent years in our schools, churches, and communities is undoubtedly due to the unique musical and spiritual values of this style of singing. Notice that the word "superior" is not used. Is singing the Pope Marcellus Mass of Palestrina unaccompanied a more satisfying musical experience than singing the B Minor Mass of Bach with orchestral accompaniment? Decidedly not! At least not for most of those people who have sung both. However, most of the monumental choral works are unsuitable for high school voices except for incidental choruses, while most of the writings of Palestrina can be given adequate performance by them.

Why have a cappella choirs become so popular in our schools? Why have they superseded in many places the established glee clubs and the general chorus? There are extrinsic as well as intrinsic factors which have influenced this choral awakening.

First of all, the name a cappella is so imposing. Few people know what it means. Many musicians cannot even spell it correctly. Then a cappella choirs look so lovely in their robes! These choirs were something new in the schools during the last two decades even though they had existed for several centuries in the churches. Secondly, due to the forward vision of several music educators, instrumental music found its rightful place in the life and activities of the school immediately after the first World War. Instead of bands playing "First Prize March" from the *Beginners Book,* we can now hear a full concert high-school band play the "Overture" to *Tannhäuser* by Wagner. Instead of "Over the Waves" presented by a limited orchestra, we find many high school orchestras with full instrumentation giving creditable performance of symphonic masterpieces. What has this to do with a cappella singing? Only this! Instrumental music was progressing by leaps and bounds. The devotees of vocal music awoke to the fact that the chorus had lost its predominating place in the high school activities. "What can we do to hold our own?" they asked themselves. There was only one move possible. The standards of choral music had to be raised in order to compare favorably with the quality of work being done by the instrumental groups. The development of a cappella singing, the purely vocal art, was the solution to which they turned.

Values of A Cappella Singing

Permanent values exist only when there are intrinsic qualities of merit. Unaccompanied singing, first of all, approaches a pure means for vocal expression. It enhances the meaning of an idea expressed musically. It is personal, intimate, and sincere. It is less trammeled by externals. A cappella singing requires careful and complete use of the voice, because the voice alone must carry the burden of expression. The singing is not carried along by an accompaniment. The singer feels the responsibility of expressing the musical idea. He is stimulated by this direct and personal approach to tne song. He is freer to express himself sincerely and beautifully.

Secondly, unaccompanied singing facilitates more careful listening. The true musical experience must be approced through listening. There are many opportunities for listening to music. Too many people can hear, but never listen. Listening is the completion of the musical experience which is approached through hearing. It is in this approach that the unaccompanied choir justifies itself and gives richer rewards than those offered by choral units that sing only accompanied music. The human voice has very individual tonal and musical characteristics. These personal qualities of the human voice are intensified in pure choral combinations. When there are no external distractions, the singer is freer to listen to what is going on tonally, harmonically, and dynamically. Heavily accompanied choral singing may even impair a young singer's sensitivity to accuracy of pitch, quality of tone, unified articulation, and delicate shadings of dynamics and nuance. Truly, if the young singer is to receive a genuine musical experience through beautiful vocal expression, the psychological procedure is to introduce him early to unaccompanied singing. The richer palette of accompanied singing may follow. This approach should be used before the student reaches the senior high school and unaccompanied singing should continue to be an important part of his musical experiences.

A third value which is significant in a cappella choirs lies in the type of material available. A large percentage of unaccompanied music is from the literature of the church. The great musical contribution of sixteenth and early seventeenth century's composers such as Palestrina, Orlando di Lassus, Byrd, Morley and others, was the perfection of small vocal forms. The motet and madrigal are the highest musical expressions of these composers. By more modest means they express a musical idea as complete as the fugue, the cantata, the opera, and the symphonic forms of the eighteenth and nineteenth centuries. There is a wide difference in the scope of the musical idea, but the earlier forms are the equal of the later forms in quality. Therefore, the a cappella choir has a wealth of beautiful music especially suited to its needs. Nor is it necessary to search the archives of modal music for a cappella literature. An increasing demand for unaccompanied choral music has produced striking and effective arrangements of a wide variety of folk songs, as well as the best musical efforts from some of our contemporary composers.

Scheduling the Choir

The a cappella choir should rehearse during school time. In smaller high schools one period a day should be cleared for choral activities. If there are no glee clubs, the choir may alternate with the general chorus. If there are glee clubs, the choir may alternate with them. The choir should rehearse at least three times each week for the usual school period. If many performances and concert trips are planned, a rehearsal every day may be necessary.

If daily rehearsals are scheduled, more time should be devoted to vocal development and reading through beautiful music that may never be performed at concerts. Daily rehearsals devoted entirely to assiduous practice on a few numbers for a concert or a contest may become tedious and lose their educational value.

Arranging the Voices

A cappella choirs should sing on elevated platforms. Collapsible platforms may now be purchased at a reasonable price, and are indispensable if many trips are made. For selected choirs that sing on risers the following two arrangements of the voices are favored.

CHART NO. 1

1st Tenor	2nd Tenor	1st Bass	2nd Bass
2nd Soprano	1st Soprano	2nd Alto	1st Alto

The objections made to this arrangement for the general chorus, namely, the flatting in the boys' voices, have been eliminated by selecting qualified singers and by elevating the male voices. It should be noticed that the first and second parts alternate. This arrangement gives a point of contact of the vocal parts in numbers that call for a double choir.

CHART NO. 2

2nd Bass	1st Bass	2nd Tenor	1st Tenor
1st Soprano	2nd Soprano	1st Alto	2nd Alto

Some conductors prefer this arrangement for voices. It places the inner harmonic parts—the tenors and the altos—close together. These parts often have harmonic phrases together. It is claimed that the fundamental tone of the basses assists the sopranos in maintaining pitch and, consequently, the intonation of the entire choir is improved. It can be said that the arrangement in Chart 1 has an advantage in the fact that in eight-part music the first and second tenor parts often double the first and second soprano parts.

No one arrangement, however, is the panacea for all vocal ills. The conductor should experiment and should depend upon his ear to get the best results for different choirs and possibly for different selections. These seating plans seem best suited to the choir that will stand during a performance. Theoretically, singers should be able to sing as well sitting as standing. Practically, however, most singers seem to prefer to stand. Psychologically, it seems more difficult to continue a good singing posture while sitting. Naturally, during a long performance singers should have opportunities to sit and rest.

Selecting the Voices

It should be considered an honor to belong to the a cappella choir, and the members should be carefully selected. Applicants should be sincere in their purpose and should give evidence of an ability to:

1. Sing an easy song rhythmically and expressively, with a pleasing quality of voice.
2. Vocalize over an extended range of approximately an octave and a fifth.
3. Carry a voice part independently.
4. Read music of moderate difficulty, employing diatonic progressions.

These requirements are exacting for high school students. Adjustments can be made in view of the quality of performance expected and in light of other musical opportunities in the curriculum. At this point we should like to suggest that in choosing between character and an exceptional voice for a selected group, choose character. A more serious type of student is needed for this work, one with integrity and a sense of responsibility. Also, it should be added that singing is largely emotional but mentally controllable, and one cannot stress too much the necessity of the right mental attitude for a successful a cappella singer. Mental stability is far more important than vocal ability.

We have heard beautiful singing by choirs ranging in size from sixteen to fifty voices. We prefer a choir of approximately fifty voices. A choir of this size is capable of attempting all types of unaccompanied choral compositions without becoming so cumbersome that some delicacy and finesse are lost.

Rehearsing the Choir

A suggestion should be made for choir rehearsals in addition to those ideas for rehearsing the general chorus. That refers to the "bugaboo" of pitch. Perfect intonation must be the goal, but don't make a fetish of it. If a chorus gradually drops a few vibrations in the singing of a number, few listeners or singers, or even conductors, will ordinarily be the wiser. The important thing is for the various parts to be in tune with each other. This implies that the singers must learn to listen to each other. If the choir is "in tune" in spirit, it is remarkable how often the pitch and harmonies are "in tune." Poor intonation arises from carelessness, inertia, and faulty tone production. There is a high correlation between good diction and good pitch. This does not mean that good diction, good tone quality, and good pitch are synonymous terms. Sing smaller intervals in descending passages; longer intervals in ascending passages. Be ever alert for those semitones! Sing on top of the notes! On a series of repeated notes have a sense of rising! Rehearse the same number in different keys. Flatting can often be avoided by raising the pitch a semitone. Why all this mystery about concealing the starting pitch, anyway? Where is the artistic point? Isn't it merely a stunt? Eliminate these handicaps and poor intonation disappears. The teacher is often as guilty of hanging these millstones around his neck as the students are.

Selecting the Music

These young singers can do most of the standard choral music written for unaccompanied singing. We plead for a wide variety of material. Do not confine your selections to

Brooten (Minnesota) High School A Cappella Choir, 120 pupils in high school, 75 in choir. Carl E. Sutherland, Director.

A Cappella Choir, Ogden, Utah.

Girls' Glee Club, H. P. Harding High School, Charlotte, N.C. Mary Brockwell, Director.

music of the modal polyphonic school. Also, sing something besides negro spirituals. You will not be condemned to purgatory if you select some material for the a cappella choir which is accompanied. Let us suggest those lovely waltz songs by Brahms, the "Liebeslieder," which have a two-piano accompaniment. Some of the Bach cantatas with a string accompaniment are most effective.

Plan your programs and select your music carefully. Ask yourself several questions. Is the music suited to immature voices? Is the range of any voice part too extreme? Does the text have poetic quality? Is it singable? Does the music enhance the poetic idea? Will it be a joy to rehearse the number? Is the music worth the amount of effort and rehearsing necessary for artistic performance? Will it appeal to an audience? And finally, does the composition have a place in the permanent repertoire of the individual singer and the choir?

Boys' Glee Club

Is the glee club on the wane? If so we are reluctant to see it go. We believe in the values of coeducation as practised in this country, but occasionally boys like to participate in activities undisturbed by the fair sex. One of these activities is singing. The spirit of "when good fellows get together" has often awakened in boys an interest in music. The agreeable quality of the close harmony in the range of changed voices is fascinating. The school and community audiences take a special delight in the singing of the boys' glee club. It is true that there is a shortage of first tenors, not only in high school but everywhere. Make a specialty of developing them. Only a few are needed to balance the glee club.

The term "glee" originally meant an unaccompanied song for three or more voices. It was not confined to boisterous songs of merriment. By all means let us have merry, rollicking songs, songs with "barber-shop" harmony, songs with harmony that is "faked." But also, let us have beautiful legato songs with poems of unquestionable merit. Make the rehearsal a social occasion as well as a time for work. Schedule the glee club to meet at least once each week and alternate with the general chorus or the a cappella choir.

The Associated Glee Clubs of America are doing commendable work in sponsoring junior glee clubs as well as senior glee clubs. The music educator should back such movements. Musical and social opportunities must be provided for young men after they leave the high school. The junior male glee club is one answer. We can nurture interest in this style of singing in the high school. By all means let us have a boys' glee club!

Girls' Glee Club

Do girls as well as boys like to sing alone? Our experience seems to point to the fact that girls prefer the mixed choir. It may be due to their interest in young men, though we are fearful of the personal results of such a statement. It may be more reasonable (and tactful) to attribute it to the lack of variety in an ensemble of girls' voices. The "silly" little songs that they have so often been asked to sing also contribute to their preference for mixed groups.

There is an abundance of material for girls' glee clubs, much of it questionable. Don't forget that these young ladies on the whole are more mature than the young men. Study carefully the beautiful songs of Brahms for ladies' voices. Three-part songs seem to be the most suitable for high school. In senior high schools, however, many four-part songs are possible. Do not purposely avoid them. *They are richer in harmonic texture and more satisfying in unaccompanied singing.* Many girls may sing the second alto part if they do not sing with forced chest quality. It is true that most music for treble voices is accompanied. The popular rage for "blues" singing may develop more second altos than we want.

Give the girls an opportunity to enjoy a glee club if there is evidence of interest in this form of music. It should be scheduled for at least one rehearsal period each week to alternate with general chorus or a cappella choir. The celestial quality of these young lyric voices often provides the high light of a musical program.

Small Vocal Ensembles

There must be singing experiences for students of all degrees of musical ability. The general chorus invites all students to participate in expression through song. The choir and the glee clubs are more selective. Small vocal ensembles, such as madrigal groups, boys' quartets, and double quartets, girls' trios and double trios, provide opportunities for students of superior talent.

Public education must provide for three levels of student ability: the handicapped, the average, and the exceptional student. If music educators achieve their ultimate aim of making America musical, they must develop leaders in music. *Small ensembles in the high school can serve as one means for developing these leaders.*

Small singing ensembles have values other than giving the student with superior musical ability an opportunity for more extensive study. First of all, these groups contain the core of a program that will develop a musical America. What is happening to all the young students who play in our large high school orchestras and sing in our large choruses? After graduation do they put their music on the shelf and their instruments in the attic? Too often they do, even when opportunities are provided for participating in musical organizations sponsored by the community. Experience in small singing ensembles in the high school stimulates the desire to keep this form of expression alive after graduation.

It is much easier to organize small groups in the community than large choruses which involve considerable expense and superior leadership. It is much more convenient to gather with a few friends in various homes and enjoy the intimate association that comes from making music together in small ensembles. This point of view indicates that these small groups in the high school should emerge from participation in the large musical organizations instead of the latter developing as a result of small groups. It also implies that there will be more than one madrigal group, one boys' quartet, and one girls' trio in the high school. There should be many such groups for different levels of artistic musical performance. There may be one selected group of each type of vocal ensemble which will represent the school in the community. But many other small groups of singers should be encouraged, and the teacher should give his assistance and advice in the organization of such groups. Formation of singing groups can be stimulated by presenting a plan to the general chorus, the choir, and the glee clubs. This plan should include a description of various small ensembles such as the madrigal group, mixed quartet, girls' trio and sextet, boys' quartet and octet.

Regular rehearsals should be planned to be held weekly, bi-weekly, or even once a month in various homes by members who are in the habit of meeting together socially. Each group should have a student leader who sings with the group. Occasionally time should be taken from chorus and choir rehearsals for these groups to present numbers that they have been practising. Large numbers of such small informal groups carried into adult life will nurture a singing America.

The small ensembles which are selected to represent the school can be very effective in contributing to the musical life of the community. These groups are composed of the most talented students in the school. They should do artistic work. Moreover, on account of their size there are no difficult problems of organization. This fact is very important in filling singing engagements. Rehearsals are easily arranged. Transportation is no problem. The singing of these groups is most appropriate for club meetings and informal gatherings. A small meeting place is not only adequate but actually advantageous. If they sing well, they will be in continuous demand. But this demand can be overdone. In addition to these selected groups, various members can be assigned by the instructor to small singing groups to represent the freshman, sophomore, junior, and senior classes. These groups should sing for various social, classroom, and assembly programs. In this manner all the groups can make a real contribution to the musical and social life of the school.

Selecting the Voices

The type of singer that should be selected for the small ensembles representing the school has been indicated. Although the instructor will probably be well acquainted with the superior students, a try-out is not only fair but is also tactful. This try-out should include all the suggestions offered for selecting members of the a cappella choir, but the test should be even more exacting. It should include reading and singing part-songs. A natural blend of voices is very necessary for these small singing ensembles, and the instructor should hear the voices together before making final selection. Great care should be taken to select students who will work together. Often students will form such groups on their own initiative and come to the teacher for help.

Scheduling and Rehearsing

Small ensemble groups should be scheduled to rehearse during school time at least twice each week. In small schools it may be necessary to schedule rehearsals during study periods. Members of the groups should arrange other meetings in various homes at frequent intervals. As suggested before, each group should have a student leader who will not conduct but who will sing with the group. Each group should also have an accompanist who might serve as leader in some groups. This student leader is directly responsible to the teacher. The ensembles must be trained to practice alone, without supervision by the teacher. They have become acquainted with rehearsal techniques by their membership in the larger choral organizations. They should be serious students who know when to work and when to play. The instructor should arrange to meet with each group every week for part of a rehearsal, at least. At this time he can make suggestions for improved musical performance and guide procedures for future rehearsals. Members of these highly selective groups can assist the instructor in supervising the work of all other small singing ensembles in the school, both the class groups and the informal groups who are meeting in the homes. This plan educates students for leadership and cooperation.

Selecting the Music

In these groups the students will naturally have a greater voice in the selection of music that they are to sing. If they do not enjoy the music, singing rehearsals will be a failure. If a good job has been done in building a repertoire of fine music in the chorus and choir, there need be no fear for the music that they will select for themselves. Undoubtedly, the teacher will need to guide them continually in developing criteria for the selection of music. He will carefully analyze the musical merit of the compositions that they choose. At times it may be necessary for him to point out the inadvisability of including a certain number in their permanent repertoire. The teacher remains the guiding spirit in the picture, but he should give the students as much freedom in the selection of music as their discriminating power warrants. They must be made to realize that they are building a permanent library for the school.

This last statement leads to the question of material for the informal singing groups. They should be permitted to check out music from the choral library of the school, but the instructor will need to advise each group in the matter of selection. The life of these groups depends largely upon attractive material. Music that is too difficult or not suited to the group will cause tedious rehearsals. A few rehearsals that lack the joy of a musical experience will ring the death knell for a group.

Conclusion

All these small singing groups should be encouraged to study the music and text, and to bring their interpretation to the teacher and class for suggestions. After consideration such suggestions may be accepted or rejected by the ensemble. The students will understand that the teacher, because of his wider experience and richer musical background, is more fully qualified to grasp the meaning of a composition and re-create it in better taste and style. However, the suggestions made by the teacher will not take away the joy or value of creating something of their own. After students have worked a thing out themselves, they are usually more responsive to the suggestions of interpretation by the teacher.

Singing in these small ensembles is often a more satisfying musical experience than singing in a large chorus or choir. Students develop independence, leadership, responsibility, and cooperation that is more active and personal than that resulting from participation in larger groups. By all means let us as music educators direct some of our attention and energy to these small singing ensembles.

Topics for General Discussion

1. Do you feel that the a cappella choir movement has been overdone in our schools? What has been its effect in your high school? Give reasons for your answer.

2. Discuss thoroughly the respective values of the a cappella choir, boys' glee club, girls' glee club, and small ensembles. In which organizations would you prefer to sing? Why?

3. Formulate a list of two-, three-, and four-part songs for male voices which could be used in a beginning boys' glee club.

4. Examine a number of the standard duets for treble voices written by master composers. Do you find them suitable for high school girls' glee clubs? Do you believe these numbers preferable to many three-part songs on the market?

5. Make a program for the first public appearance of a high school a cappella choir.

6. Name various types of music appropriate for small vocal ensembles. Give examples of each.

THE VOICELESS

A few can touch the magic string,
And noisy Fame is proud to win them:—
Alas for those that never sing,
But die with all their music in them!

OLIVER WENDELL HOLMES

Chapter 8

SINGING ACTIVITIES: THE VOICE CLASS

Most music educators approve of the voice class as an activity for the senior high school. However, there is usually very little done about it. The choral organizations demand so much of the music instructor's time that the values of the voice class do not seem to compensate for the extra effort necessary for its development. It is pointed out that students receive vocal training in the group organizations and that the voice class would only extend this training beyond the obligation of the public schools. Then, frankly, we believe that many music instructors realize their inadequacy for teaching a voice class, while they may be fully qualified to conduct a choral group. Teaching the voice class does require special training. The teacher must have a thorough knowledge of the principles of singing which include voice production, and style and taste in the interpretation of song.

Values in Voice Classes

Let us examine a few of the educational values of voice classes. Recently we heard one music educator express his disapproval of such classes on the principle that they were undemocratic. Can any democracy survive without leaders in all fields? Are we developing musical leaders in our secondary schools? One of the evils of our present educational system is the lack of advantages for the student of superior talent and ability. Such students must have the opportunity to pursue their interests to a fulfillment of their own artistic performance. We heartily approve of all types of listening activities. But we thoroughly believe that the musical nation will be a singing and a playing nation. Voice classes can raise the standards of singing by developing artistic singers.

In the second place we do not believe that the vocal training in choral groups is sufficient to give singers a feeling of confidence in their own individual efforts. In fact, almost the reverse is true. Except for the small singing ensemble, a feeling of dependence may be engendered which will determine a student's future participation in the making of music. Most of the time spent in choral practice is devoted to the voice problems of the group and the preparation of numbers to sing on various programs. This is as it should be. Not enough time can be devoted to individual singing to give students a thorough understanding and command of their voices. Moreover, the problems of group singing and individual singing are not identical. In fact, the former restrains the individual expression of personality and voice for the good of the group, while the latter stimulates individual artistic expression and generates a confidence in one's own musical ability. There are many individual vocal problems in these young singers that need more attention than is possible in large choral groups. There are also many interested students with good voices who should have more opportunity for extended study than is possible in the choir and the glee club.

Did you ever listen to the songs that high school students sing when they are gathered together in their homes on informal social occasions? What do they sing on their hikes and picnics? Occasionally one may hear a folk song, a carol, a negro spiritual, or even a part-song if the voice parts are represented. Usually it is the popular song, the jazz song, the "swing" song. The social value of popular music is excellent for relaxation, although the words are often ridiculous to the point of absurdity. But we do wish that teachers as music educators could lead these young people in the desire also to sing the art songs of Franz, Schubert, and other master composers of song, together and for each other. When students discover that they can express their deeper feelings through really beautiful songs, they will cease to be content with the frivolous qualities of the current popular song. The voice class will inspire familiarity with the great songs of music literature. Since these songs have lasting quality, familiarity will breed, not contempt, but a desire on the part of these young people to include the singing of such songs as part of their common experiences. Critics often bewail our lack of appreciation for better song literature. The voice classes will stimulate this appreciation. An appreciation of better songs will create a demand for a better type of music. Our American song composers will devote more time to composing beautiful songs when they receive more recognition for their creative efforts.

Finally, the voice class can serve the school and community by preparing young artist singers who can perform in small ensembles and as soloists. It is often more expedient to have a solo, a duet, or a vocal quartet for some program or social occasion than to attempt to enlist the services of large choral groups. Church choirs are continually searching for singers who are musicians; singers who can give an artistic performance of incidental solos in the anthems. Musical and vocal standards in the volunteer choirs of our churches have been universally low. Music

Greenwich, Connecticut. High School Opera Club presents O'Hara's operetta Little Women, *Mary Donovan, Director. Boys' Voice Class, Miss MacLean, instructor. Voice Trials.*

educators can be of real service to their respective communities by developing young singers who can bring more artistry and musicianship to the service of worship in the churches.

Organization of Voice Classes

In introducing voice classes into the high school curriculum it is probably best to admit all students who are interested in this study, but to encourage only those with the better voices. It has been pointed out that the aim of these voice classes is to develop individual singers. The class should be scheduled for at least two periods each week and outside practice should be expected. If the class should meet for a period every day it would be quite feasible to conduct it on a laboratory basis in the granting of school credit.

Size of Classes

The size of the class will depend somewhat upon the peculiar talents of the teacher; in other words, upon his ability to teach voices in classes. If a class is smaller than eight, it almost ceases to be a class and instruction is practically on a semi-private basis. If the class becomes the size of those in other academic subjects, approximately thirty or thirty-five students, it becomes almost too cumbersome for voice study, in which case students must have considerable individual attention. However, it is natural that the beginning class should be rather large. The mortality rate will be quite high, due to such factors as graduation, conflicts as a result of change in schedules, and a realization by students that their voices do not warrant the demands on time and energy. The ideal beginning class should be approximately twenty members. As this group becomes more advanced the number would probably diminish to approximately twelve students. In advanced vocal study, more individual attention is necessary than at the beginning, when all students are attempting to grasp the general principles of singing.

Eligibility of Members

In the introductory statement it was suggested that all students who are interested should be admitted to the classes. Naturally this statement must be tempered. The aim is to develop soloists and musical leaders. It is only poor guidance on the part of the teacher if he admits students with no talent and practically no voices. Other musical experiences should be provided for them. It is best to admit only boys whose voices have changed. These voices may not have completely "settled," but at least they should not be changing. Since boys' voices change at different ages, the age of the boy cannot be a deciding factor. Although girls' voices change considerably during adolescence, they do not pass through the radical change of boys' voices, which drop an octave in range and greatly deepen in timbre. Therefore, it is usually safe to admit any girl in the senior high school voice class unless she is unusually deficient or her voice is so immature that it seems advisable to postpone vocal study.

Segregation

Many singing teachers favor voice classes of one sex. Such segregation does simplify the presentation of materials, for at this age girls' voices are usually more flexible. Moreover, boys usually favor types of songs that are different from those best suited for girls' voices. However, a more practical segregation would be a division of the high voices from the low voices. This segregation enables the teacher to devote attention to the outer range of voices. In classes composed of all types of voices many students are idle when attention is devoted to the extreme ranges. This segregation avoids, also, the necessity of much transposition, which is usually done poorly by the accompanist or teacher. It eliminates the necessity of the group's learning every song in the medium-low key in order that all members of the class may participate. This practice can actually develop harmful habits in sopranos and tenors as they approach new songs. Furthermore, such segregation retains the superior interest often found in mixed groups. High school students usually prefer mixed voice classes. There is ample material suitable for both the girls and boys in the beginning classes, as least, when divided into high and low voices.

Realistically, voice classes are usually composed of all types of voices of both sexes. The many factors involved in scheduling both the student's and the teacher's time produce this result. Such classes tax the skill and ingenuity of the teacher. The disadvantages have been suggested. Now let us look at the advantages.

The superior interest in mixed classes has been pointed out. Students become aware of the problems of others with voices that are different from their own. They become familiar with a greater variety of song material which is suited to all types of voices. Mixed classes afford the opportunity for various types of duet singing which is so greatly enjoyed by most students. Finally, mixed quartets often develop from mixed voice classes. This opens a large field of beautiful sacred and secular literature to the students and increases the interest in singing outside the class.

Teaching Procedures [1]

The voice class is a class and should not be taught as a series of separate private lessons. It is true that some suc-

[1] Alfred Spouse, "'Voice Classes in Senior High Schools" *1930 Report of the Committee on Vocal Affairs,* Music Educators National Conference.

cessful teachers of voice in private studios are not successful with voice classes. They fail to capitalize on the class situation and their procedures are often controlled by traditional practices which are the outgrowth of private teaching. A knowledge of the principle of singing, an understanding of young people, and efficient planning are the chief requisites for success with voice classes. Occasionally the inspired teacher, who loves and understands his work, can get results without careful planning. This fact is no proof, however, that more striking results would not have been produced had he planned carefully. In voice classes both teacher and students can observe the progress made when the general and specific aims are kept constantly in mind.

The Drill Approach

The traditional method of teaching singing was to confine students for several months or even several years to a group of vocalises until they had mastered the various techniques of singing. Then came the glorious day when they were permitted to learn a song. (Of course, these students had probably been learning songs all along but without the guidance of the teacher.) They were now supposed to apply their technical knowledge to the singing of the song. Too often the application was not made and learning to sing was a long laborious process. There are no short cuts to the artistry of singing but much of the mental and physical strain can be avoided.

This method of using abstract drills as an approach to singing was initiated and firmly rooted in practice by the old Italian masters, notably Porpora. These old masters were concerned primarily with developing opera singers, a style that makes great demands upon the vocal powers of the artist. Scant attention was given to the problems of the average singer. A singer who survived this strenuous period of drill might hope for some acclaim in the professional field of the opera. The music of the day contained many florid passages, chromatic runs, and embellishments which demanded plenty of surplus technique. In consideration of the demands of the music and the goal of the singers, there may have been some justification of the methods used.

The voice class in the high school has different aims. Here the goal is to develop an appreciation of song literature, a sense of power for individual expression in song, and solo singers to serve the school and the community. The songs to be used do not make superhuman demands upon the voices of the students. Although phenomenal technique is not necessary, it should not be disparaged. The drill approach is unquestionably out of step with all methods based upon modern psychological thought. An even greater censure for this approach is found in the unwillingness of students to participate in classes conducted by these methods.

The Song Approach

We hear a great deal of discussion of the functional method in music education today. One would assume that this means a method that functions or gets results. The old Italian masters would have claimed such results for their method. However, the term has come to mean the teaching of technique only from an expressive situation, from the music itself. It is a direct approach to learning songs. No drill is advocated that does not stem directly from the singing of a phrase of music.

Many teachers give lip service to this approach and then violate every premise on which it is founded. This

A Cappella Choir, Junction City, Kansas. Stage set as organ console and pipes. Combined Glee Clubs, Clifford J. Scott High School, East Orange, New Jersey, in Christmas performance of The Messiah, *Paul L. Young, Conductor.*

method is based on the thesis that technique is not built by habitual drill but through intelligent control. *Continual repetition of a song without intelligent application will not develop vocal technique.* This method is a challenge to the ingenuity of the teacher to examine carefully the technical factors in the art of singing and how they may be acquired by the most direct and musical approach.

The inability of teachers to analyze vocal problems and to offer concrete suggestions for improvement accounts for the frequent failure of this method to produce artistic singers. Vocal technique is not an end in itself but a means to expressive singing. These two components of beautiful singing go hand in hand. Singing usually lacks expressive and beautiful qualities if vocal technique is limited. Here again we mean by technique not the ability to do vocal tricks, but the ability to use the voice to produce beautiful musical effects. It is quite true that the song approach fails to give students a surplus technique. It only meets the demands of the song to be sung at a given time. Due to various physical factors, vocal control is a variable quality with many singers. Surplus technique enables singers to meet vocal demands at all times and in all situations, new and old.

The Combined Approach

As in most phases of teaching, there is no one best way to teach singing. Effective voice teachers are usually those teachers who do not use to the extreme either of the two methods described, but combine them in a judicious manner.

In our voice classes let us begin with the song! By this statement we do not mean a detailed study of the poem before the music is heard. But in popular vernacular, "Try the song over." After this introduction it is time to discuss the value of the poem and the quality of the musical setting. There is no intention to belittle the words, but it is the music that usually interests a student in a song; or more likely, the union of the words and the music. Then vocal problems are segregated and technical drills introduced to master them. Vocalises should be introduced only when the student feels some difficulty in producing a musical result. They should be introduced to gain better vocal control to better produce the desired musical effect. Vocal exercises as such occupy a minor place in developing a voice. They should be few in number and apply directly to some phase of the singing act; namely, breathing, vowel formation, articulation, extending and equalizing the range, or resonance. They should apply directly to the musical effect that the student is trying to produce and he must understand the application.

General procedures in voice classes should consist of learning and singing songs together. Poems should be studied and recited as a group. Vocalises should be sung together with an occasional interruption by the teacher to correct an individual fault. He must train his ear to detect the faults of an individual in the group. As songs are learned, time may be devoted to solo performance, while the class serves as a friendly audience to criticize and make suggestions for improvement. A record by an outstanding artist of a song being studied is often a stimulation and a challenge to the entire class.

Principles of Vocal Technique

Although instrumentalists are willing to devote hours of daily practice to gaining a facile technique, singers sometimes fail to see the necessity for diligent practice in order to develop a voice with flexibility and power. The technique of the voice is quite as difficult as that of an instrument, and because of the intangible nature of the human instrument, only intelligent practice will bring out its full beauty.

It is easy to say that the criterion of good voice technique is a free and natural production, but this is not so easily achieved. The basic principle of good voice production is the control of the coordinated act involved in singing. It includes proper management of the breath, an automatic adjustment of the vibrators, and a free and unimpeded reënforcement by the resonators of the tone produced. This complex coordinated act is not controlled by a mechanical process, but by synthetic experience. Overemphasis on separate physical factors will only destroy the coordinated control absolutely necessary for good voice production.

The Singing Tone

If we follow the line of reasoning just presented, then we will begin the study of voice by endeavoring to give the students a conception of the singing tone which should be approached directly through the use of the voice. The ideal of a good tone may be gained through demonstration by the teacher, by listening to artists in concerts, over the radio, by means of records, and by observing the work of the teacher with fellow-students. A good tone may be dependent upon the proper management of the breath; but to begin the study of voice with an analytical discussion of the diaphragm, the abdominal and thoracic muscles, and the lungs, is opposed to our conception of the singing act.

The term "voice placement" is in bad repute, and rightly so, because it implies that the voice is placed somewhere, even by force. Nevertheless, it is true that the sensation of a good singing tone is high and frontal. Normally, many physical factors impede the production of a pure singing tone, especially former bad habits of speech. *Soft* humming of songs and extended scale passages will give the sensation and conception of this free and unimpeded singing tone. This mental conception is very important for beginning students. Now we do not propose humming as a panacea for all vocal ills, for humming, if too loud, may be forced; but it will quickly give students the high and frontal position necessary for a singing tone and the free and unimpeded production of a correct tone.

A singing tone should be free and it should be resonant. Resonance implies a reenforced tone of good quality. A singing tone should ring. Not by any sense of the imagination can the anemic tone heard in many of our elementary schools as a result of continual soft singing be called a true singing tone. Such vocal production over a period of years will gradually weaken the voice for expressive singing. The same result will occur if an adult "croons" over a period of years. The voice will lose its original power and become ineffective. It is somewhat comparable to putting your leg in a cast for several months. Any muscle of the body must be used or it deteriorates. The voice needs healthy exercise to give it power and expressiveness. If young children were going to ruin their voices through a little vigorous singing, they would be ruined through yelling and loud talking long before they reached the music teacher. It is right that children should sing with the so-called "head tone," but their voices should be developed throughout their entire range.

This same devitalized tone is carried over to many high school a cappella choirs and voice classes. In the choirs, voices are constantly toned down to secure blend and balance. These qualities are sometimes obtained at the expense of vitality. The test of a voice is a beautiful full tone and the test of a choir is the blend and balance in the *forte* as well as the *piano* passages.

Voice technique is a building process. Voices should be trained throughout their complete pitch range. Average high school voices should have a vocalizing range of at least two octaves. Voices, also, should be developed throughout their complete dynamic range. A voice that is free and correctly produced can sing softly and loudly equally well.

Vowel Formation

The key to good singing is correct formation and connection of vowels. Voice production is dependent upon the ability to manage breath, but we do not learn a song by practicing the breath marks. We learn a song by singing sustained words, and the sustained quality of the words is dependent upon vowels. It is amazing how often better management of the breath results from the demands of the song phrases and from correct formation of vowels.

It has been pointed out that the full beauty of a singing tone depends upon ringing resonance. Such resonance is obtained through the use of bright vowels. Continual use of dark vowels will make the voice "hooty" and "thick." It will lose life and vitality. The *ah* vowel is the normal one to use because it will add both "brightness" and "roundness" to the voice. Moreover, through the use of this vowel students will get the sensation of a free, open jaw.

From our own observation of singing in the high schools a rigid jaw is interfering more with free tone production than any other one factor. Get their mouths open! Give the tone a chance! It is difficult to convince students that their mouths are not open and their jaws not free. Teachers must be ever alert to overcome this inertia.

If a group of twenty students is asked to pronounce the vowel *ah,* there will be approximately twenty varieties or shadings. Consequently, more uniformity will probably be secured if the *ah* found in such words as *are* or *far* is used. In using the *ah* vowel in exercises, care should be taken that it does not sound like *uh* which will deaden the voice if formed incorrectly. All vowels should have some of the "brightness" and "roundness" of the *ah* vowel. The *ooh* and *oh* vowels should not be sung too closed or dark; on the other hand, the *ee* and *ay* vowels should not be sung too open or bright. The relation of *ah* to these vowels can best be understood by a simple diagram.

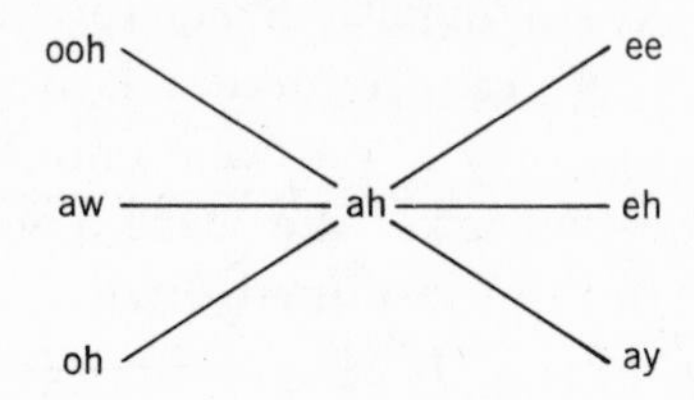

With these things in mind, individual attention must be given to the form of each vowel as it appears in song. Try repeating different vowels on one same pitch free from the hindrance of consonants. "The Monotone" by Cornelius is an excellent study song for this purpose. Any sustained song with narrow pitch range will serve as well. In singing musical phrases, if some vowels seem out of line, repeat rapidly on a single pitch the word containing the vowel. This practice has a tendency to free the vowel and the tone. The same practice is valuable in the connection of vowels. Constant attention must be devoted to the correct formation of vowels for they are the open-sesame to beautiful tone.

Diphthongs

Many words contain diphthongs or compound vowels. The reader may discover the nature of the compound vowels by pronouncing the following words: *cry* (crī-ē), *blow* (blō-oo), *day* (dā-ee), *toy* (taw-ee), and *view* (vee-oo).

Care must be taken to sustain the longer vowel of these words without changing the form throughout its duration. Singers of popular songs are often guilty of this fault. Over the radio one hears such words as: *deh-ee-uh* for day; *crah-ee-uh* for cry; and *vee-ooh-uh* for view. Changing the vowel during the singing of a word destroys a legato style and sounds affected. The safest rule for diphthongs is not to think of them as compound vowels. Treat the shorter vowel, whether it comes at the beginning or end, as a consonant and articulate it as quickly as possible. If vowels are sung open and not too dark as suggested in the foregoing paragraph there is less tendency to change the form of the longer vowel in singing words that contain diphthongs.

Breathing

It has been stated that all good voice production depends upon proper management of the breath. But to make students over-conscious of breath in the beginning usually hampers free coordinated action in singing. It is better to gradually transfer the student's attention to the part played by the breath and to encourage him to rely more and more upon the breath muscles for a steady, rich tone.

Deep breathing in some form is advocated by all teachers. Little value is derived from abstract breathing exercises apart from tone production. Long phrases in songs are more dependent on good vocal technique than upon a large amount of breath. Breath control itself is a matter of vocal technique. Some teachers interpret breath support as a pushing up or a lifting, just as the pillars support a bridge. Other teachers believe that the real sensation in singing is that of resting or almost pressing down on the breath muscles, as the bridge would rest upon the pillars. The term "breath balance" may be closer to the truth. It is very difficult to write clearly on the subject of *breath balance,* but there is no doubt that direct attention must be given to it according to the demands made by the song that is being studied.

Articulation

The American Academy of Teachers of Singing define articulation as "the action of the speech organs in the formation of consonants, vowels, syllables, and words." In singing, articulation depends upon the free action of jaw, tongue, lips, and soft palate. Songs of rapid tempo with many words assist in developing this flexibility. Two cautions may be valuable. First, the vowel form must not change while it is being sustained in tone; and second, the consonant should not interfere with the vowel form and the tone line as it interrupts the various vowels.

Americans are notorious for their slovenly speech caused by the lack of lip movement and free use of the articulators. The same criticism can be directed toward our high school students for slovenly singing. It is for this reason that much of the singing that we hear can be called, "Songs without Words." Scientists tell us that in speech the vocal cords are vibrating approximately forty to forty-five percent of the time while in singing they vibrate ninety to ninety-five percent of the time. Hence, in singing there is only a small percentage of time to pronounce consonants in comparison to speech. Still, it is through the clean enunciation of consonants that words are understood. Therefore, unless singing is to have more meaning than a melodic vocalise the consonants must be clear and distinct. As in the case of vowels rapid repetition of the words of a song on a single pitch will usually eliminate difficulties of articulation.

Flexibility

Vocal technique is closely related to flexibility of the voice, which, in turn, does not mean the ability to do tricks but the ability to produce beautiful musical effects. There is a high correlation between flexibility and quality. This can readily be understood because flexibility of the voice calls for free production. Free production means free resonance. Attempting to control vocal resonance causes some form of rigidity which, in turn, impedes a free and flexible tone. Light, flexible songs will tend to develop a more lyric quality of voice. There is no reason why men should not study songs like Mozart's "Alleluia." There are many books of exercises for flexibility, one of the most useful being Panofka's *The Art of Singing*.

Materials

There is a rich treasury of beautiful songs, but it is not so easy to select interesting and unusual songs for beginners that will enable them to grasp vocal principles while learning the song. An effort should be made to secure songs in the beginning which will seize upon the interest of both boys and girls and still have musical value. It is more economical to begin study with a collection. Suggestions for collections will be found in the appendix of this book.

A voice class book should contain songs as well as exercises. No book of exercises should be used unless supplemented with a book of songs. Likewise, a book of songs needs to be supplemented with vocalises which will assist in the development of the voice.

In the beginning it is best to select songs within an easy range of the voice. Let the students learn to sing in English first. Why should we approach singing through the Italian language? As in all phases of music teaching, so much depends upon the selection of materials. The teacher of the voice class is developing potential leaders of music in the community and much care should be taken to direct this development to greater musical heights through the selection of interesting and worthwhile songs for study.

Conclusion

We hope that, in the discussion of the various phases of the singing act, the reader has not lost sight of the fact that it is the result of coordinated control. In study, these phases of technique are not necessarily taken up step by step, but some attention must be devoted to them in the development of solo singers.

Voice classes in our high schools can develop countless numbers of individuals who enjoy singing. They can develop singers who like to express themselves individually through the medium of song. In the last analysis, the carry-over of high school music into adult life will depend upon such individuals. There will probably never be a sufficient number of community music organizations to absorb all of the graduates of high school music ensembles. Moreover, the pressures made upon adult life today leave little time for many of these graduates to participate in the existing community organizations. All too often, these organizations lack the dynamic leadership necessary to interest the high school graduate.

Therefore, the voice classes, by developing individuals who can sing for themselves and by themselves and who are familiar with a growing repertoire of beautiful songs, will contribute a large share to the articulation of high school music with adult and home life.

Topics for General Discussion

1. In the development of singing activities in our high schools have we provided sufficiently for individual differences? What activities are necessary to do this?

2. Examine some of the voice class methods listed in the appendix of this book. Which of these seem to be self-sufficient and which need to be supplemented with other material?

3. In your own study of singing which procedure was em-

phasized—the drill approach, the song approach, or the combined approach? Do you believe that you would have shown greater improvement under one of the other procedures?

4. Listen to several artists on the radio or on records. Which ones seem to sing with your idea of a good singing tone? Discuss and try to demonstrate the different tone qualities of various artists.

5. Do you agree with the statement in the Conclusion of this chapter concerning the "carry over" of high school music? Support your decision.

AT THE SYMPHONY

The 'cellos, setting forth apart,
Grumbled and sang, and so the day,
From the low beaches of my heart,
Turned in tranquillity away.

And over weariness and doubt
Rose up the horns like bellied sails,
Like canvas of the soul flung out,
To rising and orchestral gales;

Passed on, and left irresolute
The ebony, the silver throat. . . .
Low over clarinet and flute
Hung Heaven upon a single note.

ROBERT NATHAN

Chapter 9

INSTRUMENTAL ACTIVITIES: ENSEMBLES

The phenomenal growth of large orchestras and bands in our high schools during the past twenty years has special significance for music educators. It indicates that these organizations have a strong and direct appeal for young people which stimulates them to spend hours practicing and rehearsing, both in school and out. It signifies that this experience gives them pleasure and is vital to them. It is evidence that they feel the need of such a musical medium.

There is no doubt that the large instrumental ensemble is a natural product of our time and the chosen musical expression of the machine age. Moreover, it is peculiarly American, as is testified by the amazed admiration of visiting European educators. Also, there must be some correlation between big business, big orchestras, big everything. The correlation is economic, at least, if not psychological.

It is noteworthy that the initial growth of large orchestras and bands in the public schools was with pupils of adolescent age. The boy whose voice was changing found a cloistered path to musical expression—behind his instrument his self-consciousness disappears. These emotional young people discovered in the orchestra and the band an outlet for personal expression that stirred their entire being. Playing an instrument gave them a chance to transform a natural manipulative tendency into a pleasure-giving skill. *And above all, the orchestra and band filled a social need.* It has been pointed out in Chapter II that the adolescent is a social being. The "gang" spirit of the age found a wholesome outlet in belonging to the band or orchestra. Pride was gratified in the recognition which this membership brings and there was the special satisfaction in the acceptance by and fellowship with a group of students having similar interests.

Values of Large Instrumental Ensembles

At first, educators and administrators were somewhat hesitant in accepting the educational values of school orchestras and bands. These had always been extra-curricular. They were noisy. They were expensive. But with the pioneering of a few guiding spirits and the immense improvement in the organizations, the musical, social, and educational values became apparent. As a result, they have been accepted and fostered by most forward-thinking educators. These organizations make a definite contribution to the life of the student, the school, and the community.

For the Student

The excellent school orchestras and bands today give those students who participate an opportunity for a finer, richer cultural and emotional life. Filled with enthusiasm and bubbling over with physical and emotional energy, they are provided, in the playing of beautiful music, with a wholesome and controlled outlet for this energy and with a mental and spiritual training of the highest value.

Furthermore, these organizations provide a basis for establishing contacts with congenial schoolmates who have similar tastes. The friendships formed through such associations, under the guidance of a sympathetic and inspirational leader, tend to lay the foundations for finer attitudes and appreciations which prepare these young people for a more satisfying life. *A student who has participated in the performance of fine music never forgets the thrill of it.* Later in life he is carried back each time he hears a program of good music. Listening to a symphonic band or orchestra concert becomes a greater treat for him throughout life. Programs that contain music which he has studied are like meeting old friends; for such programs as these he has a keener appreciation.

For the School

A modern school without music would certainly be a dreary place. No activity, not even athletic teams, has more influence than the orchestra and the band for increasing the morale of the student body and for causing a cheerful atmosphere to pervade the entire school. The orchestra transforms the assembly from a dull affair into a delightful occasion. The band stimulates school spirit by playing at athletic games and school functions.

In a like manner, cordial relations are established between the school and the community through these organizations. The bugle and drum corps plays for open-air, patriotic ceremonies. The band plays for parades and many community rallies. The orchestra gives concerts and contributes to the musical life of the entire community. Most communities take pride in these organizations, and the wise administrator uses them to advertise the general work of the school and to foster closer ties between the school and community life.

For the Community

Interest and pride in these school organizations leave an imprint upon various bodies of citizens. The parent-teachers association may assume the responsibility for supporting orchestra concerts. Service clubs become interested in purchasing stunning uniforms for the band and in sponsoring independent community bands and orchestras. Gradually there is a nucleus of a large group of citizens who become fired with love and enthusiasm for raising the cultural level of the life of the community.

Such school organizations develop in students the desire to contribute to the musical life of the home and the church. *As these young people graduate and assume responsibility for citizenship, they form a group ready to contribute to the aesthetic life of the community, both by participating in musical affairs and by supporting musical enterprises.* They gradually form an element in civic life which sees the value of music in maintaining emotional and spiritual equilibrium and in utilizing, well and wisely, the leisure time created by the industrial era.

Organizing Large Instrumental Ensembles

There are three general methods for organizing orchestras and bands in the high school.[1] Naturally, these methods assume that there is no band or orchestra on which to build as a foundation.

The first method consists simply of announcing in some effective manner, usually in the assembly, that an orchestra or band is being organized and that all those interested are invited to meet with the teacher of music at an appointed time. A few eager individuals attend this meeting, and through personal contact of this group and the teacher with other students who play instruments, a representative organization is built up. This is an old procedure in organizing bands and orchestras, and it is still followed in some

[1] Norval L. Church and Peter W. Dykema, *Modern Band Training Series.* C. C. Birchard and Company, 1939, pp. 4-9.

places. Good results have been obtained by this method, regardless of some marked disadvantages. Let us consider some of the handicaps:

1. Students are taught individually by private teachers, the quality of instruction varying to a great degree, and frequently being of questionable calibre.
2. The resulting wide difference in student abilities and skills produces more teaching difficulties than would be the case if all were beginners. Moreover, many of the most capable players are not interested in playing with a beginning group.
3. Membership is dependent upon students who have chosen their instruments without guidance, which often results in students attempting to play instruments for which they are ill fitted, and also in bringing to the organization instruments of inferior quality.
4. Seldom is there a semblance of ensemble balance.

The second method in organizing bands and orchestras is more modern in approach and is used in many schools. A demonstration of the playing of the symphonic instruments is given in the assembly by the teacher of music. His aim is to arouse the interest of the entire school. He demonstrates his qualifications as a teacher by playing several instruments. He explains briefly their manipulation and their place in the band or the orchestra. Questionnaires are passed around and an announcement is made that immediately after the assembly there will be a meeting of those interested. These students are permitted to handle the instruments and to ask questions about them. They take home to their parents an announcement that instruction will be provided as part of their school music program if instruments are purchased for the students. Then classes are organized for the various instruments. When a certain amount of proficiency is gained, usually after one semester of instruction, a band or orchestra is organized. Let us examine the advantages and handicaps of this method:

1. The instruction is uniform, its quality depending upon the ability of the teacher of music. *Unless he is proficient, he should not try to teach these classes.*
2. The instruction is conducted to develop ensemble players, not individual soloists.
3. When instruments are purchased under the guidance of the teacher of music, there is more chance of their being of better and more uniform quality.
4. There is a greater likelihood of balanced instrumentation than under the first method, although as long as instruments are purchased by parents the teacher cannot wholly control this factor at the beginning.
5. There is evidence of social value in these classes because the students enjoy learning to play the instruments together.
6. The disadvantages of this method, however, is the tendency for instruction to become too technical; for music to be uninteresting because ensemble motive is lacking; for social value to diminish until the band or orchestra is organized; and for a consequent high mortality in the registration.

There is a decided trend toward organizing school orchestras and bands by a third method. In many ways this method is similar to that just described. The organization of a band or an orchestra is decided upon by the administration or teacher of music, often after consulting students who might be interested. A demonstration of the instruments to be used is given in the assembly. Questionnaires and letters are sent to parents. There is usually one announcement to the effect that there are a few instruments owned by the school which are available for use by certain qualified students. The teacher has anticipated the problem of securing ensemble balance and has persuaded the administration to purchase as permanent equipment some of the more unusual and larger instruments needed by the band or orchestra.

After these preliminary demonstrations and announcements, a rehearsal is called as soon as a reasonable time has been allowed for securing instruments. Direct instructions in playing is given to this group of heterogeneous instruments, without its being divided into separate classes. Such an arrangement creates many teaching problems. *A teacher of marked ability in both musicianship and the understanding of young people is essential.* This organization of all instruments together contemplates, and is usually supplemented by, class lessons where there is some segregation of the different types of instruments. The teaching of these different classes will be discussed in Chapter X. At present, let us examine the advantages and handicaps of this third method of organization:

1. It presupposes a teacher well trained in class instrumental teaching, who understands the educational principles involved, and who is familiar with the materials necessary to its success.
2. Class instruction and ensemble practice are closely interrelated and are uniform in quality. They, in turn, are more closely related to the aims of the other phases of music instruction.
3. The necessity of a balanced instrumentation induces students to purchase instruments that are needed, not merely those in which they are personally interested. It also demonstrates the need for financial assistance from the board of education.
4. If care is taken to assure a balanced instrumentation, students have a more delightful musical experience

in a much shorter time than under the second method, where small instrumental groups are taught separately.

5. Since there is greater interest in immediately playing in a band or orchestra than in an instrumental class, the social motivation is stronger.
6. Immediate membership in the band or orchestra gives the student a sense of responsibility and challenges him to improve his playing and musicianship. This fact probably accounts for the lower mortality in registration than occurs under the second method.
7. Under a qualified teacher this method seems to have all the advantages described in the second method, plus a sounder psychological, educational, and musical basis.

The Orchestra

The best method for organizing an orchestra, like all best methods, is a debatable question. If the teacher is unskilled in class instrumental instruction, the first method is undoubtedly the best. Almost any group of orchestral instruments will sound fairly well together if the piano is brought in to support them. Although a couple of violins, a 'cello, a saxophone, a trumpet, and a piano is some distance from a symphony orchestra, nevertheless it is a beginning. Moreover, materials can now be secured which, by simplifying and cross-cueing of various parts, enable performers of different degrees of skill to play together. Use of these materials will assist in no small measure in using all available players.

Even though a teacher is skilled in instrumental class teaching, the problems which arise in combining string instruments and wind instruments are almost insurmountable. Therefore, teachers in some situations combine the first and second methods. An orchestra is formed from the material available and instrumental classes are started simultaneously. As soon as a player is qualified to enter the orchestra, he is admitted.

Other teachers combine methods one and three. An orchestra is organized, beginners are admitted along with those students who have some skill. Material is used that enables the advanced students to play the more difficult parts while the beginners play very simple parts, often just open strings for the violins. Combinations such as these are made possible by use of the piano to fill in the harmony and missing parts. As soon as a balanced instrumentation can be developed, the need for piano support will diminish, until, under symphonic standards it can be dispensed with.

The actual method used in organizing an orchestra depends upon several factors. The teacher must realize his own powers and limitations as a conductor and an instructor of instrumental classes. He must study the situation carefully and have some idea of the students who can play instruments before he makes the announcement. He must have the support of the administration and must adjust his method to the financial aid that he can expect from the board of education. Regardless of method, he must keep ever before him the goal of developing an orchestra that will provide real musical experiences for the members and contribute to the musical life of the school and community.

The Band

The organization of a band presents a slightly different problem from that of starting an orchestra. The piano is seldom used to support the instruments and the missing harmony parts. This might be possible, as, for instance, in a dance band, where scores are published with piano parts. However, it is doubtful procedure for military or symphonic band development. Moreover, since there are not the same difficulties in teaching all wind and percussion instruments that one finds in combining strings, wind, and percussion, the third method is not only feasible but seems to be the best approach in organizing bands. Some teachers have had almost miraculous success in forming bands and in teaching them as an ensemble. In a relatively short time the band is able to play a program for the assembly which creates spontaneous enthusiasm, enlists new recruits, and stimulates added support from the school, the administration, and the community.

Which should be organized first in a school, the band or the orchestra? Music educators differ on this question. Some of them say that the band should be organized first because wind instruments are easier to play than strings, the mainstay of the orchestra. Consequently, a better showing can be made in a shorter time, greater enthusiasm can be aroused, and the entire music program will be improved as a result. Practical experience shows that in such schools the orchestra in many cases is never organized, and that if it is, it seldom has the support, the prestige, or the preference that is given to the band.

Other educators insist that, if the orchestra is organized first and put on its feet, the band will be a natural outgrowth of it. This was the normal procedure before the present widespread enthusiasm for bands. When the orchestra is organized first, in a short time there is an overflow of wind instruments. This is natural because they are more easily played and have a close affinity with the popular dance band. In a short time this group forms a nucleus, and so a band is organized. As soon as the band plays for a few athletic games there are many new recruits. The development of a symphonic band is a natural outgrowth.

Many teachers follow the latter course. However, there

is no doubt that the band, when organized first, will arouse early enthusiasm and secure support. The best procedure is to organize string classes in the grade school, and then a fine symphony orchestra can also represent the school in a few years.

Marching Band

More and more stress is being placed upon the marching band. It can be functional in several phases of school life. At the athletic games it assumes an importance second only to the school teams. It is a means by which high school music can be brought directly to the community without waiting for the public to attend school concerts and to take a responsive interest in musical activities in the high school. In fact, the marching band may serve as the stimulus for creating community interest.

The world has not become so sophisticated that it fails to thrill to the sounds of a stirring march played by a band outfitted in colorful costumes. Led by the drum-major, or the more modern drum-majorette, it presents a thrilling sight to young and old alike. There is a danger that the drum-majorette fad may be carried to the extreme, but we are in favor of anything that will improve the appearance of the marching band.

It is only natural and right that the school band should participate in patriotic parades and community celebrations of festival days. Problems which may arise with the local musicians' union when bands play at civic functions are discussed in Chapter XVI.

The marching band in the high school will usually consist of the same personnel as the symphonic band. Players of double reed instruments, such as the oboe and bassoon, should be able to play clarinets or saxophones for the former instruments are too difficult to play while marching.

In fact, it takes quite a skilled player on any horn to march and maneuver and still obtain something from the bell of his instrument that represents music.

The band should be able to execute all of the movements required by the marching competitions sponsored by the National School Band Association and published in the School Music Competition-Festivals Manual, 1941, by the Music Educators National Conference. They are as follows: (1) Forward march—while playing and while not playing; (2) Halt—while playing (continue to play after the halt) and while not playing; (3) Column right—while playing; (4) Column left—while playing; (5) Countermarch—while playing; (6) Diminish front—while playing; (7) Increase front—while playing; (8) Choice of right oblique, left oblique, column half right or column half left —while playing; (9) Start playing and cease playing—while marching.

Movements 3, 4, 5, and 8 are to be executed with an interval of not less than two paces (60 inches), measured from center of the position to center of next. The scoring chart includes the following items: required movements, playing, cadence, alignment, carriage, precision, inspection, discipline, special maneuvering, general effect.[2]

A suggested practical and efficient procedure for bands which spend only the minimum time on marching is as follows:

1. Rehearse the music (one or two pieces) indoors.
2. Drill on maneuvers outdoors, not playing, paying careful attention to drum-major signals.
3. Play the music while standing in formation.
4. Combine marching and playing.

High school bands should use a cadence of from 120 to 128. Faster cadences cannot be justified because they result

[2] Special aids in developing the marching band may be secured from such sources as: "Getting Results from School Bands," Gerald R. Prescott & Lawrence Chidester. Carl Fischer, 1939.

in bad playing. Correct playing, with good breath control, gives carrying power, whereas loud overblowing is of no value either in concert or marching band. Good rhythm, good accent, and clean articulation are vital to good playing on the march. Good tone and intonation are as desirable in the marching band as in the concert band.[3]

Fife, Bugle, and Drum Corps

This spectacular organization serves a real function in some communities and is often a stimulus to the development of bands and orchestras. It is easy to organize, easy to train, and contributes to patriotic parades, ceremonies, and general school and community functions. The third method of organization seems to be the most feasible. Class lessons on these instruments without the incentive of the ensemble are not very satisfying.

We still hear of some band instructors who insist that the marching band should include only boys as members. We fail to see any visual, physical, or educational reasons for this argument. We believe that all school orchestras and bands, including the marching band, should have membership of both boys and girls. As a rule, fife, bugle, and drum corps should also be co-ed. However, in some situations we would not object to a colorful corps composed of only young ladies as members.

Rehearsing Large Instrumental Ensembles

There is no intention of giving detailed procedures for the rehearsing of orchestras and bands. Only a few principles will be suggested that are often overlooked.

The Set-Up

Every teacher knows that the rehearsal room should be properly heated, lighted, and ventilated. Every teacher

[3] *Course of Study, State of Oregon, High Schools, MUSIC*, edited by Bain and Emerson. 1940. State Printing Department.

knows that the rehearsal room should be neat and not cluttered with music, unnecessary equipment, and extra chairs. Every teacher knows that student representatives from the orchestra or band should arrange chairs, stands, and music before the members arrive. Too often through carelessness and inertia these things are overlooked and slovenly rehearsals result. *These factors are very important for efficient rehearsals.*

Seating Procedures

A seating plan should always be designed to give musical results. Standard seating plans for orchestras and bands of various sizes can be found in many sources.[4] If the teacher is not familiar with these plans, we suggest that he attend a concert of some fine organization, see for himself, and judge the musical results. We further suggest that before he experiments with other seating arrangements, he try these established plans which have been adopted by outstanding conductors for many years. It is quite possible that a more balanced musical result can be secured by shifting the players of certain instruments. If so, there is nothing sacrilegious in changing these accepted practices.

There is some controversial opinion regarding the procedure to follow in assigning chairs in certain sections of the orchestra and band. Some teachers place it on a purely individual and competitive basis, and they remain the sole adjudicator. Some permit the remaining students in the organization to judge the better player. These teachers argue that this democratic procedure motivates more practice at home. Occasional individual performance without the competition for chairs would do the same thing. There is a trend toward assigning chairs on a musical basis by dis-

[4] Recommended seating plans and instrumentation for orchestras and bands of various sizes will be found in the Appendix.

tributing the better players among the poorer players. Some teachers go so far as to give every member of the first violin section a chance to be concertmaster at rehearsals. It would create more interest if players in different sections were exchanged occasionally. We favor these trends because it is better education and the musical results do not seem to suffer.

Discipline

There are several factors in the band or orchestra rehearsal which sometimes cause our old enemy "discipline" to arise. Instruments are noisy, students are eager to play, a feeling of fellowship is prevalent, and there is a sense of release and freedom from academic tasks. This is a perfect situation for developing constructive attitudes toward discipline. Remember, discipline comes from inner control, not from imposed authority. Students can be made to keep quiet through fear, but that is not discipline. When they are quiet through a desire to cooperate, a desire to learn, or a desire to make music together, that is discipline.

The two factors which usually control disciplinary problems are: first, gaining the respect of the members of the organization, and second, keeping them interested in the thing that they are doing. The teacher gains the respect of the students by proving that he is qualified in every phase of instrumental music and by being sympathetic, reasonable, and just in his relation with them. Interest is created through enthusiasm and careful planning.

Teaching and conducting are not synonymous. Many fine conductors are not good teachers. They fail to take advantage of teaching situations. The conductor with no love or ability for teaching makes a pedestal of the podium. He beats time for the students with little concern for their rhythmic development. He imposes an interpretation without elucidation. At times he becomes so enamored with his own performance that he fails to see and hear what is going on and loses contact with the performance. The sympathetic teacher is quite different from this type of conductor in rehearsal. He arranges chairs with ample space between them so that he can spend most of the rehearsal period among the players, watching and listening. He encourages the students to keep their own beat by counting inaudibly, or in their mind. He builds musicians who can follow the expression marks and can contribute to the interpretation of their own music. His corrections are short and to the point. He is ever present—correcting, helping, and encouraging. In the high school, conductors must be teachers, and teachers, in turn, must be conductors who can inspire the students to finer performance after they have learned a composition. The teacher-conductor will have few problems of discipline.

Performance

As in all music education, appreciation is the aim of band and orchestra rehearsals, not the vague appreciation that results from desultory listening, but the keener appreciation that usually accompanies participation in the adequate performance of great music. To the music educator, performance is not the primary value of these organizations, but rather, the effect upon boys and girls of membership in these organizations. The instrumental ensemble exists for the benefit of the individual student, not the individual student member for the benefit of the orchestra or band. There need be no conflict between these aims because boys and girls will develop finer attitudes and appreciation during those rehearsals which strive for a more musical performance. Such performance involves two things, technique and expression.

Sault Ste. Marie (Michigan) High School, Class "A" Band.
Brooten (Minnesota) H. S. Girls' Drum Corps.
Wahoo (Nebraska) H. S. Band, Class "C".

Technique. Everything that was said about technique in the singing act applies to the present discussion. Indeed, many successful high school instrumental teachers approach the technical programs in instrumental performance through singing. As with the voice, technique must not be taught as an end in itself. We are not concerned with tricks of agility, but with the making of music. Students learn to play the violin, clarinet, cornet, and other instruments not to demonstrate their mechanical possibilities, but to produce musical effects. Technique on instruments should be approached from an expressive situation. This means approaching technical problems from the phrase, which is the heart of musical expression.

Certain technical factors need some attention at every rehearsal as they relate to producing ever better musical results. Most important of all is tone quality. Students must be made tone conscious. Sensitivity to tone is necessary for both the performance and the appreciation of music. Students must realize the effect of rich tone in playing a Bach chorale or a sustained passage. Technical problems of embouchure and bowing must be pointed out and corrected. Teachers must be ever alert to the rough and raucous tone. Problems in rhythm must be attacked directly as they arise, and devices used to develop a bodily response to rhythmic patterns. Styles of tonguing and bowing and difficulties in reading are eliminated through an understanding of phrase structure. These problems are not treated in isolation but in their relation to phrasing. Harmonic balance is developed through training the ear to hear other parts and other instruments. Can the first trumpet players hear the note that the second trumpet players are sounding? Can they sing it? Such devices will develop a listening attitude.

Expression. The expressive factors in musical performance must not be neglected in the rehearsals. Technique and expression should be taught at the same time. They are dependent upon each other. Expression facilitates technique and technique makes expression possible. *Quality of tone* is again our first consideration. There is more than one "good" tone, as evidenced by the many different kinds of voices and the variety of timbre in the orchestra. Attention must be continually directed toward producing the kind of tone that will bring out the most meaningful expression. *Tempo* means the rate of speed with which a composition is to be played. Few people have the ability to set a good tempo. Tempo terms give us a clue but they are so variable. A Handel "Allegro" is certainly not the "Allegro" of the contemporary composer. The inner content of the music must disclose the tempo to the student and the teacher alike. Students must "feel" the true pulse of the music. *Dynamics* are not some phase of expression that should be dictated by the teacher. The student should sense the dynamic level if he senses the meaning of the music. This does not mean that the teacher, with his greater experience, cannot demonstrate the powers of musical expression through a wide variety of dynamics and delicate nuances. But the teacher must always lead the students to greater sensitivity in the factors that bring out the fullest expression of the music. They must realize that expression is not arbitrarily imposed upon the music by the teacher, but that it grows out of the musical structure itself.

Aim of the Rehearsal

Finally, we are not concerned about the order of pieces played at the rehearsal. It is not necessary always to open with a number that is familiar and to close with a "peppy" march. It would seem better psychology to vary the rehearsal programs. But one thing is sure, every rehearsal should give the students a few genuine musical experiences. It may be reviewing and improving a familiar number. It may be reading a new composition. It may be listening to a record of a familiar piece or a number to be learned. *But no rehearsal, to be educationally valuable, should be devoid of at least one musical experience which sends the students to their other activities in a better frame of mind and heart.*

Values of Small Instrumental Ensembles

There is a striking trend toward more small instrumental ensembles in the high schools. We believe that this is a move forward from spectacular education to sound musical education. The values and problems are similar to those found in the discussion of vocal ensembles, but it might be well to review them in the light of the instrumental program.

One of the most challenging doctrines of modern education is that of individual differences. Music educators are obligated to recognize this doctrine. One of the most effective ways to apply it in the high school music program is through the organization of small instrumental ensembles. One expects fairly talented students in the bands and orchestras; but the small ensemble provides for students of superior talent, the musical leaders in the school, and the future leaders of music in the community.

The educational and musical values to the members of these groups cannot be measured. Playing in such groups fosters a brand of musicianship not possible in playing only in large ensembles. First of all, playing in these ensembles develops the aural sense. Players become aware of slight variances in intonation and learn to make pitch adjustments for chord blending, tone qualities are more easily distinguished and thereby improved, a sense of balance of parts is achieved, and a finesse of phrasing and nuance is developed. Surely this is a most favorable musical recommendation. Just as important is the development of self-reliance in playing parts individually, and at the same time making the playing of individual parts conform to the improvement of the ensemble. In this way members of the groups develop responsibility and self-discipline, musically and otherwise. They may become the most valuable members of the orchestras and bands, providing they do not lose their perspective and sense of values in their association with the members of the large ensemble.

These smaller groups, moreover, have definite social values. They tend to bring the music of the school to the home. They fill an important part in the social life of the community by appearing at various functions. And finally, they are developing the kind of music which will carry over into adult life, keep the music amateur alive, and develop a musical nation.

Organizing Small Instrumental Ensembles

Although these small ensembles are designed especially as projects for students with superior talent, they should not be limited to such students. They are a natural outgrowth of the large instrumental organizations—the orchestra and the band. To these organizations a plan is introduced whereby students are encouraged to organize into small groups and meet in each other's homes for an evening of music once each week or even once in two weeks. The different kinds of combinations are explained, such as string quartet, string trio, piano trio, woodwind quintet, brass quartet, and other combinations. The teacher assists in the assigning of members to various groups. It is quite possible to arrange for groups to represent various classes such as freshman, sophomore, junior, and senior. These groups should be asked to play at various times for orchestra and band rehearsals, assemblies, social occasions, and class activities.

Special combinations may be selected by the teacher

Springfield (Mo.) High School Orchestra.
Topeka (Kansas) High School Band.
Mt. Kisco (New York) High School Band.

which will represent the school in making appearances in contests, civic clubs, churches, and other community activities. These latter groups should be closely supervised by the teacher.

String Ensembles

There is practically no limit to the number of string combinations and the literature that is available for such combinations. There should be several string quartets and string trios of different levels of advancement. One superior string quartet in which the teacher may even play can contribute in no small way to the musical life of the school.

Wind Ensembles

The best known of the wind ensembles is the woodwind quintet and the brass quartet. In the past the quintet has usually consisted of a flute, an oboe, a clarinet, a French horn, and a bassoon. Many teachers are replacing the French horn with an alto clarinet, but this is questionable in view of the variety of timbre secured when the horn is included. Woodwind ensembles are by no means limited to these instruments.

There are many types of brass quartets and ensembles. Some teachers use a combination of two trumpets, a trombone, and a bass trombone; others use two trumpets, a French horn, and a baritone or E♭ tuba. But there are numerous possibilities and music is being published for nearly all combinations.

Jazz Band [5]

The problem of incorporating "jazz" and "swing" in the high school is becoming more and more an issue that high

[5] The practice of students, who are members of dance bands, accepting professional engagements is discussed in Chapter XVI under the section entitled, "Earning Money."

school teachers must face. There is no doubt that most high school students are interested in popular music. In many instances this is a passing fancy of adolescence. Moreover, we believe that the ardent "swing" fans are in the minority. Nevertheless, music teachers cannot deny this interest or avoid it. What can be done about it?

Students should develop discrimination in popular music as well as in the classics. Therefore, it behooves the teacher to know something about popular music. What are the various styles? What are its limitations? What is its appeal? What is its place in musical development? Discussions of such questions will bring about a closer musical understanding between teacher and student. The teacher so often lives in his musical heaven of Bach, Beethoven, and Brahms that he forgets the earthly beginnings of his own musical development. Some teachers who have taken such an unrealistic attitude have tried to forbid "jazz" music in the high school, but their efforts have, of course, merely driven the stream underground. The young people have continued to enjoy their jazz music sub rosa, and the teachers have lost a valuable human point of contact with their students.

We doubt the validity or advisability of approaching folk songs and the classics by way of a "swing" version in an effort to interest students. We doubt, for instance, that the "swing" version of "Sweet and Low" will lead high school students to prefer the quiet flow of the original song. We doubt that the singing of the "Song of Love" from *Blossom Time* will develop a keener appreciation for the beautiful second theme from the *Unfinished Symphony* of Schubert. Some relationship may be possible if the moods of the compositions are similar; otherwise, *approach the popular song and the classics directly, each for its own worth and enjoyment.*

We believe that one way to develop discrimination in

the popular song is to organize a jazz band or bands. Symphonic bands should avoid the "swing" arrangements. It simply is not the type of music for this combination of instruments. A jazz band need not be sponsored by the teacher; but if a group of students express a desire to organize one, the teacher should be willing to assist them. The jazz band, like all popular music, should be employed for amusement, recreation, and dancing. For these activities it has a place. It can be used at times in the assembly. A pep meeting should have an appropriate musical setting, but do not use the symphony orchestra on the same day. *The mood of the music should set the mood of the assembly.*

Cowboy and Hill-Billy Bands

As students hear these combinations on the radio they often show a genuine desire to have such organizations themselves. Again the teacher should express a willingness to cooperate and assist in every way possible. These groups must not, and need not interfere with the development of more standard musical organizations, for our educational aims will be achieved only if we permit the best in music to permeate the life of the school.

Rehearsing Small Instrumental Ensembles

Naturally it is impossible for the overworked teacher of music to supervise the rehearsals of these groups. If rehearsals in the orchestra and bands are enjoyable experiences, the students will probably approach the problems of rehearsing in small groups in the same manner. Each group should have a student leader who is responsible to the teacher and who reports to him at regular intervals. He is also responsible for the music checked out from the school library. When these groups play for the orchestra or band they will receive the constructive criticism of both the teacher and the students. The teacher will visit rehearsals as often as his time schedule permits. When there are a number of small instrumental ensembles in the school, which are led by responsible students, the teacher of music can feel assured that his program is getting educational results.

Selecting Music for Instrumental Ensembles

The success or failure of a music program depends largely upon the materials that are available. The teacher must be a genius to interest students in dull material. He must not underestimate the value of this phase of his study and he should continually be on the search for new material which will fit his needs. Publishers are more than willing to cooperate and they have made rapid strides in recent years in the quality of music published for small instrumental ensembles. Examine the materials used by a school and you can pass fair judgment upon the value of the music program.

Conclusion

Practically nothing has been said of the relative value of school orchestras and bands. At present there is a tidal wave of enthusiasm for bands. Sponsors for bands capitalize upon the spectacular nature of the organization and the quick results obtained, due to the fact that wind instruments, to a certain level of accomplishment, are much easier to play than strings.

It is in the matter of materials that the problem is brought to the surface. There is no question but that the great composers have devoted their most serious and most musical efforts to the symphony orchestra. This is easy to understand when we consider the natural expressiveness of the strings and the variety of tone color in the instrumentation. There is no denying that band material of the better quality is extremely limited. Transcriptions are not an adequate substitute for the real thing. Better music is being written for the band, but the outstanding composers still turn their major attention to the symphony orchestra. To say that it is too difficult to organize orchestras in schools is begging the question. If we place a premium on developing string players, we shall have string players. Many fine orchestras exist in our high schools today and they are giving adequate performances of symphonic masterpieces. There is a place for both organizations, and when a school neglects either of them something is missing in the music program.

Topics for General Discussion

1. Compare the relative values of choral and instrumental activities in the high school. Chapter II will give you some assistance in the approach to this question.

2. Have you ever used any of the methods for organizing orchestras and bands suggested in this chapter? Which method have you found to be the most successful? Point out specific reasons for your answer.

3. Do you know a successful instrumental teacher who is an excellent conductor as well? What are some of the procedures that he uses in orchestra or band rehearsals?

4. List a number of suggestions which will foster better discipline in large instrumental organizations. Which ones agree with the discussion of discipline in this chapter?

5. Were small ensembles developed in your high school? Point out the relative values of small and large instrumental ensembles in the high school.

6. What has been your experience with jazz bands? Is the organization of them a crucial issue in your high school music today? What is your attitude of using jazz music in the schools?

7. If you were teaching in a high school and there was neither a band nor an orchestra, which would you organize first? What has been the procedure in introducing instrumental music into some high school with which you are acquainted?

From *LEAVES OF GRASS*

All music is what awakes from you when you are reminded by the instruments,

It is not the violins and the cornets, it is not the oboe nor the beating drums, nor the score of the baritone singer singing his sweet romanza, nor that of the men's chorus, nor that of the women's chorus,

It is nearer and farther than they.

WALT WHITMAN

Chapter 10

INSTRUMENTAL CLASSES

It is very significant that the rapid and extended growth of school orchestras and bands was accompanied by a similar growth of instrumental classes. In fact, the development of these orchestras and bands has undoubtedly been contingent upon a similar development of instrumental classes. For educational and economic reasons the system of private teaching had to be supplemented by class instruction on instruments. In truth, this change from the old style of dependence on private lessons to the newer emphasis on class lessons is one of the most far-reaching innovations in music education in the past century. What are the essential differences between the two types of lessons?

Trends in Teaching Instruments

The traditional type of private lesson was seldom a thrilling adventure. At first, the student played scales and arpeggios; then the assignment in the exercise book was played; and finally, attention was turned to a "piece of music." It is true that the private teacher today has adopted more modern methods. He has been forced to do this through competition with class lessons and because he has seen the advantage of adopting the functional approach so successful in classes. The traditional private lesson emphasized abstract technique out of all proportion; and, although more consideration is now given to the relation of technique to expression, it is still difficult for some private teachers not to pay undue obeisance to technique which is abstract and has little application in the making of music.

Students like to do things together. It is much more fun to make music with a group of friends than by one's self. Also, in the class lesson one does not have to spend most of the time on those scales and exercises. The music is interesting. Part of the time is spent on the band or orchestra music. It makes one feel more like practising technical exercises when one is doing it with friends and when one can see the reason for it. No wonder the class instrumental lessons became more popular than private lessons!

Criticism is often leveled at the class lesson. The charge is made that it does not develop musicians. Progress is slow. It is too cumbersome to give adequate instruction. It is impossible to give sufficient individual attention to obtain results. In answer to such criticism let us compare the shortcomings of the meager school orchestra before the introduction of class instruction with the quantity and quality of school orchestras and bands since its inauguration. The difficulty of understanding between the private teacher and the music educator is found in the difference of their aims. The aim of the private teacher is chiefly professional, while that of the music teacher in the school is primarily social and educational.

Numerous problems arise in the class teaching of instruments in the schools. Shall the classes be composed of individual or heterogeneous instruments? How large shall the classes be? Shall they be preliminary to membership in the orchestra or band? Shall more than one student use the same instrument? Shall there be classes on different levels of advancement? We shall discuss these questions in relation to the first one which, at present, is the most controversial.

Classes of Individual Instruments

These classes are composed of the same kind of instruments, such as the violin, clarinet, or cornet. Classes in instruments were first organized in this manner. Such classes are in contrast to those of heterogeneous instruments, where all types of instruments are taught together.

The type of class will often depend upon the size of the school and the number of instrumental instructors available. It is easier to segregate instruments in a larger school. If classes in individual instruments are favored, they should not serve only as preparation for the existing orchestra or band, but a beginning ensemble for them should be organized at the same time. Exponents of this type of class claim the following advantages.

1. Progress is more rapid since students can be checked more closely.
2. Good habits in playing are more readily formed since the teacher has greater opportunity to anticipate and avoid faults.
3. Technical problems are so peculiar to individual instruments, *i.e.,* tone color, fingering, bowing, and embouchures, that it is almost impossible to give instruction on all types of instruments at the same time.
4. Problems of key and range make it difficult to secure sufficient materials suitable for all instruments in the beginning.

Classes of Heterogeneous Instruments

For beginners there is a decided trend toward classes of mixed instruments. This fact in a measure speaks for itself. Many musicians who at first scoffed at the idea of instrumental class lessons have become one hundred per cent converts after seeing results and learning to teach the classes themselves. Experiments showed that five trumpet players meeting for group instruction five times per week would learn faster than five trumpeters meeting for individual instruction once per week each.[1] This evidence was too convincing to ignore. As music teachers began to teach instruments in groups, they discovered that they grew in their ability to teach increasing numbers. The next step was the combining of different instruments. Gradually many teachers developed their skill to the point where beginners could be taken as a full band or orchestra and developed into a creditable organization without additional instruction.

There seem to be three valid reasons for beginning classes in heterogeneous instruments; namely, (1) educational, (2) social, (3) economic. The first two were discussed in Chapter IX in conjunction with the methods of organizing bands and orchestras. The possibility of securing a more balanced instrumentation, the greater challenge to the student, the richer musical experience, and the stronger social motive in these mixed classes were pointed out.

The economic factor is without doubt a strong argument. Segregated classes in instruments will be relatively small, at least in the high school. It is not easy to get together twenty-five or thirty instruments of one kind, even saxophones. It is doubtful that, in our public school system, small individual class instrumental lessons are a justifiable use of teacher time. One of the best arguments to the tax-payer for retaining instrumental music in the schools is the ability of the teacher to get results with large groups of mixed instruments. These classes can stand shoulder to shoulder economically with other subjects in the curriculum.

Another indefensible practice, at least under present

[1] Lockhart, Lee M., "Classes of Heterogeneous Instruments," Music Educators National Conference. *Yearbook 1936*, p. 242.

conditions, is that of permitting expensive school-owned instruments to be used by only one student. To eliminate this expensive practice, the "Multiple Use" plan has been introduced to many schools. This plan simply provides several mouthpieces for each instrument. Each student has a different mouthpiece and uses the same instrument. This plan presupposes classes on different levels of advancement. Of course these instruments are supplemented with privately-owned and privately-played instruments. The school-owned instruments remain at the school but may be checked out in the evening for practice at home. This plan is expedient in introducing and developing large instrumental classes of heterogeneous instruments.

The criticisms leveled at the mixed instrumental groups cannot be disregarded. It *is* difficult to teach strings and winds together. Technical progress is often slower when wind and percussion instruments are used together. Another detail in the total picture is the need for classes composed of members of the advanced band and orchestra. In consideration of all these factors, it seems educationally and economically sound to organize classes at different levels for certain homogeneous types of instruments which will supplement the instruction received in the bands and orchestras and where problems of technique and expression can be given more individual attention.

Types of Instrumental Classes

The outstanding problem in instrumental classes is to balance the economic factor with educational and musical results. Many kinds of segregation have been demonstrated as practicable. In view of the problems present, there is a growing tendency to divide the instruments into strings, winds, and percussion sections. The resulting classes will form a balanced string orchestra, a wind band, and a drum corps. Further segregation may be feasible with advanced groups.

The String Orchestra Class

This group should be as far as possible a full string ensemble with balanced instrumentation. The advanced level functions as a vital and regular part of the school symphony orchestra. The beginning level has the dual advantage of both technical and ensemble instruction as well as sectional preparation for playing in an orchestra. Although the technical problems of violins, violas, 'cellos, and double basses are different, still they are all strings and they are sufficiently related that a class of such instruments does not present an impracticable teaching problem. Moreover, there is good material for beginning groups and the master composers have devoted some of their most serious efforts to the string orchestra.

Because of the greater difficulty in playing string instruments than in playing winds, some music educators fear lest school orchestras will be largely replaced by bands. *This need not be!* The educational value of developing strings is decidedly worth the effort. It is true that there must be more efficient teaching for string instruments; also that instruction should usually begin before the high school, preferably in the elementary school. The technical problems of violins and other strings must be analyzed carefully by each teacher to avoid the pitfalls and detours that so many string players have encountered. Closer supervision of practice, especially at the beginning, is necessary to prevent the fixing of bad habits of position and bowing.

Tone. It is usually expected that beginning string players, especially violinists, will "scratch around" for about two years before any sound that resembles a musical tone

Upper left—*Milam Quintet—First Chair players from Beaumont (Texas).*

Upper right—*High School Orchestra, small ensemble, Beaumont (Texas) H. S. Dr. Lena Milam, Director.*

Lower left—*Bells, Elkhart (Indiana) High School.*

Lower right—*Proviso High School (Maywood, Illinois). Brass ensemble.*

is forthcoming from the instrument. In many cases this is a great waste of time. The development of tone should be approached by giving the student a conception of good tone. He must be made "tone conscious." The student must, first of all, form his ideal of good tone mentally. *He must first think tone*. Listening to great artists and to fine symphony orchestras will be a decided help to students in forming the right concept of tone, entirely practicable in this era of the radio. The teacher can assist greatly in this development by being able to demonstrate a good string tone himself.

Technique. Tone depends largely upon a bow technique, which is as essential to the string player as breath control is to the singer or the wind instrument player. Without bow technique the full beauty of the composition will remain hidden and obscure, regardless of the care taken in other phases of study. It is the bow that gives to the string instruments their dignity, their individuality, their power of expression, and that distinguishes the artist from the amateur.

The left hand technique on the violin involves both the position of the arm in supporting the instrument and the position of the wrist so as to place the fingers in the right relationship with the finger board. The violin must be held up so as to secure the freest resonance, and forward, in order that the bow may be drawn at the correct angle across the strings. This insures ease in moving from one position to another on the keyboard and allows freedom for finger dexterity and control without which good intonation is impossible.

The same considerations apply to the playing of the viola, 'cello, and double bass, namely, the holding of the instrument, bowing, position of the left arm, and finger control. There are definite differences in the technique of playing these other string instruments and the teacher must be well grounded in the fundamental technical principles of each.

Teachers must continue to analyze the technical difficulties and eliminate hazards. A student progresses to the degree in which he *understands and puts into practice the fundamental principles involved in playing the instrument of his choice.* The art of producing musical tones on string instruments is not a mystery; it can be taught to students with average intelligence and sensitivity. The teacher can easily point out that playing a string instrument is a satisfaction that continues throughout life because of the wealth of literature available and the many opportunities for continued playing. If students are given a conception of a beautiful string tone and devote some time to intelligent practice, there need not be a scarcity of string players.

The Wind Band

When all the wind instruments are instructed in one class, the resulting ensemble is a complete band except for the percussion section. This arrangement affords greater opportunities for more interesting material and greater musical enjoyment than when woodwind and brass are taught separately; it also presents more teaching problems for the instructor. However, in many places these problems are now being overcome by the teacher who "knows his business." There are many books on the market that give detailed instruction in the individual peculiarities of the different wind instruments. In our discussion we will refer to only a few basic principles.

Tone. As with the development of string players, it is important that wind players become tone-conscious and that each player have the right conception of the timbre of his own instrument. To develop this tone, attention must be given to breath control. It is very similar to the control in the singing act, and so singing can be used to good advantage in developing wind players. The embouchure must be developed, but too many wind players are "lip-conscious." Much of the work of the lips and throat muscles must be transferred to the larger muscles of the abdomen. Careful attention to posture tends to facilitate the use of these muscles. Although the more intricate phases of tonguing should be postponed until sustained tone can be produced, the importance of a clean attack from the beginning cannot be over-emphasized. A feeling of pronouncing "toe" as tones are attacked has a tendency to employ the larger breath muscles and to produce richer and fuller tone.

Technique. Flexibility is dependent upon several factors, including posture, embouchure, tonguing, and fingering. The importance of posture for wind players in producing a musical tone has been pointed out. It is of equal importance in attaining a flexible technique. It is through the embouchure that the instrument becomes a medium for personal expression. Embouchure means more than merely the position of the mouthpiece on the lips. It involves the coordination of all the muscles used in producing tone. A faulty embouchure will defeat the purpose of teacher and player, regardless of the attention given to other factors of technique. Fluent tonguing, which is equivalent to articulation in singing, is largely dependent upon a correct embouchure and an intelligent understanding of the difficulties involved. Fingering is flexible in proportion to freedom from muscular tension. A thorough study of the details involved in these basic principles will reap rich technical rewards.

The Drum Corps

The percussion class may well include more than drums, but it is recognized as an organization if called a drum corps. All rhythmic instruments should be included in the class, but special instruction is usually needed for such instruments as the xylophone, orchestra bells, triangle, tambourine, gong, and chimes as they are used in ensemble performance.

The percussion section, and especially the drummers, are often the forgotten members of the band and orchestra. After a brief lesson on how to hold the sticks, the players in this section are left to shift for themselves. The teacher is so involved with developing strings and winds that this section is neglected. Indeed, in high school ensembles throughout the country, the percussion section is often the weakest. That this is a musical tragedy is often demonstrated in results of ensemble performance.

Most teachers realize the importance of the tympani in the orchestra, but limit their instruction to desultory suggestions as to tuning, tone, and technique. Another mistake is the erroneous assumption that anybody can play the bass drum. To keep a steady beat on the bass drum demands a player with keen rhythmic sense. Moreover, many leaders seem unaware that the bass drum is capable of a great variety of musical effects. It is the side drum players that often suffer the most neglect. Many times there is no training in developing an even beat or a roll. Every teacher should make sure that these drummers understand the rudiments of drumming and are able to execute them.[2] Attention must likewise be given to the effect that can be gained from the proper use of the cymbal, tambourine,

[2] A sheet containing thirteen rudiments of drumming may be obtained from Ludwig and Ludwig, Chicago, Illinois.

triangle, gong, and other accessories. *Percussion instruments are important!* A class devoted to their development will pay dividends in musical results.

The Piano Class

Various teachers of music have taken a census of their respective schools to determine the students who would like to play a musical instrument and also the instrument which they prefer. The number of students who wish to play the piano is always surprising. And yet it can be understood when we consider the versatility of the piano. It provides keen musical satisfaction when played alone for one's own enjoyment. It is indispensable for accompanying instrumental and vocal solos. It gives added zest to group singing. It is used in the orchestra to support and to supply missing harmonies. And finally, nearly all social gatherings in the home, school, church, and community use a piano and welcome a pianist.

The introduction of piano classes in the schools was a decided break with the traditional method of teaching piano in this country. The private piano lesson followed the same routine as private lessons on other instruments; namely, scales, exercises, pieces. Although Liszt often met his pupils as a group to play for them, to have them play for each other, and to make suggestions for the benefit of all, still, this group did not resemble the modern piano class, especially beginners. Moreover, this practice of Liszt's was not adopted by many teachers except to form a few "master" classes.

There is no doubt that piano classes should begin in the elementary grades or the junior high school. However, if there are students who wish to begin piano study in the high school, it should be provided. Moreover, instruction should be continued for those students who have begun their study in the earlier grades. Piano classes offer an ideal medium for developing a keener appreciation of music. Students of piano classes are often the leaders in other musical activities of the schools. Finally, a large share of extending and perpetuating the spirit of music in adult life will depend upon those people who can play the piano.

The introduction of piano classes in the schools has affected private teaching in two ways. First of all, it has been proved that classes have stimulated wider interest and that private teachers who are qualified have received their share of the greater number of students. Secondly, the private teacher has been led to examine his own methods of teaching, to study class piano methods, and to adopt more modern procedures with his own students.

Piano instruction in the schools can be sponsored only in classes. The advantages of class lessons over private piano lessons are similar to those in the study of other instruments. It may be well to review these educational advantages in the light of piano study.

Economic. Piano classes are inexpensive and thus they make possible the study of the piano in the schools. With one piano in the room, a qualified teacher can take care of a class of from ten to twenty students. Two or even three pianos are an advantage but not a necessity. The other students can be supplied with silent keyboards, which are very useful in many phases of the work.

The fact that piano class instruction is inexpensive has led to certain abuses which should be recognized and corrected. For one thing, it has led many teachers to feel that the class is more a means for testing aptitude than for actual instruction in piano playing, and that in the class the capable pupils may be discovered and then diverted to individual lessons where real progress may be expected. Needless to say, teachers who have this attitude seldom give the problems of class instruction their best study, and the results of their work are not likely to be strikingly successful.

In some places the teacher transfers pupils from the class to her own private instruction. Indeed, certain school systems approve this plan for augmenting the teacher's salary, even though obviously it cuts into the livelihood of the community's private piano teachers and opens the way to questionable practices.

Few high schools are prepared to offer individual lessons in piano playing excepting where the teachers use the high school building and equipment to give private lessons, for which the students pay them. While it has been demonstrated that class instruction in piano can be carried to a high level of performance, it is quite evident that many students need individual instruction, and these students should be recommended to good private teachers.

Piano classes should be supported by the board of education in the same way as other instrumental classes are and for that matter as all instruction is. There is never a charge for sewing or shop lessons, so why charge for piano lessons? In some places this seems impossible at the present time. We hold the view that if it is necessary to charge a nominal fee of from ten to twenty-five cents for each lesson, this arrangement is better than no lessons at all. Even this arrangement aids many interested students who otherwise could not afford to study the piano.

Social. Young people like to work if they are working together. For many students, the private lesson was drudgery. The piano class now is composed of their friends and they enjoy studying with them. Therefore, the piano class is popular with students. This enjoyment of working together should not be interpreted as meaning that piano playing, class or otherwise, is all "fun." It is fun, but it is also hard work. The initial interest of the class is transformed into sustained interest through the enjoyment that comes from cooperative and serious effort.

Musical. Early criticisms of piano classes discredited the quality of performers produced. Piano classes have answered these criticisms by producing more performers, better performers in many cases, and finally, what is more important, better musicians. The nature of the piano class engenders this musicianship. It was necessary for the class to adopt procedures which were conducive to the development of a broad and discriminating musicianship. Let us examine some of the procedures which produce these better musicians.

Ear-Training

It is amazing how often the average pianist fails to actually hear music that he plays. This failure is due to the mechanical workings of the piano. When a key is pressed with the finger, a definite pitch is sounded. There is no need for an adjustment of finger or embouchure as one finds in string or wind instruments. As a result the pianist is not compelled to listen for the tones to be played. For this reason he may fail to develop a sense of auditory imagery.

The piano class took the right step in the beginning by encouraging students to "play by ear." To the traditional private teacher this was a sacrilege. Their motto was, "stick to the notes." By the practice of essential listening, the piano class forces students to hear a melody before it is played. Later students begin to hear simple harmonies that accompany the melodies. Gradually the thematic relationships are classified until a better understanding of the structure of the music is reached.

Another phase of ear-training is developed by the practice of having students listen carefully while other members of the class are playing. They learn to recognize harmonies, cadences, phrase structure, simple forms, and variations in style. Thus, through "playing by ear" and listening carefully, pianists are trained to hear the music that they play. *Better musicianship results.*

Eye-Training

Another woeful weakness of the average pianist is his lack of ability to read music readily at sight. The average private lesson of scales, exercises, and prepared pieces gives little opportunity to develop this important skill, which is the mark of a musician. Of course there are private teachers who are achieving this objective, but the class lesson by its very nature facilitates it. Reading music means more than playing the right notes in correct rhythm at sight. Music reading involves the ability to do this plus the ability to bring out the expressive qualities of the music. Eye-training is a natural corollary of ear-training; musicians should be able to "see what they hear and hear what they see."

The piano class devotes considerable attention to this phase of musicianship through: (1) rote work, (2) listening as one follows the score, (3) studying pieces with appropriate reading drill, and (4) encouraging students to spend a certain amount of practice time at home reading through new material.[3] Rote work develops a sense of anticipation of what normally is to come, a skill so valuable in reading music. Listening as one follows the score helps to associate the printed page with the musical sound. Opportunity for reading in the class and at home provides the actual practice needed to develop this skill.

[3] Raymond Burrows, "The Positive Approach, a Significant Opportunity in Piano Class Instruction." Music Educators National Conference, *Yearbook 1936*, pp. 267-272.

Technique

The reader is referred to the discussion in the preceding chapter on technique and expression in connection with rehearsing musical ensembles as prefatory and relevant to our present discussion. We repeat that technique and expression are separated only for the sake of emphasis. Their development should coincide in actual practice for they are dependent upon each other.

The principle presented in our discussions of "function before technique" does not mean that there is no place for study of special technique in the piano class. It does mean, however, that students will understand how they are to profit by technical practice. Varying conditions in the class will determine the most advantageous time to introduce the study of scales and arpeggios to develop flexibility. It may arise from a recognized need of a student to make runs and scale passages more fluent in the composition that is being studied. As the other members of the class become aware of his need to make the musical effect more artistic, they will recognize a similar need in their own performing difficulties. This is the psychological time to introduce technical exercises. With high school students the opportune time may occur relatively much earlier than with younger children.

A caution may be added concerning the use of the damper pedal. The various uses of the pedal must be studied and analyzed. The pedal is designed to produce better musical effects, not to cover up mistakes. We wish to go on record as saying that the one most prevalent and inexcusable fault of the amateur pianist is the overuse of the pedal.

Expression

There have been many deprecatory remarks made about the expressive inadequacies of the piano. For one thing, there is no control over the tone after the key has been pressed. Therefore, the expressive qualities of the piano are the result of control of the balance between tones rather than the qualities of a single tone. This balance includes the relation between melody and harmony, between different contrapuntal lines, and between the notes of a chord. The piano touch determines the range of dynamics, and, in part, phrasing and nuance. The duration of the tones marks the style of playing as staccato or legato as well as phrasing and nuance. Control of these various factors in expression is needed for artistic piano playing.

One of the delights of the piano is its power to produce marked rhythms. When this power is added to the possibilities of artistic pedaling, and to the variety of tonal possibilities described above, we fail to see how anyone can deny the musical and expressive qualities of the piano. It stands supreme as the most accessible and universal instrument from which one individual can obtain complete musical satisfaction. It encompasses all the elements of music. The great masters truly realized its expressive qualities by devoting some of their most profound musical ideas to the medium of the piano. *The literature for the piano is rich in quality and quantity.*

Accompanists

We often hear the statement made that "accompanists are born, not made." The same statement is often made about teachers. This book was written on the hypothesis that (paraphrasing George Gershwin), "It Ain't Necessarily So." In fact, we would defend the thesis that born accompanists and teachers must also be trained. *If someone would say that the training of accompanists is the most neglected of all musical preparation, we would heartily agree.*

When one considers the need of excellent accompanists,

it is surprising that one finds practically no systematic training for their development. If choral conductors were honest, they would have to admit that, on some occasions and in some situations, the accompanist is more needed than they themselves are. The good accompanist can create enthusiasm in group singing, he can "make or break" an artistic musical performance, and he can contribute in countless ways to the musical life of school and community.

It is true that the accompanist must be a sensitive musician. A common instruction to an accompanist is to "follow the soloist." Too often he does just that. No, he must be so sensitive, so musical, that he will anticipate the intentions of the soloist in order that the combined performance of the two may be an artistic whole.

By all means there should be a class in accompanying. In the class, students would receive practice in this art. Difficulties in accompanying choruses and different types of soloists would be studied. Think of the musical literature that could be covered by such a class! In the light of its contribution to the musical life of the school, such a class might well be the most important instrumental class in the curriculum.

Guidance in the Selection of Instruments

Nothing has been said about the ability to prognosticate success on different types of instruments. The usual approach to this problem by music teachers is through a priori reasoning, chance observation, or reference to instruction in orchestra and band manuals. The factors often considered are pitch, tonal memory, and rhythm "senses," as measured by standardized tests, and in addition, such physical characteristics as slenderness of fingers, evenness of teeth, thickness of lips, and alignment of jaws. The existence of professional violinists with short fingers, woodwind players with uneven teeth, and French horn players with thick lips have caused some teachers to question this usual procedure in predicting success on various instruments.

One of the most interesting investigations that we have found is reported by Charles Lamp. He reports these findings in light of the experiment conducted with high school students in San Francisco.[4] The findings of the experiment were also reported in the *Journal of Educational Psychology,* November, 1935. These findings are of sufficient importance to include here:

(1) Each of the three "mental" measurements, namely IQ (Terman) and the Seashore measures of pitch and tonal memory, show positive correlations with importance on each of the three types of instruments studied. However, no one of the nine coefficients is high enough to be of practical value for individual guidance.

(2) Pitch as measured by the Seashore test appears to be more essential for success in brass performance than in string performance, the coefficients being .49 and .35 respectively. The difference between these correlations, amounting to but 1.7 PE, is too small to be reliable, but the finding is suggestive. While it is true that a violinist must produce notes which are accurate relative to others sounded, the player of a brass horn, having no strings of fixed pitch as reference points, needs something resembling a sense of absolute pitch. The ability required to image a tone accurately before its production in relation to the tone just produced is doubtless somewhat akin to the trait measured by Seashore under the name of "tonal memory."

(3) Neither of the physical traits listed reveals any significant relationship with success on any of these instru-

[4] "Can Aptitude for Specific Musical Instruments Be Determined?" Music Educators National Conference, *Yearbook, 1936,* pp. 246-250.

ments. Slenderness of fingers, so far from figuring largely in success on violin, shows a correlation of only .17 plus or minus, .09 in the case of beginners. Similarly, evenness of teeth appears to have no significant bearing on either brass or woodwind playing, despite the confident assertions in band and orchestra leaders' manuals.

(4) Of the physical measurements studied, only lip thickness behaved at all as expected. This was found to correlate .28 plus or minus, .088 with diameter of mouthpiece favored by brass players. How low this relationship is, however, may be illustrated by the fact that the boy having the thickest lips in the entire experimental group and the one having the thinnest lips, both became professional French horn players of marked ability.

Experiments of this nature indicate that there are other factors to be considered in predicting instrumental success, aside from those that are usually accepted as a basis for prognostication. Such elements as motor reaction, innervation, digital dexterity, lip texture and lip musculature have been overlooked entirely, or it has been assumed that they are either evenly distributed or non-selective. Whereas the truth of the matter is that these elements may be the real selective elements, varying with each individual. A student may test high in pitch and still not have the lip texture and lip musculature necessary to become a successful brass player. Another may test high in pitch and have long, slender fingers; still some condition of the anatomical structure of the hand may interfere with the dexterity of certain finger movements necessary for the violin.

Another finding of the foregoing experiment has significant importance; namely, if a student fails on one type of instrument he has three chances out of four to do normal or superior work on one of the other two types of instruments included in the experiment. What a consolation that should be to one who is deeply interested in instrumental study but has failed on one type of instrument!

In the light of these findings and the findings of other experiments, the music teacher should give every consideration to a student in his choice of an instrument. It would even appear that the predilection of a student for the tone quality of an instrument bears distinct relationship with his success in playing that instrument. Elimination from study for some slight physical handicap is dangerous practice. Students who fail to do normal work on one type of instrument should be encouraged to try another. *Until better measures for prognostication are devised, every student should have the opportunity to pursue his interest in instrumental study to ultimate success.*

Conclusion

Instrumental study is one of the more expensive activities in the high school curriculum.[5] But playing instruments in a group has such a hold on these young people and appeals so directly to the parents and the community that the wise administrator gives whole-hearted support to instrumental organizations.

When a vital need arises the human mind finds ways to meet this need. It is a tribute to the music educator that he had the vision to utilize the instrumental class as an answer to the economic criticism of the tax payer and board of education. Not only did he utilize the instrumental class as preparation for ensembles but he discovered in it superior educational values of its own. Through the development of class work instrumental study has been made available to all students and the expense of this study has been reduced to such a degree that its inclusion in the curriculum at public expense is not only feasible but also expedient.

[5] Russell V. Morgan, "Analysis of Teaching Costs by Subjects," Music Educators National Conference, *Yearbook, 1933*, pp. 313-318.

Topics for General Discussion

1. Is class teaching equally successful for all instruments? Which instruments seem to give more difficulty than others? Give reasons for your answer.

2. Examine several instrumental class methods suggested in the appendix of this book. Are most of them designed for heterogeneous or homogeneous grouping of instruments? Do they contain materials which follow the principles suggested in this chapter? Be specific in your answers.

3. Some instrumental teachers advocate piano classes as preparation for other instrumental study. What is your opinion of this idea?

4. Did the good accompanists that you have known have special training or did they just "grow up" like Topsy? What practices would you advise to train accompanists in the high school?

5. Point out some of the accepted practices in the selection of instruments with which the report of the study by Charles Lamp disagrees. Did this study support or contradict your own opinions? Explain.

6. A young lady applied for the position of music instructor in a high school. When asked if she could play the piano "by ear," she replied, "I used to 'play by ear,' but my professor has corrected that." What is wrong with this story?

APPRECIATION

Hold this sea-shell to your ear,
  And you shall hear,
Not the andante of the sea
Not the wild wind's symphony
But your own heart's minstrelsy.

You do poets and their song
  A grievous wrong,
If your own heart does not bring
To their high imagining
As much beauty as they sing.

THOMAS BAILEY ALDRICH

Chapter 11

LISTENING ACTIVITIES

Throughout this book we have emphasized the primary aim of music education as appreciation. We do not mean an appreciation which is superficial. We mean an appreciation which pierces the rim of understanding about music and reaches the core of the inherent beauty in music. Such appreciation will make music a part of living, a recognized force in human and cultural relationships.

The Meaning of Appreciation

When music teachers talk of music appreciation, they usually speak in such vague terms as a "love for music." Is it not true that one can also appreciate an enemy? From some teachers one hears the expression that appreciation is the "understanding of music." Too often this simply means "knowledge about music." If we had to choose, we would prefer a lover of music with little understanding of it to a person well versed in the factual aspects of music, but with no apparent love for it.

But if these things in themselves are not appreciation, what are the things which are involved and intrinsic in appreciation? First of all, it seems to us that there should be joy in listening to, or participating in, music. We use "joy" rather than "pleasure," for it seems to imply deeper feeling. Secondly, appreciation does involve understanding. This understanding, however, is more than mere knowledge, although it involves "knowing." Knowledge implies recognition, cognizance, and an acquaintance with fact. Understanding includes knowledge, but also implies discernment, discrimination, clear comprehension, and judgment. Appreciation has this element of appraisal in it. *Webster speaks of appreciation as knowing and feeling the worth of something*. It is difficult to improve upon this definition. It might be applied to a particular composition without implying that one "loves" that number.

Furthermore, when something is appreciated, it increases in value. One's appreciation of music is a process of seeing and feeling a gradual increase in the value of music. Consequently, when one appreciates music, one must be able to evaluate it rightly; but this evaluation is the result of both feeling and knowing its worth.

The Meaning of Listening

"He that hath ears to hear, let him hear." Listening means just that—giving ear to something, giving heed to something. It involves attention. We hear much of active and creative listening. These terms are often vague, but they point in the right direction.

Active listening endeavors to overcome a passive attitude. It includes marked attention. But it also means acting upon the music rather than being acted upon by the music. Training in active listening may involve bodily response to music, such as clapping to its meter, dancing to its rhythms and forms, singing and playing its melodies, and reacting to its moods. Creative listening may include active listening, but it also involves recreating the music in terms of one's own experiences. It seeks to feel and understand the emotional experience which brought the music into being. It embraces the various qualities of the creative act; namely, assimilation, clarification, selection, and expression. It searches for the message through a greater comprehension of the language in which the composer expresses himself.

Types of Listening

Although we often speak of types of listeners, it is probably more correct to speak of types of listening, since few people listen consistently with one type of response. Listening responses usually vary with external conditions, inner feelings, and familiarity with the music which is being heard. And so when we speak of types of listening, we refer to those responses to which people conform with more or less consistency until they can almost be classified into types of listeners.[1]

Sensuous

Many people, while listening to music, are "lost in a sea of sound"; others bathe in the "sweet concord" of melody and harmony. Such listening limits appreciation. Such appreciation is naïve. The baby is soothed by the lullaby, primitive man responds to the beat of the drum, the warrior thrills to the fanfare of trumpets, and the heartstrings are touched by the nostalgic melody. People who listen to music in this way only do so in a manner similar to that of the persons who sees and listens to a French comedy without understanding the language. The gist of the play may be grasped, but the jest is entirely missed.

Associative

Probably the second most prevalent type of listening is based upon the connotation of music. Music is peculiar in its ability to evoke from memory pleasurable experiences and associations. Sousa's "Stars and Stripes Forever" vivi-

[1] James L. Mursell, *The Psychology of Music*. New York: W. W. Norton and Company, 1937, p. 218.

fies the image of "Old Glory" flying in the breeze; the Overture to "The Flying Dutchman" brings to mind that trip on the ocean; a favorite melody of Tschaikowsky's recalls that other person with similar tastes. *Few people listen to music who do not at some time enjoy the pleasurable associations which it evokes.* And yet this type of listening is usually belittled by musicians. It certainly is not the acme of appreciation but it has its place in the development of a more discriminating type of listening.

Intellectual

To have a clearer understanding of the language of music it is necessary to study the agencies of musical tones and the structure of music. The intellectual type of listening consists of devoted attention to these factors. It is the type of listening which is emphasized by trained musicians. No less a personage than Stravinsky, during his varied musical career, has stated that it is the only aspect of music with which the composer should be concerned. This seems to be carrying things too far. Such an attitude will relegate music into an esoteric art for the limited few. Composers and musicians will find themselves separated from people and life, the source of their support and inspiration.

However, even with musicians, listening responses are not confined to this intellectual type of listening. They, too, are thrilled by the trumpet call in the "Lenore Overture"; they, too, are "reminded by the instruments," paraphrasing Walt Whitman; and they, too, enjoy a descriptive program such as the one that accompanies "Till Eulenspiegel," by Strauss.

Listening to Music

It has been pointed out that few people listen to music with only one type of response. It is natural and necessary for us to enjoy the sensuous qualities of music because by this response our entire physical and emotional being is stirred. The associations and memories which may accompany a piece of music often endear it to us. If these types of listening are supplemented by the study of music as a language and of the elements that compose the organization of that language, then listening to music can become one of the most delightful and satisfying of aesthetic experiences.

The Message of Music

If music is a language, it has meaning; it has a message for human ears. There is much divergence of opinion as to the manner in which the composer works, but it seems to be similar to that of other creators except for the medium. Our conception of music creation is that of a composer who, having an experience with beauty, wishes to share it with others. This creative expression may grow out of a single incident or it may be the result of cumulative experiences of several years or of a lifetime. His desire to share it may grow out of inner compulsion, desire for recognition, or definite commission. By using the medium of tone, he endeavors to arouse in others emotions similar to those that have stirred him. *True appreciation is the reverse of this path.* Seeking for the message of the music, the listener traverses the maze of tone and endeavors to reach the emotional quality of the experience which inspired the music.

Sometimes the composer gives clues which will assist the listener along that path. The title may furnish a clue. The music may tell a story, paint a picture, or awaken lovely memories with harmonious sounds. Musicians call this "program" music, often in a deprecatory sense. And yet this type of music includes such masterpieces as "Ein Heldenleben" by Strauss, "Sixth Symphony" by Beethoven, and the Prelude to "Lohengrin" by Wagner. It is true that the music can be enjoyed for itself alone without the accompanying program. But if the composer furnishes a program, the listener should know what it is as an introduction, at least, to the message of the music.

Very often titles are limited to "String Quartet in G," or "Theme and Variations." There is no semblance of a program. Musicians call this music "pure" or "absolute." Although the message of such music will have different meaning for various people, the tonal patterns in themselves offer a means of pure, aesthetic enjoyment apart from literal association. Only through a study of the materials and structure of the music will one grasp the message of the music. Emotional reactions will be determined partly by understanding.

The message of music is often made more meaningful when approached through some life experience with which it seems associated. *War* will make more vivid the fervor of patriotic music associated with a country. *Worship* will make more reverent the music of the church. *Work* will make more intimate the qualities of music which sing the song of labor. An approach to the message of music which speaks the language of our own daily lives strikes a sympathetic chord in the listener who is beginning his journey in the land of music.

The Musical Tone

The material and medium of music is tone. To understand the language of music the listener must become sensitive to tone. This sensitivity includes a recognition of the various physical factors of tone; namely, pitch, volume, and quality. What is the difference in effect of a song sung by a high voice and a low voice? What is the effect of a delicate *piano* and a full resonant *forte?* What is the effect of singing or playing a composition at different levels of dynamics? And finally, what is the effect of the different qualities of tone which the composer uses to express himself? The amorous voice of the tenor usually makes him the hero of the opera, although the baritone voice has the more heroic quality. A melody played on the strings differs in meaning and emotional quality from the same melody played on the French horn.

To be able to discover the subtleties of tonal shadings and colors is one of the first steps toward a more discriminating listening and a keener appreciation. It is not enough to be able to recognize the different voices and instruments. We must ask ourselves these questions: What are the characteristics of the different kinds of voices and what styles of songs are best suited to these voices? Why did the composer use the oboe to play a particular melody and why did he use certain combination of instruments in other situations?

Design in Music

The architectonic quality of music is expressed through its design. We use the word "design" instead of "form" because we conceive of form as being the synthesis and fusion of all the musical elements and means which are used to produce an harmonious and expressive whole. Design contributes to form by arranging and bringing ordered relationships among the many constituent elements.

There are three common methods of expressing an idea through the medium of language: (1) by continual repetition of the same idea, (2) by stating the idea in several different ways, and (3) by contrasting the idea with other ideas to clarify and vivify it. In music, the first method is exemplified by the rondo form which is a continual reiteration of a dominant musical idea separated by intervening sections. The second method is exemplified by the theme and variation form where the dominant musical idea is expressed in various styles by various means. And finally, the third method is exemplified by the two-part song form, three-part song form, classic-dance form, and the sonata allegro form. The contrapuntal forms in music, such as, the canon, invention, and fugue, also employ all three of these methods of reiteration, variation, and contrast, utilizing them to weave intricate tonal patterns from the basic idea or theme.

To the average listener these terms sound academic and technical. However, it is not beyond his grasp to recognize these designs, if a little diligent study is applied to them. *Learning to follow a score is a great asset because it employs visual as well as aural perception.* It is necessary to understand design in music if one is to sense the full import of the great masterpieces based on pure musical form.

Rhythm in Music

The unique quality of music is tone, but the life and flow of music is determined by the organization of tone into rhythmic patterns. The two aspects of musical rhythms are the variety of patterns and the pulse or beat of the music which brings order to these patterns.

To sense rhythm is not a matter of recognizing time signatures, but rather of experiencing through bodily response the accents of the pulse of the music and the variations in the patterns. "Active listening" is a decided aid in experiencing rhythms. Conducting the meter and clapping or walking to the rhythmic patterns are devices which direct attention to feeling the rhythm of music.

Melody

Everybody loves a good tune. The tune is about as far, however, as most people go in their appreciation of music.

The tune is the principal melody of a piece of music. But most compositions contain many melodies either succeeding one another or sounded simultaneously. Sometimes there is a counter-melody which is usually called an obligato or descant. These counter-melodies are easily discernible because as a rule they lie in a higher range than the tune. But in choral compositions the alto, tenor, and bass parts are also melodies. A little concentration is necessary in order to hear these melodies. Contrapuntal music consists of combining two or more different melodies. The various movements of symphonies are based upon melodies, often called themes or motives. These themes are continually heard in toto or in part. If the listener learns to sing and to recognize these melodies, his enjoyment of music will be greatly enhanced. Theodore Thomas once said, "Popular music is familiar music." There is no better way of becoming familiar with the great masterpieces than by learning to sing their melodies.

Harmony

The study of harmony seems to be the most difficult for the average listener, yet it is necessary for complete appreciation. The musician has clothed this phase of study in such esoteric terminology and with such confusing rules that the relationship between the study of harmony and actual music is often lost.

If the listener realizes that all harmony in music is based upon three primary chords in somewhat the same manner as color combinations are based on three primary colors, an adequate understanding of it may not seem impossible. The study of these three simple harmonies (the tonic, dominant, and subdominant chords) as they are used in simple folk songs, their expansion by the classic, romantic, and even modern composers, is a delightful adventure. Playing a familiar folk song in different harmonic styles is an excellent device for introducing listeners to the possible effects of harmony and musical expression.

Radio and Listening

For the development of the appreciation of music by the masses, radio is a great blessing but it also has its attendant evils. Never before has there been so much "good" music readily accessible; and as a corollary, we might add that never before has there been so much "bad" music available. So the first problem in radio listening is the vast quantity of music, much of it inferior in quality. American broadcasts are supported by commercial advertising. The primary use of music by industries is to advertise their products. They must provide music which will reach and entertain the largest number of people in order to increase their sales. Needless to say, this policy causes programs to be built largely of music that has obvious appeal. Our best approach to the problem of a higher standard of music on the radio is through education. As appreciation grows, students will become more discriminating in their tastes and will turn to the "better" programs.

The second problem is radically different. Regardless of the great number of disappointing programs on the air, many stations are devoting more time to fine music and are producing excellent programs. The problem here concerns the kind of listening which is prevalent. In many homes the radio accompanies every activity. Listening becomes desultory and passive. The finest programs are only half-heard. *As a result sensitivity to music is actually dulled.* Of course, it is not necessary to listen to every radio program stiffly and formally, with undivided attention. One of the delights of radio is the comfort and informality with which we can listen. Still certain programs should be selected and listened to with the same care and attention that one gives at a musical concert where interruptions are frowned upon.

Many high schools, especially in rural districts, will find great stimulation in using the programs of music appreciation that are now available on the air. Every school should spend some time in helping students to select the finest programs, to discuss them in class, and to encourage a more attentive and discriminating type of listening for these programs.

Phonograph and Listening

For years, many teachers have seemed to consider the phonograph and appreciation as synonymous terms. We are happy to notice a trend in accepting other musical activities as contributing to appreciation. We do not aim to belittle the value of the phonograph in music study. However we do feel that no phonograph is better than a very poor one. An excellent phonograph and a fine collection of records can be a musical blessing. Music can be played to fit mood and choice. Favorite records can be repeated many times. Direct attention can be given to the elements of musical structure which we have discussed. Musical scores can readily be followed while listening. And so we encourage the use of phonographs and plead for better ones.

Self-Recording and Listening

A word should be said about portable recording equipment which enables students and teachers to obtain an estimate of their own performance. In the past the results of most self-recording equipment were very discouraging due to mechanical imperfections, and they failed to give reproductions which were sufficiently accurate to be of great use. At present, however, equipment is available which gives reproduction that is faithful enough to be of considerable value in teaching.

It is often said that a singer cannot hear himself. Of course, this is only one of those half-truths frequently used in educational circles. It is true, but not quite to the same degree, of the instrumentalists. It is often shocking, and at times disconcerting to hear oneself sing or play as reproduced on a phonograph record. The self-recording machine may serve as a means for self-analysis and make clear in a few minutes points of tone and interpretation that can not be clarified by hours of "talking about them." If the instrumental teacher uses such equipment to make records of his band and orchestra, he can quickly convince the students of their good points and shortcomings. If a composition is being studied and a record is made during a rehearsal, the students hear those bad attacks, poor intonation, lack of balance, and failure to follow dynamic markings. When this record is immediately compared to a professional record of the same composition, they are inspired to improve their own performance. In this manner the highest type of discrimination is being taught, and not only is performance being improved but appreciation of the keenest kind is also being developed.

The same procedure may be used with choral groups and with individual soloists. Recording equipment can be used to the following advantages: (1) self-analysis by the student, (2) check-up of the teacher's instruction, (3) periodic record of student progress, (4) opportunity for experimentation in performance, (5) development of appreciation through keener discrimination.

Students display genuine interest in self-recordings and often wish records for themselves. However, teachers must be careful not to infringe upon copyrights in the recording of published music. Publishers, as a rule, have no objection to making records for teaching purposes. But making records for sale to students is a different matter, and teachers should receive permission from the publisher to use any music for this purpose.

Sound-mirror

A new device, called sound-mirrors, is now available for use in teaching. This machine makes a recording on a magnetic tape of one or two minutes' duration, depending on the type of machine. It has been used for several years by speech teachers, but it has only recently been perfected sufficiently to be used for recording music. This machine dispenses with records and needles. The recording is played back immediately and can be repeated as often as desired. As a new recording is made the old one is erased. Its advantages are found in the simplicity and speed of operation. It can be used to check quickly on interpretative and technical details in performing various parts of a composition. Its disadvantages lie in the brevity of the recording that can be made and the fact that the recording is not permanent so that an accurate check of progress cannot be made. It is extremely valuable for individual vocal and instrumental practice and also to clarify quickly certain points during rehearsals. The sound-mirrors that are available are still rather expensive, but their possibilities as a teaching device should be studied by every music teacher.

Performance and Listening

Performance is one of the surest and happiest roads toward the summit of appreciation. However, one is not led over this road by thoughtless and careless performance. Listening must accompany all performance—listening to yourself, listening to the other parts of a chorus, listening to the other sections of the orchestra, listening for the message of the music.

Besides listening that accompanies performance, there should be listening to supplement performance. The young student finds great inspiration in listening to the virtuoso. Teachers will find that it pays in musical and educational dividends to interrupt a rehearsal long enough to play an excellent recording of the number that is being studied in chorus or orchestra.

It has been estimated that, in the high school, such musical organizations as the band, orchestra, and chorus reach about thirty per cent of the student body. What about the other seventy per cent? Cannot these excellent organizations be made to serve this larger part of the student body? Do not confine the efforts of these organizations to concerts and entertainments. Use them to develop appreciation programs in the assemblies. It is one of the best ways to interest the entire student body.

Classes in Appreciation

Music appreciation is a synonym for music education. And it is true, that every music lesson should be a lesson in appreciation. Of course, in practice this is only a half-truth.

Performance does not necessarily lead to an intelligent appreciation. Many people who never perform seem to have a greater joy in music and keener appreciation of its beauty than others who have acquired the technical skill necessary for performance. In fact, the acquiring of this technical skill seems to present a barrier to some students toward developing the most important thing of all—a love for music itself. Other performers become so involved in their own technical performance that they seem to forget the message of the music. How often do you find students who are unable to name the composer of the piece they are studying!

Without disparaging the intimate musical experience that comes from performance, we can see that it is not the whole story. Musical activities that stress performance will reach only a limited number of the students. Music educators must reach the remaining large per cent of the student body. The answer is the general course in music or the special classes in music appreciation which emphasize listening, utilize performance, and encourage composition.

This kind of class was described in Chapter III in the discussion of integrating experiences in music. Such classes should be organized in units that emphasize the elements of music as discussed in that chapter. If the curriculum is organized in broad fields for the first two years and music is presented in relation to the other arts, then such a course in music appreciation should be offered later in the curriculum to students who wish to devote more direct attention to developing a broader and deeper appreciation of music. A class in the history of music is not vital to the high school curriculum, but if it is included in the later years, it should be offered to students who have had a rich experience in listening.

It so happens that musicianly listeners are not born; they are made. Many of our best listeners have developed through their own efforts. This fact does not relieve the school of the responsibility of providing guidance for that great body of musical consumers, the listeners. These classes in appreciation have a specific purpose—the cultivation of intellectual enjoyment of music. This kind of enjoyment will be attained through two types of knowledge—knowledge about music and knowledge of music itself.

Knowledge about music is music history; knowledge of

music is music theory. Both the history and theory of music are sciences, while appreciation is an art. Therefore, in teaching appreciation only the historical facts that are pertinent to discussion, criticism, and interpretation of the specific music under consideration should be included. It is not necessary to know every small detail of a composer's life; but a biographical sketch which gives one a better understanding of the man behind the music, the times in which he worked, and his contribution to the development of music will be pertinent to appreciation. It is not necessary to be able to analyze every chord and cadence of a composition; but to be able to hear a striking change of key or mode, a subtle rhythmic pattern, or to follow the broad outlines of the musical design—these things mark the difference between fondness for music and appreciation of music.

It is true that music appreciation developed through intelligent listening has not made the impression on school or community that has been enjoyed by our bands, orchestras, and choirs. Of course, the activity is not so spectacular. And also, the happy thought that anyone could learn to appreciate music, at least to some degree, led to the current belief that anyone could teach the appreciation of music. Chadwick's statement that "a teacher must not only present his subject matter clearly, he must illuminate it," is especially cogent here. Success of classes in appreciation will depend upon the ability of the teacher to share his greater knowledge, keener insight, inspired enthusiasm, and general musicianship.

Music Clubs

An activity encouraged in many high schools is the formation of music clubs. These groups of students in some cases meet in the school building, and in other cases meet at different students' homes. The club members sing and play for each other, prepare papers on musical topics, discuss current musical events, listen to radio programs, attend local concerts, and in other ways stimulate a deeper interest in performing and listening to music.

This form of music activity is usually described as extracurricular. The clubs have their own officers and plan of organization, and, with advice, work out their own program of musical activities.

Conclusion

It seems that nearly every human being likes music to some degree. The chief difference between people lies in the kind of music they like. "There's music in the air" is more than the title of a song today. That this music is having a decided effect upon people is found in the increase of concert attendance even during periods of economic difficulties. One more evidence is the large number of books appearing on the market that are devoted to music appreciation. One of the missions of the music educator is to serve as a guide to this ever growing mass of musical consumers.

Topics for General Discussion

1. Do you believe that the primary aim of music education should be appreciation? Will this aim contribute to the desirable changes in students stated on page 6 in Chapter I.

2. What is the difference between listening to music and appreciating music?

3. Whose opinion of a new composition would you give the most consideration: an elderly lady who does not play an instrument but who has spent a lifetime attending concerts, or a young lady who is an excellent pianist but who has had little opportunity to hear great music?

4. Can a person appreciate music without any knowledge of it? Give reasons for your answer.

From *ABT VOGLER*

(after he has been extemporizing upon the musical instrument of his invention)

But here is the finger of God, a flash of the will that can,
Existent behind all laws, that made them, and, lo! they
are!
And I know not if, save in this, such gift be allowed to
man,
That out of three sounds he frame, not a fourth sound,
but a star.
Consider it well: each tone of our scale in itself is
naught;
It is everywhere in the world—loud, soft, and all is
said:
Give it to me to use! I mix it with two in my thought,
And there! Ye have heard and seen: consider and bow
thy head!

ROBERT BROWNING

Chapter 12

CREATIVE ACTIVITIES: AN APPROACH TO MUSIC FUNDAMENTALS

In discussing the "message of music" in the last chapter we brought out the relationship between appreciating and composing. In appreciating music one retraces in terms of one's own experience the path that the composer trod in creating the music. This conception of appreciation presents a challenge to the listener and tends to show the affinity between the composer and the listener.

The word "composing" instead of "creating" has been used throughout our discussion to mean the production of original music. There is an aura of confusion around the word "creative" in music education as in all education. We do not belittle the musical activities often labeled "creative," but we have attempted to define the term for the sake of clarity.

Composing as a Creative Activity

We distinguish three types of creativity in music. *Listening* is creative perception when in terms of one's own experience new meaning is discovered in any composition. *Performance* is creative interpretation when this new meaning finds expression. *Composition* is creative expression when we embody this new meaning or new experience in tonal-rhythmic patterns. All listening and all performance are by no means creative. For that matter, not all composition can be called creative expression. However, when new meaning is disclosed in musical forms, old or new, we are inclined to call it creative.

Music educators have probably avoided the word "composing" because it seems such a formidable task for young people. And, undoubtedly, it is if we think of it in terms of what others would consider valuable. It is an unusual child that does not improvise little tunes to express his daily experiences. This natural medium of expression must be encouraged and nurtured. With richer musical experiences and greater command of techniques, this medium can be a normal means of expression for the high school student.

After all, are not the results of education determined by where you place your emphasis, by the things you set as a premium? Who would have thought twenty-five years ago that high school orchestras could give effective performances of Brahms' and Tschaikowsky's symphonies, or that school choirs could give thrilling performances of eight-part choral masterpieces? We have seen this come to pass in some places because we have placed a premium on performance by large musical organizations. A study of primitive cultures discloses the fact that variations in these cultures are dependent upon placing a premium on certain activities. As a result we find in some cultures that all men were warriors, while in others, all men were artists.

Modern educators are placing great emphasis upon the creative in education. As a matter of fact, they recognize an element of the creative in all learning. W. H. Kilpatrick makes a strong point of this attitude in the following summary:

"Now let us ask the question: Can the gifted alone create? I say no. Before man was man, the first instance of learning took place far down in the life of the amoeba. Creation has ever been present in the world from eons before man was a man. So we have no right at all, as I see it, to say that here are a few people who stand at the upper end of the human line and they are the only ones who can create. They may be the only ones who can create great creations but not the only ones who can create. Every one of you, every child that you have, in my opinion, is capable of creation, and in fact does create every day." [1]

We do not mean to imply that all students in the high school should become composers. However, we do believe that all students in the high school should have the opportunity to objectify their emotional experiences into tonal-rhythmic patterns. As with little children, we feel that the emphasis should be placed upon the creative process rather than upon the actual product. On the other hand, the process will become more meaningful and will have more value if command of technique is acquired which will produce a better art product.

As Kilpatrick vigorously asserts, we are all endowed with some ability for creative expression. However, the degree of this ability differs with individuals as abilities vary in all phases of human activity. And so, opportunities for composing in the high school will bring to light those students to whom creating in tonal design is a natural self-expression. The future American composer may be among them. Many other students will have a very limited ability to express themselves in tonal-rhythmic patterns. It may be that their most natural medium of expression is in another art field. Nevertheless, some sensitivity to the medium of tone is unmistakably present and should be encouraged and nurtured. These students are easily discouraged because they compare their own efforts with the

[1] "Some Basic Considerations Affecting Success in Teaching Art." Eastern Arts Association *Proceedings,* April, 1929, p. 4. Quotation taken from, *Creative School Music,* Lillian M. Fox and L. Thomas Hopkins. New York: Silver-Burdett, 1936, p. 17.

music that they have experienced through listening and performing. For such students composing should be an experience in appreciation. There is no better way to understand the creative process of composers than to experience that process ourselves, even though it is on a much lower scale of artistic creation. One of the best ways to appreciate the "Well-Tempered Clavichord" of Bach is to try writing a few fugues yourself. This is perhaps the place to make a plea for all teachers to continue to develop their own creative efforts in musical composition. Only then will there be full sympathetic understanding of the creative efforts and problems of the students.

The mystery which surrounds musical composition must be dispelled. It is not different from other creation. It is true that the techniques are more intricate. But these techniques have been encased in a set of formidable rules which bewilder the student and inhibit any free individual expression. They have been developed on the assumption that students must have a thorough knowledge of traditional practice before attempting anything original. Traditional practice should be followed when music is written in traditional style. We must never forget that rules are made from great music; they serve the composer and do not restrict him. In fact, the contemporary composer is trying to do the very thing that children do so naturally, namely, express themselves without regard to traditional practices.

The teacher's aim should be for the student to gain an understanding of chord connection, phrase structure, and style without inhibiting the desire for free and original expression. Such understanding is best acquired by continual reference to the music of the masters. A study of the music of Beethoven will reveal the manner in which the design and form emerge from the style and are not imposed on the music. These procedures do not eliminate technique, but simply give it more meaning for the student.

We do not mean to give the impression that creating musical masterpieces is a simple accomplishment. Musical composition is creation of the highest order. But if the esoteric veil that surrounds musical composition can be lifted, the average student will experience to some small degree, at least, the process of composing, and thereby will gain a greater appreciation of the masters as well as having the joy of creating something of his own.

TYPES OF COMPOSING

There are three types of creative work in music which we recognize as composition. We refer to *improvising, arranging,* and *composing* in original and written forms.

Improvisation

Although most composers caution against the use of the piano in the act of composing, still we find most of them very proficient at improvising on the piano. We know that some of Beethoven's works were first conceived as improvisations. Even a master with the auditory imagery and sensitivity of Mozart preferred to have a clavier in his room when he was composing. Although there is danger in learning to think and hear through the fingers instead of with the imagination, still improvisation will often release many musical ideas. Improvisation is seldom as well organized as written composition is, but in this indetermined quality lies much of its charm.

There is no doubt that improvisation has been greatly neglected during our century. The old masters placed a premium upon the art of improvising. As the "stick to the note" practice in piano playing became dominant, both "playing by ear" and improvising were frowned upon. If we seek guidance in the practice of the masters, we will encourage our students to improvise for the added harmonic knowledge it will foster, the keener appreciation it will develop, and the sheer joy that it will bring by enabling students to express themselves freely in something that is original. Perhaps the success of "jam" sessions and other forms of improvisation in popular music lies in the opportunities for free self-expression.

Arranging

Some people have original ideas and are not able to develop them completely. Other people disclose great originality in taking an idea and creating something new by adding and expanding it. In the realm of music the latter people are the arrangers. They have been of untold service to the music educator. Very often, although the original musical idea seems complete, still it may not be in the medium that is usable in various situations. The arranger adapts the music to serve the needs of different kinds of performing groups. If the arranger faithfully retains the mood and structure of the original idea, he has made many great masterpieces accessible which would otherwise remain unheard by many students.

Arranging is not as high an art as original composition, but it certainly should not be cast aside as of little importance. Many professional organizations exist largely through the cleverness and musicianship of their arranger. If we again seek guidance in the practice of the masters we find many of them changing the original versions of some of their compositions to a different musical medium. Moreover, we should not forget the transcriptions of Liszt. Ferde Grofe's masterly orchestration of George Gershwin's *Rhapsody in Blue* is a landmark in the recognition of arranging as a field of art. And also, many composers' literal use of folk songs is a type of arranging. In fact, in some music it is difficult to determine where original composition ends and arranging begins.

For the student in the high school, arranging is an interesting and useful practice. In fact, as an arranger works with musical ideas, he absorbs them as his own, so that the final result gives him the same satisfaction and thrill as an original composition. A few student arrangers in the school can be of invaluable assistance to the teacher in making music adaptable for various organizations and occasions. Such projects in arranging pieces for various ensemble groups large and small, in making choral arrangements of songs and in scoring instrumental accompaniments for choruses, as well as selecting and arranging music for pageants, are among the most practical approaches to the study of harmony and composition. It will give the student an increased knowledge of the structure of music, thereby increasing his appreciation of music in general.

Composition

The most satisfying and absorbing of all musical experiences is original composition, a topic which is developed in the next section. Harmonic exercises scarcely deserve this unstinted tribute. In truth, composition which emerges painfully from a mathematical treatment of the rules is seldom a joyful experience. Unless high school students are given an opportunity to indulge in free composition, their musical experience is not rounded. It is worthwhile if only to gain a greater appreciation of the composers. It is a sad commentary on the achievement of our goal in music education that the composer is all too often the least important figure at our concerts, and that memory contests are necessary to give him his deserving recognition.

Opportunities for Composing

Our next step is to consider the opportunities that can be given high school students for original composition. Although creative activity of any kind can be encouraged, it cannot be forced. It defies a time clock. It is highly individualized. However, that does not deny the possibilities of the group as an agency for the encouragement of creative effort on the part of the members.

General Music Classes

In Chapter III we discussed briefly the introduction of original composition in certain types of integrating classroom activities and in classes of appreciation. We see no reason why the group creative work carried on in the elementary schools should not be continued in the high school. It may provide a stimulus for much individualized creative effort.

Furthermore, we contend that the average student can grasp the technical problems in the choral relations of the tonic, dominant seventh, and sub-dominant harmonies. These three chords offer wide possibilities for free and individual composition. It is amazing how often just these three chords are used in folk songs and short instrumental compositions. They are the basis of all harmony. Other chords are a substitution or an extension of these three fundamental chords.

The problem of introducing harmony and composition into the general music classes is one of reducing technical discussion and difficulties to the minimum. People have written good tunes without knowing that the antecedent ends with a semicadence and the consequent with a perfect authentic cadence. If students learn to hear the uses of the three fundamental chords, they will tend to compose

Upper—*NBC Orchestra, Walter Damrosch, Conductor.*
Lower left—*Class listening to NBC Appreciation Hour.*
Lower right—*Individual Recitation in Voice Class, Collinwood Senior High School, Cleveland, O., Fred Lake, Instructor.*

"by ear" rather than by rule. There is no reason why two or three students cannot compose songs and other musical numbers together. It is being done in the popular field every day. One student may be able to play or improvise on the piano, a second may have the ability to sing tuneful melodies, a third may be able to write the words. Such combinations may produce music. At least they are having the joy of "making up music," and they cannot fail to approach the work of the masters with more respect and with pertinent questions relating to musical structure.

Classes in Harmony

The high school should provide classes in harmony for students who wish to devote more time to original composition than is possible in the general music classes. Of all music subjects that are hidebound by traditional practice, harmony wins the prize for maintaining the *status quo*. For over a hundred years harmony has been taught on the assumption that no student should attempt creative work until he has completely mastered all the rules. It is the same basic error that has accompanied the teaching of techniques of performance. *Harmonic rules should serve creative effort, not obstruct it.* Why not begin with composition, however simple, and use the accepted rules to perfect the product? The student, in turn, will better understand these rules and accept them.

To retain some order in a creative approach to the study of harmony, would it not be wise to introduce chords in some sequence based upon the frequency of their use in music? Simple pieces could be written which would utilize the chords that were being studied. Original work, however, should not be limited to this sequence.

On the contrary, students should be encouraged to employ any chords which voice the musical ideas they wish to express. While the student should be expected to handle with technical accuracy the chords or chord progressions which have been the subject of class instruction, the teacher's criticisms of the more advanced harmonic effects should be based chiefly on the question of whether or not the student's written expression accurately reflects his own musical intentions. The balance between directions which the student is required to follow and the stimulation of individual freedom and spontaneity is a delicate matter, involving real teaching skill. But the advantages awaiting both student and teacher who follow the modern creative approach to music study are rich and rewarding.

In an approach of this nature passing and neighboring tones will be introduced immediately. Earlier compositions will be easy folk tunes with accompaniments, piano or violin pieces, and children's songs. Four-part choral writing will probably be postponed until there is better command of harmonic technique. Isn't it strange that we have based our harmonic study entirely upon four-part choral writing, ignoring the fact that this style of composition demands real skill?

A creative approach to harmonic study demands a resourceful teacher, one who readily sees the technical skill needed by the student to improve his creative efforts. It is time for a revolution in the teaching of harmony. The high school is psychologically the place to make a beginning.

The School Project

Is the school project worthwhile? We say, "Yes, but not too often!" For the high school of moderate size nothing will so integrate the efforts of the entire school as the writing and producing of a musical play. The services of many departments are enlisted—music, dramatic art, English, history, industrial arts, fine arts, home economics, and the administration. The contributions of these departments are not incidental, but are vital to the educational success of the project. It is very likely that the school project will have greater educational values than the regular routine of classwork. Careful planning will distribute the responsibilities of various departments so that one teacher will not be overburdened with work. However, the music teacher will undoubtedly carry the brunt of responsibility.

An operetta, musical play, or pageant composed and produced by the entire school involves many of the evils attendant upon the production of a published operetta. In Chapter V we pointed out these evils to be chiefly the monopoly of the music teacher's time, the disruption of the remainder of the music program, and the poor materials available. Furthermore, not only is the music program sacrificed often for the sake of the project, but inroads are made upon the activities of many other classes.

Weighing the advantages and disadvantages of the school project, we must recognize that the students have the joy of creating something and the responsibility of producing something. Of course, the educational values are dependent upon the quality of the story and the music. Unless the creative work is of superior calibre, it would probably be more profitable to spend the time in becoming acquainted with great masterpieces of literature and music. However, original operettas have been composed by students which are superior to some of the operettas on the market. And so we commend to all teachers of music in the high school the consideration and possibility of creating and producing a musical play which will utilize the entire school.

Conclusion

As long as music educators consider musical composition a medium of expression for a limited few, it will be a neglected activity in our schools. When composing is considered in its rightful function as an experience toward the development of the highest appreciation, it will be given an equal and as universal a consideration as the activities of listening and performing. A more direct approach to composition will allay the fears of many as to the technical difficulties. If teachers of music take this attitude toward composing it will not be necessary to defend many of their other activities with the word "creative." Creating music will be synonymous with composing music. Technical difficulties will cease to be a barrier, and with Browning, the poet, we shall say:

> Ah, but a man's reach should exceed his grasp,
> Or what's a heaven for.

Topics for General Discussion

1. Write a short paper expressing in your own words the psychological factors involved in the music creative process.
2. Do you believe with William Heard Kilpatrick that everyone has creative ability? Does a person have to be especially talented to compose music? Discuss.
3. Explain the creative elements found in composing music. Performing music. Listening to music.
4. When you were studying the piano were you encouraged to "play by ear"? What are the differences between improvising and "playing by ear"?
5. In the study of harmony should chords be introduced according to their frequency found in music? Analyze the harmonies of twelve folk songs to discover the frequency of the diatonic chords. In your study of harmony were chords introduced according to the frequency as indicated by the analysis of these twelve folk songs?

Los Gatos (California) Union High School Music Building, showing large windows in band and orchestra room.

New Assembly Building, Sacramento (California), Senior High School, Charles F. Dean, architect.

Part Three

ADMINISTRATION

THE PRESIDENTS ON MUSIC

Because music knows no barriers of language, because it recognizes no impediments to free intercommunication, because it speaks a universal tongue, music can make us all more vividly aware of that common humanity which is ours and which shall one day unite the nations of the world in one great brotherhood.

FRANKLIN DELANO ROOSEVELT

We cannot have too much music; we need it—the world needs it—probably more than ever before, and I am the friend of every effort to give it its rightful place in our national life.

WARREN G. HARDING

The man who disparages music as a luxury and nonessential is doing the nation an injury. Music now, more than ever before, is a national need. There is no better way to express patriotism than through music.

WOODROW WILSON

Let the love of literature, painting, sculpture, architecture, and, above all music, enter into your lives.

THEODORE ROOSEVELT

Chapter 13

ADMINISTRATION AND SUPERVISION

The first two parts of this book have been devoted to the teaching of music in the high school. We shall now consider those problems of administration, supervision, organization, and management upon which the effectiveness of music teaching depends. To introduce and support our statements, we shall quote freely from the writings of educators in the field who are closely associated with these problems.

In the present chapter, we direct our discussion toward the administrator, the supervisor, the teacher, and the professional relations between them. First of all, there are some phases of the music program which may seem difficult for the administrator to understand. Reference will be made to the support of the program for which he should feel responsible. Secondly, the relationship between the supervisor and the administrator, and the supervisor and the teacher, are often strained. Accepted practices in regard to this problem will be considered. Finally, there are many aspects of administration which the teacher of music not only fails to understand, but of which he also neglects to make himself sufficiently cognizant to appreciate the point of view of the administrator. As a result, the music teacher may lose the sympathy and support of the administrator. If the music educator will make a sincere effort to understand the point of view of the administrator rather than criticise him for lack of appreciation of the music department, the aims toward which this book is devoted will be much nearer realization.

Purpose of Administration

"The fundamental criterion of efficiency in the administration of schools is to be found in the provision of educational opportunities for children and youth. The arrangements which make for high efficiency include freedom from partisan political control, the services of a competent professional staff, adequate support, satisfactory buildings and equipment, and curriculums adapted to the needs of pupils and to the society which the schools are organized to serve." [1]

Administration has but one purpose—to enable a school to perform the functions described in the quotation above. Administration is not an end in itself. Insofar as it makes possible better teaching, better guidance of students, and better practice based on adequate research, it justifies its existence. When it becomes so involved in detail or adopts policies which interfere with these processes, it cannot be justified.

If the primary function of administration is to make teaching more effective, then it is the responsibility of the administrator to acquaint himself with the problems of the music teacher and help him to make his teaching more meaningful to the students. Chapter II was devoted to the place of music in the high school curriculum and the chapters following this one discussed the nature of the activities which should be included in a representative music program. Chapters XIV and XV will discuss problems of the music teacher to which the superintendent can lend an

[1] Educational Policies Commission, "The Structure and Administration of Education in American Democracy." National Education Association, Washington, D. C. 1938, p. 41. *Note:* This little book is recommended to all music teachers to enable them to secure a concise knowledge of the general problems of school administration.

active hand in enabling the music teacher to do a better job.

There is nothing incomprehensible about the teaching of music that the administrator cannot learn to discuss intelligently. In fact, it is the duty of the music teacher to make him conversant with the aims and practices of the music curriculum. When a music teacher continuously claims that administrators do not cooperate, he is covering up inefficient teaching, or admitting that he has neglected his responsibility of enlightening them.

Administration and the Music Program

The various divisions of personnel in school administration must be unified to achieve the primary purpose of it—namely, better teaching. Each administrative officer has certain responsibilities to assure the success of the music program, if it is to contribute its share in the educational process.

Board of Education

In line with the criticism by some music teachers of the lack of sympathy and understanding on the part of administrators, George D. Strayer has this to say:

"There is a popular misconception concerning the power of the school administrator. The statements made by some teachers who feel aggrieved because of lack of support for their particular enterprises would lead one to believe that the superintendent of schools was all-powerful. Such is most certainly not the case. No superintendent of schools makes the budget, selects the teachers, develops a time schedule, buys equipment, or in any other respect determines the place in the school program which shall be given to any particular subject. Decision with respect to the development of each area of work in the schools may be made in accordance with the recommendations of the superintendent of schools, but if his recommendations are to prevail over any considerable period of time, it will be by virtue of the fact that they are supported by citizens, by teachers, and by the children enrolled in the schools. The lay Board of Education is influenced by all of these groups. The Board acts over any long period of time in accordance with the judgment of the community, as a whole. One who desires to change the situation in any significant manner in the schools of the United States must work with the entire community. . . .

"In the statements made above it has not been my intention to propose that the administrator does not have an important place in influencing the decisions made by the Board of Education. Those superintendents of schools who appreciate the significance of the rapidly expanding school music program and those who most certainly understand the contribution which the fine arts may make in the educational program, will be most convincing in their recommendations to the Board of Education concerning the music program. I have wanted, however, to call attention to the fact that the judgment of the administrator is only one of the many factors that enter to determine the support which may be expected for any particular phase of the educational program." [2]

There is no doubt that the music teacher has often neglected to clarify to the Board of Education of the rightful place of music in the educational program. It may be best to do this indirectly through a community music program. When a Board of Education sees the wholesome effect of music upon their children and the community at large, they will listen more willingly to the recommendations of expenditures for music made by the superintendent. Chapter XVI is devoted to a discussion of developing a community program of music which will, in turn, reflect in the music program of the school by influencing policies of the Board of Education.

However, it is often feasible to work directly with members of the Board of Education. The teacher may ask the

[2] "The Administrator Looks at Music Education," Music Educators National Conference, *Yearbook 1936*. Chicago, Illinois, pp. 45-47.

superintendent for permission to address the Board of Education briefly, at one of its meetings in support of the music program. How many music educators are sufficiently articulate of their aims to be able to convince a Board of the need for better teachers, better rooms, better equipment, and better materials? With the permission of the superintendent it is often advisable for the music teacher to discuss his problems individually with members of the Board. How many music educators are capable or have taken the trouble to do this? It is up to the teacher to convince the Board that music education is more than a few school concerts or the band parading down the avenue. Hobart Sommers sums it up in this manner:

"The music program in the secondary school is a challenge to every division of American education. There are many things we should all know by now! The president and the members of your Board of Education should know by now that good music instructors and well-planned music activities will do more to popularize the management of the school system than any other one feature. Parents and taxpayers will be brought into closer contact with the schools through an integrated music program and thus give the Board of Education an opportunity to show concretely what they have done with the public funds." [3]

Superintendent

Although the final authority of school administration rests with the Board of Education, the success of the school curriculum is dependent upon an able and far-seeing superintendent. The Board of Education turns to him for recommendations in the conduct of the schools. Attempts are being made continually to better define the relationships between the Board of Education and its executive officer, the superintendent. The Educational Policies Com-

[3] "Music in the High School," Music Educators National Conference, *Yearbook 1939-1940*. Chicago, Illinois, pp. 143-146.

mission has suggested the following rules now commonly in operation in school systems that are efficiently operated.[4]

"The superintendent of schools should nominate all employees and the Board of Education should elect only upon his nomination.

"Matters of curriculum, processes of teaching, materials and supplies, and organization of schools and classes should originate with the superintendent of schools and his staff.

"The Board of Education should hold the superintendent of schools strictly accountable for results.

"The superintendent of schools should submit an annual budget for the consideration of the Board of Education.

"The superintendent of schools should study plant and equipment needs and present the capital outlay budget.

"Administrative details should always be left to the professional executive."

It can be readily seen that, wherever these recommendations are followed, the teacher of music must look to a sympathetic and enlightened superintendent for the help needed in the matters of salary, rooms, and equipment to carry on a successful program of music activities in the high school. Such superintendents as Ben G. Graham render the music educator invaluable service by supporting school music with such statements as the following:

"In reviewing the various objectives which are set up in public school music, the administrator is impressed with three major objectives: appreciation, participation, and creative ability.

"To be able to enjoy good music by giving play to the emotions and the imagination offers perhaps one of the finest opportunities in the life of an individual. New fields of experience are opened and life is made richer through the play of the emo-

[4] Educational Policies Commission, "The Structure and Administration of Education in American Democracy," National Education Association, pp. 60-64.

tions and the stimulation of the imagination which good music affords. . . .

"Participation in the production of good music not only involves appreciation, but gives an opportunity to add to the enjoyment of the individual participating and to the pleasure of others. Therefore, the ability to sing or to play a musical instrument should be one of the major objectives in public school music.

"School administrators sometimes overlook the fact that one of the finest methods of developing team play on the part of individuals is experience in playing in a competently directed orchestra or band. Frequently we hear the athletic team extolled as the best means in a high school of developing the spirit of team play. There is an equally important field for such experience in the high school orchestra and band. . . .

"The third objective from the viewpoint of the administrator in teaching music is creative ability, a field which has been receiving growing attention on the part of music teachers and is rich in opportunity. One is amazed by what can be accomplished even in the primary grades in the field of creative music, and if latent ability is not inhibited by wrong methods of music education surprising results follow in creative music in the junior and senior high school.

"Three of the most outstanding contributions in secondary education in the last decade are found in the stimulation of creative ability in English, art, and music." [5]

The rapidly expanded program of music in the high school in the past twenty years is testimony that many other administrators have a similar point of view. Through personal association, through the students, through the community, and through producing musical and educational results, the music teacher will gain a similar sympathetic attitude from his superintendent and obtain the administrative cooperation so necessary for the fulfillment of his goals.

[5] "Music Education from the Standpoint of the Administrative Officer," Music Educators National Conference, *Yearbook 1932*, pp. 51-55.

Principal

The personality of the school usually reflects the personality of its principal. In the high school building the principal is the hub around which the wheel of educational activity revolves. If he is an enthusiastic supporter of music, one will usually find a superior teacher carrying on an excellent program of music. If he is apathetic toward music, it is usually reflected in the quantity and quality of music found in the school.

When one considers some of the responsibilities of the principal, it is readily understood how his attitude toward a subject will effect its place in the curriculum. He has the position to influence the attitude of the superintendent, and, in turn, the Board of Education. He makes out all class schedules in keeping with school policies. He signs the final program of students. He controls the number and type of assemblies. And finally, he approves budgets and makes recommendations for equipment and material.

Regardless of the initial attitude of the principal toward music, if an enthusiastic teacher can show him that music is filling a need in the lives of students and that music is popularizing his school in the community, he will find an adequate place for it in the schedule. It is wise for the music teacher to sit down with the principal, explain the unique problems in the scheduling of music, and work out a program that will get results.

The music teacher must not neglect the principal in his efforts to gain the "go ahead signal" from the administration. He is a key man and his backing is paramount. One principal has expressed in vigorous terms the attitude that principals should hold toward music education.[6]

[6] Hobart Sommers, "Music in the High School,"—Music Educators National Conference, *Yearbook 1939-1940*, pp. 143-146. *Note:* Every principal and music educator should read this stimulating article. It may also be found in "Secondary Education," Bulletin of the Department of Secondary Teachers, N.E.A., December, 1940.

"All high school principals should know by now that music activities of the school, properly articulated and integrated with a full school program, are the best media for citizenship training and the best carry-over toward later worthy use of leisure time. Harmonious acts make harmonious minds. Harmonious minds make harmonious living. . . .

"Principals should know by now that it is important for them to know as much about music and modern music movements as it is to understand a program of psychological testing, or the methods of progressive education. Administrators can no longer say 'I know nothing about music, but I love it.' They must have as much an appreciation of the goals of music as they expect their young charges to have when they leave the school."

Director of Music

The title of supervisor of music is gradually being changed to the one at the heading of this section. The duties of this position have gradually shifted from one that was almost completely supervisory to one that includes responsibilities of administration and instruction. Teaching responsibilities are usually determined by the size of the music teaching staff. When this is large, the duties are mostly administrative and supervisory.

We believe that it will be interesting to draw from the statements of two directors of music, one of a large city (Cleveland, Ohio) and the other from a small city (Ashland, Ohio), who have discussed their relative problems under similar headings. Russell V. Morgan makes the following statements about the administration problems in music departments of large cities: [7]

"Administration in the best sense combines organization and management. A department must be properly organized or its functioning will not and cannot be efficient. Good management is needed, for, without that there is no power to operate the machine. . . .

"*1. Personnel.* In large cities, the selection of music teachers

[7] "Administration Problems in Music Departments of Large Cities," Music Educators National Conference, *Yearbook 1939-1940*, pp. 147-151.

is handled by a personnel bureau, or some such office, with varying degrees of participation by the head of the music department. In some cases, the music head is responsible for the preparation and grading of applicant examinations, while in others, he is charged with the responsibility of nominating two or three candidates, with final selection by the administration. In any case, the following four points are the basis for choice: (1) Musicianship; (2) Educational preparation; (3) Classroom teaching ability; (4) Personal qualities.

"*2. Curriculum.* It is possible for the large city to present a curriculum that will preserve quality of instruction and yet provide for a freedom that is essential if proper adjustments are to be made to community differences, school purposes, and instructor's abilities. . . . If the true meaning of curriculum is the orderly sequence of successful and significant experiences, then every teacher must have freedom to discover the particular experiences that meet the needs of his specific groups.

"*3. Budget.* A school system receives a definite income each year. A superintendent and Board of Education will attempt to make a fair allotment to each subject field. Demonstrated need for more money usually receives a sympathetic hearing and an effort is made to readjust in apportionment of the budget.

"It is necessary to keep in mind, though, the definite limitations in the matter of money. A tax rate provides a specific amount of money and even the most willing Board of Education cannot add to that money. Frequently, the music department, however, can, through its development of community interest, help the Board of Education to gain more adequate support for its program through increased levies.

"In organizing a budget, the Board of Education always divides it into various headings, under which different types of expenditures are placed. In many systems the following headings are used for actual operating expenses: (1) Instructional salaries; (2) Textbooks; (3) Supplies; (4) Equipment; (5) Housing; (6) Maintenance.

"*4. Equipment, Records and Services.* It is important to have a workable record of all school and board-owned instruments which will show valuation, date of purchase, identification marks, cost of maintenance, etc. Many other types of records need to be set up so that a department will have an accurate picture of its problems—past, present, and future.

"The music department also serves as a service department and, in one sense, the supervisor's office is to be measured by the degrees of assistance it offers the classroom teacher in carrying out the daily work in the schoolroom.

"*5. Unification of School Policy.* The music department is one of many subject divisions. It has a share in the development of the whole child and, because of this must discover a way of cooperation that makes its purpose join with all in developing a complete and happy child.

"*6. Public Relations.* Public approval determines the kind of school system in which you teach. This approval is easily lost if mistakes are made. Education can lead but only slightly ahead of the understanding and consent of the community. In the end, confidence and interest won through intelligent public relations is the determining factor in the development of a school program."

In contrast to the foregoing statement is that made by Louis E. Pete who discusses music department administration in a small city.[8]

"My work is in Ashland, Ohio, a small city of 11,000 people. Whatever I have to say must be qualified by the fact that it applies to towns and small cities.

"*1. Personnel.* In most towns of this size the music department is comprised usually of two people, sometimes only one. Too often they are separate in jobs, motives, and objectives. The man handles the instrumental work, and the woman supervises grades and teaches or directs the choruses. Rarely is this a successful plan. The work is not planned as a unit and one person is anxious to outdo the other. They are two human beings, each anxious to make a mark for himself, and they are also musicians! This double-head plan can be corrected only

[8] "Music Department Administration in a Small City"—Music Educators National Conference, *Yearbook 1939-1940,* pp. 152-158.

by the superintendent, who should make one of them supervisor and the other assistant and see that the department functions as it should.

"2. *Curriculum.* In the small city the department must justify itself by producing competent performing groups. There should be a good band to go on the street. . . . This band must hold its own on the football field as well as in the competition or concert hall. There should be an orchestra to play for school functions. . . . And of course there must be a chorus, perhaps a fine a cappella choir, but surely a chorus singing good music well.

"3. *Budget.* Budgeting should always be a long-view proposition. I make it a point to ask for something at least a year before I know it to be necessary to the success of my department. It is always wise to admit limitations when they are obvious, but if you can find a way to acquire funds outside of tax moneys you have a tremendous advantage in purchasing, and the Board of Education is quite often willing to match funds secured outside.

"4. *Equipment Records and Forms.* We should always be musicians, secondly, sincere educators, but never bookkeepers. . . . Certainly records are necessary. It does take time to keep them. Let's keep as few as possible, however, and make these few only the necessary essentials.

"5. *Unification of School Policy.* We musicians too often feel that we are discriminated against when the office says we may not upset the schedule with a rehearsal we feel to be necessary to the success of a concert. . . . I make it a point never to interfere with academic classes. I rarely request an excuse from a pupil for anything, and I emphatically insist that my scheduled rehearsal periods be respected. I believe this to be the largest single factor toward friendly relationship between the music department and other departments.

"6. *Public Relations.* I am convinced that school music teachers and directors, particularly in the small cities and towns, must feel responsibility for all the music in the community. We must, if we expect to survive, supply motivation and means for our graduates to play and sing after they are out of school. Our civic groups must keep pace with our school groups . . . Boards of Education and school superintendents must make available music rooms in school buildings for these groups—summer bands, civic orchestras, civic choruses. There must be a group for every boy or girl who graduates, and who wants to continue the musical experience we helped him learn to enjoy in school."

Teacher of Music

Mention has been made of the responsibility of the music teacher to endeavor to understand the point of view of the administrator in regard to the music program. This responsibility is in line with the newer conception of school administration.

"If a spirit of democracy is to be introduced into the internal administration of schools, the principle of the responsible executive must be reconciled with the principle of teacher participation in the formulation of broad policies. . . . In education, the problem is not so much one of securing efficiency, as of determining the ends to which efficiency shall be directed and of utilizing all available professional knowledge and insight in the formulation of policies. Educational administrators must see that the exclusion of teachers from the process of formulating policies atrophies their power to think, and eventually makes of them the most unquestioning and submissive of conformists. The result is educational policies less well considered, less well comprehended by those who must put them into operation and, in the end, a less competent classroom teacher. . . .

"It cannot be too strongly emphasized that only through a larger participation in policy-making can the teacher become more effective in terms of the social objectives of education." [9]

Too often, the music teacher assumes that the administrator cannot or fails to appreciate his efforts. When administration is conceived as a function of education in which the teacher participates in the formulation of policy, a greater responsibility is placed upon the music teacher to

[9] Jesse H. Newlon, *Educational Administration as Social Policy*. New York: Charles Scribner's Sons, 1934, p. 144.

share the problems of the administrator and, in turn, to influence the administrative attitude toward music as an educational force.

Purpose of Supervision

The supreme objective of supervision, like administration, is the improvement of instruction. In fact, they are complementary activities. Supervision must be of such nature that the teaching-learning situation is made better. Supervision of music, therefore, implies the in-service training of the teacher of music. Its purpose is to benefit the teacher and, in turn, to benefit the children.

In the high school where one finds special music teachers, the effectiveness of supervision varies according to individual situations. In many places, the high school music teacher often supervises the elementary school music. In some places, the only supervision of music teaching is of a general nature performed by the principal. In large cities, the director of music, as well as the principals of individual buildings, usually supervises the teaching of the special music teacher.

It is universally accepted in modern educational circles that the purpose of supervision is the improvement of instruction. This is a general statement and for a better understanding of the meaning of supervision, it is well to examine and analyze the various aspects of it. Such analysis is an aid to thinking clearly of the techniques and procedures in supervision in its relation to improved classroom teaching. The *Eighth Yearbook* of the Department of Superintendence has conveniently analyzed supervision into four major functions: (1) Inspection, (2) Research, (3) Training, and (4) Guidance.[10]

[10] *Eighth Yearbook*, "The Superintendent Surveys Supervision," Department of Superintendence of the National Education Association, 1930, pp. 15-16.

Inspection [11]

"A. Survey of the school system, the equipment, the means of instruction, the service, the personnel, the pupils, and other items of detail:
   1. Development of means of evaluating the personnel, equipment, methods of instruction, curriculum, and all other items pertaining to efficient instruction
   2. Survey testing (use of tests to locate instructional shortcomings)
   3. Visitation of schools (for inspectional purposes)
   4. Analysis of any and all records and reports."

The *Eighth Yearbook* gives this summary of the supervisory duties and activities under the function of inspection. There has been no phase of supervision so much misunderstood as "inspection." It is probably an unfortunate choice of word. Supervision must begin somewhere and the logical place is where the teaching act is being carried on, the classroom. The fault has been in the practice of some supervisors in making inspection an end in itself. Inspection is not supervision although supervision includes inspection. For a music supervisor to merely inspect is comparable to a doctor's diagnosis that the patient is sick but doing nothing about it. Inspection at best is an evaluation which should be used for the true purpose of supervision.

Research [12]

"A. The selection and organization of the materials of instruction:
   1. The setting-up of objectives, studies of subject-matter and activities, and experimental testing of materials
   2. The making and constant revision of courses of study

[11] Ibid. p. 208.
[12] Ibid. p. 209.

3. Preparation of miscellaneous supplementary instructional material
4. The selection of textbooks, setting up standards of distribution
5. Testing the efficiency of the course of study, textbooks, and other instructional materials
6. Preparation of descriptive lists of instructional materials, supplies, and equipment with suggestions for their use and care.

B. Experimental study of the problems of teaching:
1. The construction of tests
2. The development of record forms
3. The training of teachers in the use of tests
4. The use of both standardized and local unstandardized tests:
    a. For purposes of diagnosis
    b. For purposes of classification
    c. For determining progress and making comparisons
    d. For teaching purposes (remedial prescriptions)
    e. For purposes of educational guidance.

C. Determining the desirable physical conditions of learning:
1. Expert assistance in the criticism of buildings and building plans
2. Expert assistance in the selection of supplies and equipment, writing of specifications, and setting up standards of distribution."

This summary of the function of research includes any study which will bring to the classroom teacher improvement in equipment, materials, or method. As in the case of inspection, this function pertains largely to the supervision of music in the elementary schools. Except in large cities, these duties are carried on by the special music teacher in the high school. The principal should encourage his music teacher to devote continued study to problems of research and provide time in which the teacher may carry on such study without continued interruption. Then the program of music will have unity and purpose and not be a series of haphazard and unrelated activities. In large cities the director of music will be a counsel and guide for such study. In small cities when there is often no supervision in the high school by a designated supervisor of music, it is well for the high school teachers to carry on research together under a chairman of their own selection.

Training[13]:

"A. The direct improvement of classroom teaching:
1. Classroom visitation
2. Individual and group conferences
3. Directed teaching
4. Demonstration teaching
5. Directed observation
6. Development of standards for self-improvement
7. The training of principals to supervise instruction.

B. The general improvement of teachers in service:
1. Stimulation of professional reading
2. Promotion of attendance at summer school, extension courses and intervisitation
3. Preparation of written, printed, mimeographed bulletins, circulars, reviews, or bibliographies
4. Development of exhibits of school work or other objective aids
5. Planning for participation in administration, supervision, or experimental work."

Teacher training is probably the most important function of supervision. As teachers improve, classroom teaching will improve.

The first real task for the supervisor is to secure an attitude of willingness and readiness on the part of the teachers to improve their instruction. If they consider him a "snoopervisor," they will resent his presence and his suggestions.

[13] Ibid. p. 209.

If he can assure them that he is a service agent ready to aid, to guide, and to encourage, rather than to criticize or to censure, they will listen to him. When they realize that their efforts are appreciated, not subject to sarcasm and ridicule, they will be more ready to accept advice. When they see that the supervisor's suggestions are authentic, practical, and to the point, they will seek his counsel.

Although these remarks are directed, for the most part, to the supervision of elementary grade teachers, they also apply to the supervision of the high school music teacher. It is wise for the director of music to supervise the work of these people. He should occasionally conduct a rehearsal, both as a demonstration for the teacher and as added inspiration for the students. There should be music teachers' meetings to discuss common problems. Above all, he should encourage them to continue their own musical and professional growth.

Guidance [14]

"A. Organizing programs of cooperative activity:

1. Setting up objectives which have been derived through inspectional procedures or through teachers suggestions.
2. Supplying means and guidance for achieving the objectives:
    a. Necessary information and explanation of methods and devices
    b. Necessary supplies, equipment, and instructional material
    c. Necessary physical conditions for good work, insofar as these are under the control of the supervisor
    d. Special individual help on call; the diagnosis and evaluation of teaching ability.
3. Establishing and utilizing measures of success, both in terms of pupil and teacher activity.

[14] Ibid. pp. 209-210.

B. The development and maintenance of morale, or esprit de corps:
   1. Through expertness in professional service rendered (teachers will have confidence in and give allegiance to supervisors who are known to be experts).
   2. Through a willing and unselfish expenditure of time and energy in meeting problems and in rendering service.
   3. Through administering supervision in a kindly, sympathetic, and cooperative, but none the less firm, manner.
   4. Through inviting cooperation in the solution of the problems arising within the system.
   5. Through giving full credit for all contributions from the teaching staff.
   6. Through providing opportunity for the exercise of teacher initiative in experimental work." [15]

The function of guidance in supervision, approaches more closely the newer conception of supervision and relates more closely to the aims of modern education. It brings into the picture the counsel and advice of an appreciative principal. In fact, as education has become synonymous with growth, which in turn is considered to be the result of significant experiences, the principal has assumed more and more the duties of supervision. This is natural when one remembers that he is always in the building; he is in a better position to understand the individual problems of the teacher. He knows the students of his school, and he realizes the kind of experiences necessary for them to achieve the goals that he has in mind.

More modern definitions of supervision have been formulated since the publication of the *Eighth Yearbook*. One of the most thoughtful is found in the Appleton series in

[15] Ibid. pp. 209-210.

supervision and teaching.[16] The authors attribute three major functions to supervision with a number of related minor functions as follows:

I. Studying the Teaching-Learning Situation
   1. Critically Analyzing the Objectives of Education and of Supervision
   2. Surveying the Products of Learning
   3. Studying the Antecedents of Satisfactory and of Unsatisfactory Growth and Pupil Achievement
   4. Studying the Interests, Capacities, and Work Habits of Pupils
   5. Studying the Teacher at Work and Aiding Her to Study Herself
   6. Studying the Curriculum in Operation
   7. Studying the Materials of Instruction and the Socio-Physical Environment of Learning

II. Improving the Teaching-Learning Situation
   1. Improving the Educational Objectives and the Curriculum
   2. Improving the Interest, Application, and Work Habits of the Pupils
   3. Improving the Teacher and Her Methods
   4. Improving the Materials of Instruction and the Socio-Physical Environment of Learning

III. Evaluating the Means, Methods, and Outcomes of Supervision
   1. Discovering and Applying the Technique of Evaluation
   2. Evaluating the General Worth of Supervision
   3. Evaluating the Results of Given Supervisory Plans
   4. Evaluating Factors Limiting Instructional Outcomes
   5. Evaulating and Improving the Personnel of Supervision

This definition does not limit the aim of supervision to the improvement of teachers in service, but gives it a

[16] A. S. Barr, William H. Burton, Leo J. Brueckner, *Supervision*, D. Appleton-Century Company, New York. 1938, pp. 19-24.

broader conception involving the improvement of the total teaching-learning process. The teacher is a cooperative member of this process, not the member on whom attention is focussed. Supervision is taken out of the realm of just class visitations, conferences, and teachers' meetings.

"Traditional supervision was largely inspection of the teacher by means of visitation and conference, carried on in a random manner, with suggestions imposed on the teacher through authority and usually by one person. Modern supervision by contrast is the study and analysis of the total teaching-learning situation through many diverse functions operating through a carefully planned program that has been cooperatively derived from the needs of the situation and in which many persons participate.

"The technique of teacher-training under modern supervision will be shifted from direction and requirement to cooperative self-directed improvement. In this supervisors and principals will share, thus increasing their own levels of training and insight. *The improvement of teachers is not so much a supervisory function in which teachers participate, as a teacher function in which supervisors participate.*" [17]

Supervision and the Music Program

During the above discussion of the purpose of supervision, continual reference was made to the music program. There are a few other problems which were not covered completely and which relate closely to music teaching.

Administration and Supervision

Although administration and supervision have a common aim they must not be confused as being the same thing. Administration endeavors to provide an environment in which the teaching-learning process can be conducted to the best advantage. It includes the selection of teachers, organization, management, housing, equipment,

[17] Ibid. pp. 23, 24.

materials, and maintenance. Supervision, on the other hand, works in the environment provided by the administration to improve the teaching-learning process. To do this supervision often draws upon the duties of administration, but it should never become so involved in such duties that it neglects its unique function.

Supervision and Teaching

Another erroneous conception of terms is that of considering the teaching and supervising of music as synonymous. Teachers of music teach music to children. Supervisors of music teach teachers how to teach music to children.

The music supervisor of the past has gradually become the special music teacher. As elementary schools became departmentalized, one teacher was employed to give instruction in music. Such a teacher should not be called a supervisor. Even in the more modern school where there is a return to the former practice of the grade teacher doing her own music teaching, the scheduled visits of the supervisor have been transformed to regular and requested calls by the music specialist. The practices of limiting supervision to frequent conferences of instruction and lesson plans, or teaching a round of music classes and giving suggestions for work until the next visit, is not supervision. The first is merely a modern adaptation of the monotorial system applied to music education, and the second is an attempt to make a model teacher out of the supervisor.

The titles, director of music and teacher of music, are becoming more appropriate to the profession. The high school music teacher is very often called upon to do some supervision it is true, but just because one is a good teacher of music is no sign that one is a good supervisor. Supervision requires certain personal qualities and individual techniques. The director of music is in a position to either teach or supervise as the individual situation may require.

Relationship of Supervisor and Principal

It has been mentioned that in the high school, the principal is becoming more active in subject-matter supervision. This is even true in music. Many more principals are becoming cognizant of the aims of music education. Many of them are gaining an appreciation of music and a better understanding of the techniques of teaching music. Some of our younger principals have themselves participated in orchestras, bands, or choruses, during their high school and college days.

The supervisor or director of music must not encroach upon the prerogatives of the principal. The former may be concerned about the uniformity of the music instruction throughout a town or city, but the latter realizes better how the music program must serve his school. This policy is all the more important in the modern trend of encouraging the individuality of schools depending upon the local environment. The supervisor or director must respect decisions of the principal and consult him on the problems of teachers and curriculum. Problems are best solved when the teacher, principal, and supervisor sit down together to talk them over.

Relationship of Supervisor and Teacher

What can the grade school teacher or the music teacher in the high school expect of the supervisor? [18]

Encouragement and sympathetic understanding of individual as well as teaching problems is the first requisite of the supervisor. The teacher may expect guidance in *devel-*

[18] Carol M. Pitts, "What the Classroom Teacher Wants of the Supervisor, Music Educators National Conference, *Yearbook 1936,* pp. 81-82.

opment and growth as a musician and person of culture. The supervisor should be expected to have qualities of *democratic leadership* which will be evident in his personality, capacity to impart helpful knowledge, and his own ability to teach. Through encouragement, guidance, and leadership, the grade school teacher and the teacher of music in the high school may expect *stimulation for self-improvement.*

What may the supervisor expect of the teacher?

If it is true that the supervisor should have the qualities described in this chapter, it is equally true that the teacher of music should be ready to *cooperate* with such a person. The supervisor can expect the teacher to be well-prepared for his job or willing to accept helpful and constructive criticism. He can expect the teacher to be eager to improve and to grow professionally, and finally, he can expect the teacher to seek his advice when difficulties of organization and procedure arise.

Conclusion

If administration and supervision are designed to improve the teaching-learning process, then they must be organized in a manner which will attain this purpose. So often administration is conceived as a staff and line organization with the child completely ignored. We include a typical drawing of this type of organization. For our purpose, it has been simplified.

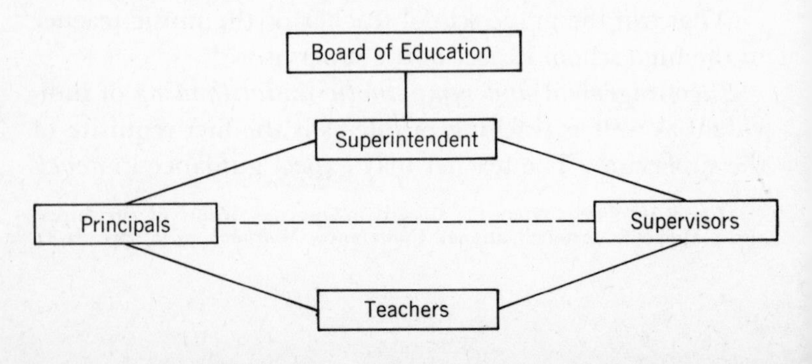

We suggest a diagram which conceives the child as being the center of the teaching-learning process with administrative officers assuming their relative nearness to this process.

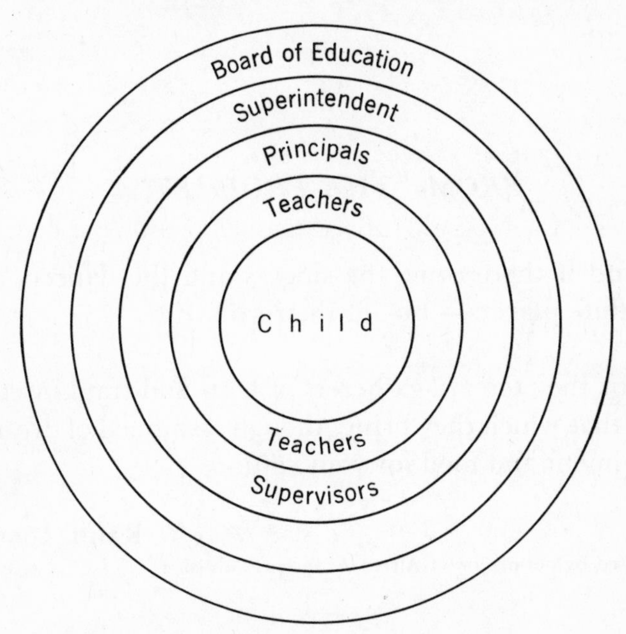

Topics for General Discussion

✓1. As a new high school music teacher, if invited to appear before the Board of Education, describe the administrative organization of the music program that you would recommend.

2. In light of their positions, whose obligation is greater, that of the administrator to understand the point of view of the music educator or that of the music educator to gain an understanding of the point of view of the administrator? Discuss your opinion.

3. Are high school music teachers becoming so well prepared that there is little place for the music supervisor in the high school? Give reasons for your answer.

✓ 4. Make a three column list of the duties of the high school teacher under the headings administration, supervision, and teaching.

FROM "THE PROPHET" *

And if there come the singers and the dancers and the flute players,—buy of their gifts also.

For they too are gatherers of fruit and frankincense, and that which they bring, though fashioned of dreams, is raiment and food for your soul.

KAHIL GIBRAN

Chapter 14

PROBLEMS OF ORGANIZATION AND MANAGEMENT

If the high school curriculum is to consist of musical experiences in singing, playing, listening, and composing, it is time that we turn our attention to some of the difficulties which may arise in programming these activities. A list of organizations and classes representing a rich offering of musical activities will probably include: general chorus, choirs and glee clubs, small choral ensembles, voice classes, orchestra and band, small instrumental ensembles, instrumental classes, general music classes, and special classes in appreciation, harmony, and composition. When we add to these the general assembly, the production of concerts, operettas, cantatas, and festivals, we can see that the administrator and musical director have no easy time in arranging schedules.[1]

Scheduling of Music Activities

Since the turn of the century music has made great strides as a recognized subject in the high school curriculum. From its status as an extra-curricular activity of minor importance, it has won recognition to such an extent that it has been accepted in many places on equal footing with the academic subjects. Musical organizations are scheduled

[1] Note: Schedules of music classes in different size high schools will be found in the appendix.

for several rehearsals each week. Rehearsals are held during school hours. This acceptance of music in the regular curriculum has greatly increased its prestige.

There are several factors to be considered in scheduling this newly created program of music. First of all, musical experiences must be provided for all levels of musical intelligence and ability. A program designed to provide these experiences intersects the various grade levels. Conflicts in class schedules necessarily result. However, several devices can be used to counteract these conflicts. If the music director works in close harmony with the administrator, the latter is often willing to clear at least two periods each day to be devoted, for the most part, to selective musical organizations. Instrumental music can be scheduled in one of these periods, choral music in another. Large metropolitan high schools, with a schedule providing many sections of the same course, have little difficulty with such conflicts in classes. Some administrators have experimented with a larger number of shorter periods per day to facilitate the programming of musical activities during school hours.

Instrumental classes, music assemblies, and even complete organizations are often scheduled on a "staggered" basis. In this system the class meets at a different hour each day of the week. In case of conflict the student attends the music class. In this way he misses his regular class only once in every five weeks.

A successful music program depends upon such devices as have been suggested. As can be imagined, they are not always received with enthusiasm by teachers of academic subjects, who fail to see why their subjects should be interrupted by the music program. The "mind-training" virtues of some of these academic subjects are now being questioned. Music educators, in turn, have extolled the virtues of their subject with missionary zeal. Naturally, subjects entrenched in the curriculum give ground reluctantly.

The Commission on the Reorganization of Secondary Education discovered that if recommendations of the committee on various subjects were followed, one would have to provide a school day about twelve hours long, and that in such a day there would be no place for elective subjects. There is only one solution. When all teachers, both music and others, set themselves to study the needs of youth and are able to estimate the value of various activities, in reference to these needs, an agreement should be possible. Then teachers will not insist that their particular subjects be taught five days per week for the entire year with never an interruption. Music teachers may have to be satisfied with two or three rehearsals a week for the choir or band. It may often be necessary to be satisfied with even fewer rehearsals with some organizations in order to reach a greater proportion of the student body. *All in all, when the evaluation of subjects is made from the standpoint of youth, and its total needs, differences of opinion with respect to the proportion of time given an activity will tend to disappear.*

Size of Classes

If music is to retain its place in the curriculum of the high school the classes must be of sufficient size to compare favorably with classes in other subjects. A safe axiom for the music teacher is to strive for quantity in the beginning and to work for quality as the music program becomes established. Many musical activities lend themselves to large groups. In fact, in terms of teacher-pupil load, music as a whole is one of the less expensive subjects in the school curriculum.[2] As various activities have been discussed in earlier chapters, the size of many of the groups have been

[2] Russell V. Morgan, "Analysis of Teaching Costs by Subjects,"—Music Educators National Conference, *Yearbook, 1933*. Chicago, Illinois, pp. 313-318.

All-State Girls' Chorus, New York State School Music Association, November, 1940, Helen Hosmer, Director.

Teaneck (New Jersey) High School Band, Etzel Wilhoit, Conductor.

indicated. However, it may be well at this point to summarize the approximate size of music classes and organizations.

1. *General Music Class:* 30 to 40 students. This number is the most satisfactory to carry on both individual and group performance and discussion.
2. *Music Theory Class:* 10 to 20 students. This number is necessary as a valid reason for including this class in the curriculum. It is not too large to prevent the fostering of individual creative effort.
3. *General Chorus:* 60 to 300 students. A large number of students is necessary to sing the repertoire most suited for the chorus. A smaller number than sixty and the chorus resembles the choir.
4. *A Cappella Choir:* 20 to 60 students. A smaller number than 20 members in the choir should be treated like a small vocal ensemble. A choir of more than sixty students resembles a chorus and often lacks precision and finesse.
5. *Small Vocal Ensembles*
   a. Male Quartet: 2 tenors, 2 basses
   b. Treble Sextet: 2 first sopranos, 2 second sopranos, 2 altos
   c. Mixed Groups: 6-12 students. When there are more than twelve students in a group, it loses its individual character.
6. *Voice Classes:* 12-30. It is necessary to work out procedures whereby 30 students may be taught in a beginning class. If a class falls below 12, it loses its group quality.
7. *School Orchestra:* 20-90 students. An orchestra less than 20 students should be treated as a small ensemble. Many schools are endeavoring to reach the symphonic standard of 90 players. If there are more students than 90, orchestras of different levels should be organized.
8. *School Band:* 20-90 students. Same as orchestra.
9. *Drum and Bugle Corps:* 20-90 students. Same as band.

10. *Small Instrumental Ensembles:*
    a. String Quartet: First violin, second violin, viola, violoncello
    b. Brass Quartet:
       (1) First trumpet
       (2) Second trumpet
       (3) Trombone or horn
       (4) Bass trombone, baritone or E♭ tuba
    c. Woodwind Quintet:
       (1) Flute
       (2) Oboe
       (3) Clarinet
       (4) Horn, English horn, or Clarinet
       (5) Bassoon
    d. Mixed Groups: 6-12 students. Includes salon orchestras and jazz bands.
11. *Instrumental Classes:* 8-20. On account of the mechanical handicaps, instrumental classes should be somewhat smaller than vocal classes. Classes may run fairly large if they are grouped homogeneously. Fewer number than eight in a class makes too great demands upon a teacher's time.

Organization in Ensembles

It may be valuable to give some consideration to the organization within ensemble groups such as the orchestra, band, chorus and choir. Some teachers follow the practice of having student officers such as president, vice-president, secretary, treasurer, etc. They base this procedure on the idea that students like ceremony and that it is democratic for them to elect officers. From our own observation, in most situations the functions of these officers are confined to having their names listed in the school annual. By far the largest majority of high schools confine the officers of these organizations to a librarian and accompanist, usually appointed by the teacher, and possibly a student conductor and business manager who may be elected.

The argument that the election of a list of officers is

democratic seems to us to be a false one. Democratic procedure is not a matter of electing officers; it is a manner of living from day to day. Unless officers have real functions that serve the electors, their election may actually be undemocratic. If the teacher is dictatorial in temperament, the election of officers will not change his conduct. High school ensembles meet together to make beautiful music. It is the cooperation within the group and the recognition individuals receive in the act of making music that gives school music organizations their value as democratic laboratories.

We do not mean to give the impression that we are against the election of officers for high school music ensembles. If they are made to serve a purpose in certain situations, the practice is a valid one. Of course, there is the consideration of the time that such procedure may take which could better be devoted to the real purpose of the organization. However, it is the setting up of false values and unearned honors that we question. In a college or community glee club where these officers serve a real function, there is no question about their necessity.

What officers can be of genuine service in high school music organizations? We have mentioned them in a previous paragraph, but it might be well to list them again. These officers have definite functions which have genuine educational values.

(1) *Business Manager*

This office should be filled by an energetic boy or girl who has executive ability. He should be elected after the teacher has carefully outlined his duties to the organization. The students will then feel more responsibility in electing a qualified person. He will cooperate closely with the teacher in all business details associated with the organization. He will handle all publicity, ticket sales, and financial problems. He will cooperate with the teacher in making arrangements for trips. He will have the power to appoint committees to assist him.

(2) *Librarian*

This office should be filled by a boy or girl who is responsible and enjoys this type of work. He may be elected but it is usually better for the teacher to appoint someone who is interested. If he is elected the teacher must impress the students with the responsibilities of the office. The librarian will have charge of cataloguing, filing, repairing, passing out, checking out, and collecting all music.

(3) *Student-Conductor*

This office should be filled by a boy or girl who has leadership qualities and musical ability. He may be elected by the students after several students have had an opportunity to conduct the organization. (Conducting by students should not be limited to the elected student-conductor.) The student-conductor should have charge of arranging the set-up for rehearsal. A rotating plan may be worked out to provide assistance for him in this duty. He should be able to take charge of the rehearsal whenever the teacher is called from the room.

(4) *Accompanist*

This very important officer should be appointed by the teacher from the students best qualified. If the accompanist is on the teaching staff, there should be several students as assistants, for they need this experience. (The training of the accompanist is discussed in Chapter X.)

Honors and Awards

The practice of granting awards and honors for superior achievement is as old as the olive wreaths of the ancient Greeks. They appeal to one of the strongest psychological motives of man, that is, the desire to succeed and receive recognition for achievement. It seems that man cannot be expected to act upon intrinsic motives but needs the stimulation of extrinsic motives in the pursuit of most educational activities.

Miss Chen found that the granting of awards of some nature was almost universal practice in the American high school.[3] Of the 235 schools on which she reported, approximately twenty per cent gave some award for participation in school music organizations. The arguments for and against the music contest apply equally to granting awards to music students. Let us list these arguments in more detail.

ARGUMENTS IN THE AFFIRMATIVE

(1) Honors and awards stimulate interest and participation in music.
(2) Honors and awards are excellent means for giving recognition to merit or service.
(3) Honors and awards encourage sustained effort in music.
(4) Honors and awards stimulate the desire for improvement in music.
(5) Honors and awards serve as extrinsic motives which may be transferred to intrinsic ones.
(6) Honors and awards are common practice in everyday life.

ARGUMENTS IN THE NEGATIVE

(1) Honors and awards are artificial stimuli and fail to interest the student in the music itself.
(2) Honors and awards develop conceit and create a false sense of values on the part of the recipients.
(3) Honors and awards may become the ends rather than the means for encouraging ability in music.
(4) Honors and awards fasten attention upon the reward and detract from a permanent desire for improvement in music.
(5) Honors and awards serve as extrinsic motivation which is not likely to lead to an intrinsic love of music.

[3] Shu-Kuei Carol Chen, *Honors and Awards in American High Schools*, The Hillside Press, 1933. p. 156.

(6) Honors and awards give students the idea that participation in music activity should lead to some form of compensation.

Undoubtedly the readers can think of many more arguments both pro and con in the question of awards for participation in school music organizations. Some schools have developed elaborate systems for the granting of awards on as objective a basis as possible.[4] The crux of the argument seems to lie in the ability to shift the extrinsic motivation of awards to the intrinsic motivation of music itself. The granting of honors and awards in music participation are valuable only so far as they make themselves unnecessary. If they become ends in themselves rather than means, they may be actually harmful. Moreover, the shift from extrinsic motives to intrinsic ones is not always easy, and teachers may use the honor and award as a substitute for inspired teaching.

It seems to the author that the privilege of playing beautiful music is sufficient reward in itself. If the teacher has enthusiasm, musicianship, and qualities necessary for leadership, he will have little difficulty in stimulating interest and sustaining effort on the part of the students in their school music organizations, without the motivation of honors and awards. If awards are given, they should not be granted to members of one organization, such as the band, at the expense of other ensemble groups. If the school has a highly developed system of granting letters and awards to members of athletic groups, it seems only fair that corresponding recognition should be given to members of music organizations. However, the honor of being a member of the school music organization, a word or letter of praise from the director, and the privilege of making music

[4] Howard W. Deye, "The Boise Award System," Music Educators National Conference, *Yearbook 1935*. pp. 230-232.

will be sufficient motivation for students who are guided by a sympathetic and understanding teacher.

Marks and Credits for Music

Shall we give marks in music? In Chapter I the inadequacy of the marking system was pointed out. Traditional marks fail to disclose the true evaluation of student progress. The subjective quality of music study increases the difficulty of giving anything that resembles a fair grading. As a result, many teachers refrain from giving, or do not bother to give, grades in music. Other teachers use high marks to attract students into musical organizations and classes, thereby boosting the student's average. Both practices may endanger the prestige of music in comparison with other subjects which grade rigidly.

It is true that music is an excellent subject with which to experiment in working out other types of evaluation, in making more adequate reports, and in setting up a more meaningful kind of record. If the music teacher does not give grades, he should be enabled to make more adequate reports and records. Both the administration and students should understand the advantages of any new type of mark or report. If traditional marking is followed, then the mark should mean something. It should not be used as a bribe. *Students should earn their marks.*

In the first decade of this century, when music was very much extra-curricular, there was little thought of granting credit for participating in musical organizations. As these organizations grew and music was accepted into the regular curriculum, much more time and work was demanded of students who were scheduled in musical activities. Crowded programs and credit requirements for college entrance caused music educators to seek credit for their subject.

As in all phases of the study, college entrance requirements [5] have controlled to a remarkable degree the amount of credit given for various phases of music study. Theory and harmony seemed to be the first subjects to be accepted on a full credit basis. Gradually requirements have become more flexible, both in the type of activities which are granted credit and in the number of credits in music which are accepted for graduation and for college entrance. Now it is not unusual for high schools to grant credit for theory, harmony, history, appreciation, orchestra, band, chorus, glee club, voice classes, and individual lessons in and out of school. Two credits out of fifteen or sixteen required for graduation is not uncommon, and in some schools the number runs as high as four out of the total of fifteen or sixteen credits required.

As long as secondary education is organized on a time-unit system, the basis for granting credits to music should be the same as that of any other subject. The most nearly universal practice is based on the plan proposed by the North Central Association of Schools and Colleges. This plan grants one unit of credit per year for each subject studied two hundred minutes each week (five days of forty minutes each or four days of fifty minutes each) for thirty-six weeks, which requires an equal amount of outside preparation. Unprepared classes or laboratory work is granted half as much credit as work which is prepared.

It naturally follows that a course in music meeting five periods a week for one year and requiring the same amount of outside preparation as any academic subject should receive one unit of credit. Such courses as chorus, orchestra, and band, which meet five periods a week for one year and do not require outside preparation, should receive one-

[5] *The Giving of High School Credits for Private Music Study*. New York: National Bureau for the Advancement of Music, 1924. A more recent summary is found in the article, "College Attitudes on Entrance Credits for Music," Music Educators National Conference, *Yearbook 1939-1940*, p. 417.

half unit of credit a year, or credit on the laboratory basis. If an activity meets for two periods per week of forty-five minutes each on a laboratory basis, a one-fourth unit of credit is usually granted for the year. In these cases, although there is a shortage of time in the number of minutes of class meeting, this shortage is made up by extra rehearsals for public performance or by outside preparation. It does not seem advisable to recognize fractional credits of less than one-fourth toward graduation.

Many controversial words have been spoken about the granting of credit for applied music. It seems only right that this study should be recognized and granted credit, if it is of good calibre. The reluctance of colleges to accept such credit for entrance has been the chief obstacle to granting credit for this study. However, many colleges are relaxing these requirements and schools are beginning to follow the practice of giving one-half unit of credit a year for applied music in piano, voice, or symphonic instruments, when one private lesson is taken each week for a year and one hour a day is devoted to practice. Applied music may be studied with a teacher employed by the school or with an outside private teacher. Work taken with teachers employed by the school is subject to the same regulations as that done in other studies. Instruction in applied music with private teachers introduces a troublesome problem.

Lessons with Private Teachers

In the past, private teachers have complained of the introduction of instrumental and vocal lessons in the schools, with the cry that they were deprived of pupils. However, over a period of several years these same teachers have usually discovered that the result of school music is larger classes and better students for the private teacher, more students taking music seriously, and home practice that is bringing better musical results. Consequently, with the phenomenal growth of school music, the private teacher has endeavored to ally himself with the school music teacher and also to secure recognition and credit for his pupils. The wise music educator has, in turn, enlisted the services of the private teacher and has made an effort to secure credits for applied music taken outside school, since these pupils have greatly improved the calibre of his own organizations.

The situation presents two problems. If credits toward graduation are to be granted, the private teacher should be qualified. Secondly, there must be some check-up or evaluation of the work done to assure the school administration that it is comparable to other work credited by the school.

It is indeed a sad truth, that all private teachers are not qualified to give music lessons. For that matter, not all school music teachers are qualified to teach school music. However, the school music teacher must be certified by the state, which represents a certain amount of training. It is only right that the private teacher should be as well trained in his field as is the teacher of music in the school. Certification can be set by state requirements, or certain standards can be fixed by the local school authorities which will insure that the private teacher is qualified. Proof of qualification can be determined by a degree, certificate, examination, training and teaching experience, or a demonstration. When school credit is given for outside study, the private teacher becomes an extension of the teaching staff. Therefore, the school administration must take definite steps to assure itself that the private teacher is qualified to supplement the school work.

Assuming that the private teacher is capable, nevertheless, a definite check on work should be made at least once each semester. This should be in the form of practice sheets signed by parents, and reports by the private teacher with recommended grades. These reports may be supplemented by examination conducted under rules formulated by the board of education. Any expenses that are incurred should be met by the school, although there are many places where students are charged a small examination fee.

The problem of credit for applied music study under outside private music teachers has not been completely solved, but by following such procedures as those suggested, the teacher of school music and the private teacher can be of mutual assistance to each other.[6]

Music Tests in the High School

At this time let us turn our attention to the better known standardized musical talent and achievement tests. We intend to discuss, not the psychological value of these tests, which is of utmost importance, but rather the practical value of their use in the high school, which is definitely limited. Musical talent tests must still be regarded as being in the experimental stage.

Many musicians have often disparaged and even scoffed at musical talent tests. Nevertheless, with all the limitations of these tests, they represent a spirit of experimentation, a spirit of inquiry and diligent research which commands respect and commendation. When one studies the slow, painful growth of tests that are given to measure general intelligence, one sees the long experimentation still necessary to attempt the measurement of a more complex and intangible quality, namely, musicality. It is not the object of these tests to discover something new, but to develop easier and quicker methods of determining musical ability which lies dormant or which is apparent only after long "trial and error" experimentation. Every teacher of music

[6] See Appendix A for a summary of states certifying outside private teachers and for forms used in granting credit to students for outside study.

or prospective teacher should study these tests for their reliability and validity in order to enable themselves to interpret the scores with intelligence and understanding.

Music Talent Tests

Of the music talent tests the Seashore "Measures of Musical Talent" is the oldest and probably the best known and most scientific battery of music tests. Their practical value is found in testing large groups to discover latent musical capacities. For the purpose of organizing high school classes into homogeneous groupings, they should be used together with a general intelligence test. This battery may be used to supplement and verify personal judgment, but alone the tests should never be used for negative findings. No student should be denied the opportunity for participation in music on the basis of such tests. It is dangerous to give either negative educational or vocational advice without a closer association and better understanding of a student than is possible through the medium of tests alone. It is rather unfortunate that this battery of tests has become known as music "talent" tests. It undoubtedly measures special abilities in music usually found in talented students, but it should not be assumed, nor is it claimed by its author, that musical ability as a functioning unit can be measured by testing these few specific elements.[7]

Another battery of tests which endeavors to measure innate abilities in music is the Kwalwasser-Dykema (K-D) Music Tests. These tests are somewhat similar to the Seashore battery, but they are shorter and more interesting to most students because some of them use actual music material. They are especially serviceable for quick preliminary surveys.

[7] James L. Mursell and Mabelle Glenn, *Psychology of School Music Teaching*. New York: Silver Burdett Company, 1938. Chapter XIII is devoted to a description of the best known standardized tests.

One great danger in the use of music talent tests is found in the assumption that anyone can give them and can interpret the scores. We have pointed out the danger of using them for negative findings. Much lack of understanding is shown in what can be expected of music talent tests for purposes of prognostication. In the first place, special training is necessary in administering these tests to assure their reliability and validity. Secondly, the teacher must be able, both through training and experience, to interpret the scores accurately and make a practical diagnosis. Thirdly, the essence of the whole matter lies in the educational application of the findings of the test. In other words, what are you going to do about it after you have made an accurate study of your students? What changes will you make in your course of study to meet the situations which your tests have disclosed? How will it affect your teaching procedures? To what degree will it better enable you to guide your students professionally and educationally? How will it affect your selection of music materials? How would it affect your assignment of the student to various types of instrumental study? These and other questions should be the direct result of the administration and interpretation of music talent tests.

Music Achievement Tests

The second type of standardized musical tests are those which attempt to measure achievement as a result of training.[8] It is quite obvious that they deal with a much more tangible, and a much more measurable quality than the music talent tests do. It is a debatable question how much standardization there should be in music education. Overstandardization will undoubtedly handicap many teachers and cause many music educators to miss the point of the

[8] Ibid. Chapter XIII.

value of music. Moreover, most studies and tests seem to show that we are far from knowing what standards to expect of boys and girls who have had public school musical training.

Most of the available achievement tests attempt to measure aural perception, technical abilities, and skill in reading the notation. The best known tests of this type are the Gildersleeve Music Achievement Tests and the Kwalwasser-Ruch tests of musical accomplishment. The Gildersleeve tests are shorter, more interesting, and more practical in most situations; the Kwalwasser-Ruch test is longer, more thorough, and serves better in testing advanced groups.

It might be well to mention one test designed to measure knowledge, namely, the Kwalwasser Test of Musical Information and Appreciation. The test is questionable in its validity to measure the appreciation of music, except to the extent that knowledge of certain facts of music is assumed to enhance appreciation of it. Moreover, many of the questions of fact are ambiguous. However, students like to take the test and to compare themselves with each other and with students of other high schools. If the teacher realizes that the test measures musical information, not appreciation, it can serve as a valid learning experience.

This brief discussion mentions only a few of the music tests that have been standardized. Many others are available, but few have developed norms to insure their validity for educational work. Tests of voice and tests to determine instrumental ability have been discussed in the chapters devoted to these activities.

The Guidance Program

In the past, the high school teacher's responsibilities were largely confined to the presentation of subject-matter and the evaluation of students' work with a definite grade. In recent years a new function of the teacher and the school has arisen on the educational horizon in the word "guidance." As with many modern features in education, it is not a new function, but elaborate procedures have been adopted in many places to emphasize the importance of guidance in the total scheme of education.

Many psychological discussions have been written on the meaning of "guidance." But the opinion most often given presents guidance in education as the procedures used in helping students solve the problems that arise in their present physical and social environment and in preparing them to meet the problems of future living. This statement includes both educational and vocational guidance.

The guidance program often includes a staff of specialists, but there is a decided trend toward expecting the teachers themselves to fulfill the functions of the guidance program, as far as they are able. Since teachers know the students better than other members of the school staff, this trend is undoubtedly advisable if guidance is going to truly function in most places. A guidance program usually involves a complete cumulative record system and it is the duty of the music teacher to familiarize himself with these records so that he can better understand his students. Any vocational guidance in music must usually be done by the music teacher, because specialists in vocational guidance are seldom cognizant of the opportunities in this profession.[9]

A list of standards which the music teacher should have in order to fulfill his part in the guidance program will include:

An understanding of the place of the music teacher in the guidance program.

Ability to guide students in their choice of musical activi-

[9] An excellent book on the professional opportunities in music is Howard Taubman's *Music As a Profession*. Charles Scribner's Sons, New York, 1939.

ties which will assure continued interest and musical growth.

A knowledge of opportunities in the various professional fields of music (radio, concert, theatre, composition, arranging, and teaching).

Ability to guide the student in his choice of music courses in his preparation for college.

Ability to evaluate personality, character, and performance proficiency in guiding students in musical interests and ambitions.

Ability to use various standardized tests in musical aptitudes and achievement.

Ability through tests to advise students in the selection of instruments.

Ability to advise parents on the desirable music education of their children.

Ability to advise parents on the price of various types of instruments, reliability of manufacturers, and plan of payment.

Music Guidance Tests

There is a possible kind of test which seems to have received scant attention. It is a test which would help the teacher in guiding the music studies of senior high school pupils, particularly those who show some definite musical interest or ability. Such a test necessarily would be largely subjective rather than objective, and would help the student to discover his own urges as well as help the teacher to form opinions as a basis for giving advice.

A music guidance test should help the pupil to explore his own attitudes toward music as a hobby, an avocation, or a vocation. It should help him to discriminate between daydreaming and wishful thinking and actual devotion and determination, both as to quality and degree. The test should enquire as to what musical activities the student is pursuing, the degree of advancement, or achievement, reached in each of them, and the amount of time and effort given to them. It should help the student determine the degree of satisfaction which his efforts have brought to him, both with respect to music as such and in comparison with his activities in other fields of interest. Further, it should sound out the possibilities open to him for further pursuit of his musical development, should such appear sufficiently attractive and worth while either as a professional or an amateur activity.

Such guidance studies need not be elaborately standardized or graded. The teacher can develop them from his own contacts with his pupils and through discussions about the things which have made music a worth-while part of their lives. They are necessarily a part of a cumulative record system. Out of such tests, or possibly they might better be called investigations or studies, a guidance program may be given of highly material assistance.

Where a cumulative record system is established, beginning in the grades and continuing on into the high school, much data for the guidance test will be available. The test itself might well be in the form of a series of questions organized according to the various topics with which the musical young student is concerned, and with ample space for replies to be written in which will be more than mere "yes" or "no." It will give some clue as to the student's likes, preferences, interests, activities, failures and successes, frustrations and hopes, obstacles and ambitions. Such guidance tests as well as the cumulative record system should serve not only for high school purposes, but may become an invaluable means for maintaining the student's interest and participation in music when he goes to college and afterward when he becomes an adult member of his community.

TRIPS

Attendance at contests, festivals, and conference meetings involves trips. Often large groups of high school students travel great distances. The stimulation which comes from performing before distant audiences, if properly developed and directed, can be of great benefit to the school music organizations and to their individual members.

The organization of such trips involves many details of preparation, conveyance, housing and feeding, chaperonage, and financing. It is interesting and illuminating to record that in the thousands of trips taken by high school music organizations instances of mismanagement and misconduct are so rare as to be almost negligible. There seems to be such a spirit of absorbing concentration on the primary purposes of these trips that the resultant self-control and self-discipline bring out the best in the youthful participants.

In Appendix A, page 404, a study of the problems of financing trips will be found. It shows how varied are the means for raising the necessary funds, and how readily school authorities and community cooperate in such an enterprise.

Conclusion

There is no doubt that teaching music in the high school today involves more than a knowledge of music and the ability to present it. This chapter has attempted to point out most of the problems of organization and management that confront the teacher. Failure to accept and solve such problems may cause many trials and tribulations for teachers who are otherwise adequate. The problems associated with business management, such as budgets, ordering of music, and observance of copyright laws, have been reserved for Chapter XVII under the discussion of the business attitude of the teacher.

Questions for General Discussion

1. Make out a schedule of music classes for some high school in which you are interested. Defend this program for the situation you have in mind.

2. Examine various types of report cards which are being used in some high schools. Organize a report card for music study which you think would be helpful and informative to students and parents.

3. Study the manuals of the Seashore and Kwalwasser-Dykema battery of talent tests. Take these tests personally and consider the correlation between your score and your own opinion of your musical ability.

4. Formulate and discuss the kind of information and types of forms necessary for a cumulative record system which would be valuable in the guidance program.

5. Work out a guidance test as suggested in this chapter. In your own experience what questions would be pertinent in such a test? How does your test differ from the available standardized achievement tests?

6. Of the arguments on Honors and Awards in this chapter, which seem to you to be the stronger—those in the affirmative or those in the negative? Why?

7. Make a report on the plan of granting credit for outside music study in your community.

When we mean to build,
We first survey the Plot, then draw the Modell,
And when we see the figure of the house, 11-2
Then must we rate the cost of the Erection,
Which if we find out-weighs ability,
What doe we then, but draw a-new the Modell
In fewer Offices (Or at least, desist
To build at all?

WILLIAM SHAKESPEARE
King Henry the Fourth, Second Part
Act I, Scene III

Chapter 15

MUSIC ROOMS AND EQUIPMENT

Many good music teachers have been forced to do a mediocre job through lack of adequate rooms, equipment, and materials for carrying on their work. Proper equipment and materials furnish the means for superior teaching. The ends toward which this book is dedicated are futile without these means.

When one visits schools throughout the country, one is appalled at the physical conditions under which many music classes are taught. Through lack of adequate insulation, music classes are often relegated to some part of the building where they will prove the least disturbing and where, all too often, there is poor light or ventilation. Even in new buildings lack of careful planning has made rooms unusable which were originally designed for music classes. In planning music classrooms and their equipment, several factors should be considered: (1) location of music rooms with relation to other classrooms; (2) size of music rooms; (3) type of music rooms for various uses; (4) music instrument and uniform storage; (5) acoustical treatment; (6) lighting and ventilation; (7) equipment, and (8) auditorium stage and equipment. These factors are described in detail in the *Music Education Research Bulletin No. 17*, "Music Rooms and Equipment," published by the Music Educators National Conference.[1] Every music teacher

[1] 64 East Jackson Boulevard, Chicago, Illinois. Price $.25.

should have this bulletin in his library for his own enlightenment as well as for a guide in discussing classrooms and equipment with his administrator.

The Music Unit

In planning the music unit, the relative values of all those activities discussed in this book must be considered. Educators are using music to affect the lives of young people and to make their lives more beautiful. This aim will be reached by providing opportunities for young people to sing, play, and listen to great music. In this way they will learn to love music to such a degree that they will continue their contacts with beautiful music after graduation, and ,live more complete adult lives because of the emotional and aesthetic satisfaction derived from their musical experiences.

If music education has this power to affect our lives, then much thought should be given to the rooms and equipment necessary for carrying on a program of fruitful musical activities. Ordinary classrooms are usually inadequate for the special requirements necessary for musical activities. Even when remodeled they are often found wanting in such considerations as convenience in location, interference with other classrooms, unhealthful conditions caused by poor lighting, ventilation, and chairs, and finally, acoustical treatment which is a real factor in the successful teaching of music.

The Auditorium

First of all, let us consider the auditorium, which in so many high schools must serve as a general meeting place as well as the one and only music classroom. In many situations the auditorium may be made quite serviceable for a general classroom for musical activities if interference of other activities is not permitted. Too often, however, it happens that various parts of the auditorium must serve for other classes. Also, there is often preparation on the stage by other departments for assembly programs and public performances. Because of these interferences, the use of the auditorium as the complete music unit is rendered unsatisfactory.

In the event that the auditorium must serve as a general music classroom, certain provisions should be made. These include a stage which will be adequate for performances by the largest music organization of the school, whether it be instrumental, choral, or combined, or operettas and pageants. Adjacent rooms to the stage should be available to serve as storage space for uniforms, instruments, stands, and risers. Dressing rooms may be equipped for practice rooms. The orchestra pit, if there is one in the general layout, should be large enough to accommodate an orchestra of at least forty players. It should be wider than the average theatre pit and not so deep. This makes possible performances by the orchestra as an independent organization for assemblies and other programs. Approximately twenty electrical outlets should be provided with hooded music stands. The auditorium should be provided with all the equipment, such as pianos, radio, phonograph, and lantern, needed for the activities which will be taught.

To avoid shifting of chairs and equipment, it is better for daily purposes to use the auditorium seats for school and class activities so that the stage will be permanently set up for instrumental rehearsals.

Some schools have made the auditorium more available for general music activities by using folding doors to separate the stage from the main auditorium. Sufficient lighting and ventilation have been provided and the walls of the stage treated acoustically. Under these conditions, if music classes are scheduled with due consideration for other demands upon the stage, the teacher of music is much freer to continue his work without interference.

Types of Music Rooms

In the preceding paragraphs, we have discussed the use of the auditorium as the only available space for carrying on musical activities. In this case the auditorium is the music unit as well as serving for sundry other functions. This is not ideal. Although the music departments in most schools use the auditorium for ensemble rehearsals, there should be other rooms in the music unit where certain activities can be conducted with better results. The number, size, and types of these rooms are determined by the musical activities which are to be included in the curriculum. All of the preceding chapters have been devoted to discussing the various musical activities needed in the high school.

General Room for All Activities

By far the most common practice in smaller and average size high schools is the use of an all-purpose room for musical activities.[2] In such cases the music unit consists of the auditorium and this room. This plan is often an economic necessity. If the high school building is old or small, perhaps only one room can be spared for music. When there is only one teacher to carry on the entire music program one room may be designed to serve his needs.

An all-purpose music room must make provision for housing all the various activities, namely: singing, playing, listening, and writing music. It must be large enough to accommodate the largest number of students expected in any activity. There should be three or four floor risers, espe-

[2] See Appendix A for diagrams of all-purpose music rooms.

cially in the rear of the room, wide enough for chairs to seat members of choral or instrumental ensembles. There should be ample space in the front of the room for all the equipment needed for different activities. Small rooms for storing equipment and instruments should be adjoining the music room. Cabinets for storing the music that is being used should be available in the room. Lighting and ventilation of this room as well as other types of music rooms will be discussed shortly.

In many instances the gymnasium must also serve as an all-purpose music room. This combination is not desirable, but it is often an economic necessity. Schedules must be worked out carefully so that the physical education and music classes do not conflict, or misunderstandings between the teachers or the students may arise. In this arrangement, the attitude is usually taken that the gymnasium belongs first to the physical education department and the music department can take whatever time is left. When the gymnasium is used for music the walls and ceilings should be treated acoustically and storage space made convenient. Above all, there should be a grand piano reserved specifically for the music classes, which can be covered and kept in good repair. The combined gymnasium and music room should be considered a temporary condition. The administration should make efforts to find quarters for music classes where all activities can be carried on without interference. In some places it is possible to have separate rooms for both choral and instrumental activities.

Rooms for Singing

In preceding chapters we have proposed that singing activities should include a general chorus, a cappella choir, glee clubs, small vocal ensembles, and voice classes.

It is very likely that the general chorus will be of such

size that it will be forced to rehearse in the auditorium. However, it is highly desirable to have a special choral room, which will accommodate the other choral groups and even the general chorus, if it is not too large. This room should be at least twice the size of the average classroom. It should be considerably wider from side to side than deep from front to back. It is best for the windows to be in the back of the room. A series of floor risers should start about the middle of the room and proceed to the back. These risers must be wide enough to accommodate one row of chairs on each. There must be sufficient space in front of the room for a piano, teacher's desk, and music cabinet. Although voice classes and small ensemble groups may meet in rooms of the ordinary classroom size, a room of this type for the larger choral ensembles is invaluable.

Rooms for Playing

Activities in the high school which provide opportunities for playing instruments should include orchestra, band, instrumental classes, small ensembles, and piano classes.

The orchestra and band room should be similar to the chorus room in shape, that is, wider from side to side than deep from front to back. Windows should be in the back. There should be a series of floor risers in semi-circular form and each riser must be wide enough to accommodate a chair and a music stand. As in the chorus room there should be sufficient space for a piano, teacher's desk, and music cabinet. Separate rooms for band and orchestra are not necessary unless these organizations must practice at the same time. It is evident that the chorus room and the orchestra room are very similar except that the risers for the latter room must be wider. The orchestra and band room should be large enough to accommodate the largest instrumental ensemble ever expected in the school. The standard size high school orchestra or band is ninety players and most large high schools are endeavoring to reach this standard.

Piano classes are usually held in one of the regular music rooms. There should be wall space for a number of upright pianos, as well as one grand piano for solo performance.

Room for Listening and for Writing Music

The ideal room for the study of music appreciation and theory should be approximately the same size as a large classroom and as a rule the same shape, that is, longer from front to back than from side to side. There should be several electric outlets in the room for the radio-phonograph and lantern projector. There should be sufficient space in front of the room for a grand piano. A room devoted to listening to beautiful music should be susceptible of artistic treatment in decoration and equipment.

Rooms for Practicing

It is a decided asset to the music program if the high school provides practice rooms. These rooms are usually built in a series along a corridor or along one side of a music room. Practice rooms should be made available to piano, voice, instrumental, and theory students. One of these rooms should contain two pianos for ensemble practice. Rooms for band and orchestra players need not have pianos. These rooms should have outside ventilation or air-conditioning, and should be insulated against sound transmission to other rooms. It is well to have soundproofed windows or doors facing the corridor or music room so that students may be easily supervised without interrupting the practice.

Rooms for Storage

Ample storage space must be provided for individual and school owned instruments, band uniforms, and choir robes. The instrument storage room should be very accessible to both the music room and the auditorium, and, if possible, adjoining to each. It is best to have lockers of sufficient size and number to care for the instruments to be stored. Shelves are not nearly so satisfactory as lockers because removable parts of various instruments are continually being lost. Steel lockers are the best, although wooden ones can be built into the room much more economically. This room must have ventilation and be protected from excess moisture, heat, and extreme changes of temperature, since many wooden instruments crack or the joints become unglued when stored in rooms that do not retain a normal temperature and humidity.

Band uniforms may be stored in the same room in specially built wooden cabinets. Choir robes are best stored in a separate cabinet which is accessible to the chorus room. Care should be taken in the storage of uniforms because one educational value of music organizations is the responsibility students can be made to feel for the appearance of the ensemble of which they are members.

A small shop adjoining the instrumental room equipped to make minor repairs on instruments is being included in the music unit of some schools. The shop provides a handy place where students may learn to make reeds, polish their instruments, replace wornout pads, and remove small dents. It is not only a means to save money but also has educational and vocational value.

The proper care of musical instruments is indeed a matter of deep importance. Every instrument of the orchestra and band has one or more vulnerable points which easily

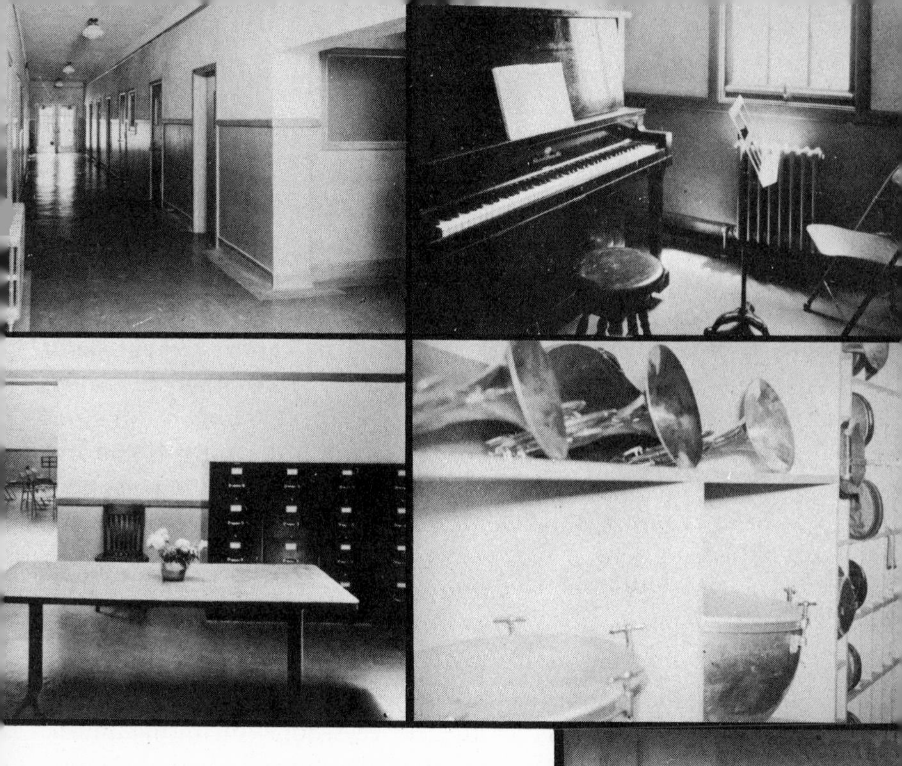

Los Gatos (Cal.) Union High School, Music Building—corridor, practice room, instrumental library.

Teaneck (New Jersey) High School—instrument and uniform storage.

get out of order and make artistic performance impossible. Reeds wear out, pads come off, strings break, valves stick, drum heads crack. These are only a few of the matters which students should be taught to expect and to know how to handle. The ponderous double bass is really one of the most difficult instruments to keep in good condition. It is astonishing to discover so many carelessly kept band rehearsal rooms, where instruments, sheets of music, chairs, and music stands are permitted to lie around in unkempt confusion. Pride in appearances and in keeping rooms and instruments in orderly repair is one of the outcomes of a well organized and disciplined instrumental group.

Music Library Room

If the music department is to function efficiently, there should be a music library which is conveniently located. It should be large enough to serve as a workshop as well. The general library serves the entire school, including music reference books. On account of the difficulties in filing music and the continuous use of these materials, it is not as efficient or convenient to include the music repertoire as part of the general library.

The music library should have four-drawer steel filing cases in which the music can be stored. Uniform folders should be secured for different types of music. The folders for instrumental ensemble music should show a list of the instrumentation and the number of each part. The parts should be filed in the folder in an organized sequence. Music should be carefully checked in and out. A complete record of music as it is used in performance should be kept because this data is valuable to the music teacher in the selection of music for future concerts. There should be space for a series of shelves on which the music being rehearsed can be stored. If the library adjoins the music room, a window or half door between the two rooms through which music can be passed causes less confusion and expedites the work to be done by librarians. Leaders of each section of the orchestra should be assigned to call for the music for their section. There should be a librarian for each ensemble organization who is responsible to the person in charge of the music library, or to the director of his organization. Each librarian should be responsible for keeping the music in good repair. He should be able and ready to mark fingering, bowing, and phrasing in the parts as directed by the conductor or concert master.

The music teacher can save himself many headaches if he gives some thought and energy to organizing an efficient music library. There is nothing more disconcerting at a rehearsal or concert than to find some player without his part. If room space is limited, the library may also serve as office space for one of the music teachers who is then in a position to direct the activities of this all-important unit.

Location of Music Rooms

The first section of this chapter is called, "The Music Unit" in order to imply that the various types of rooms described should be, as far as possible, a compact unit. When the music room is in one corner of the building and the auditorium on the other side, there is much inconvenience, a great amount of time is lost, and even considerable disturbance is caused to other rooms by music students passing through the halls during classes. There is one school that we have in mind where the piano must be moved across the entire building whenever there is to be a music program of any kind in the auditorium. Even when buildings are old, a little thought to the location of the music room in relation to the auditorium can help immeasurably the functioning of the music department.

The music room or rooms should not only be adjoining or near the stage of the auditorium but the various types of rooms should be in close proximity to each other. It has already been mentioned that rooms which serve large ensembles should be adjoining the music library. Likewise, storage rooms should be adjoining the rooms of the organizations that they are to serve. Also, practice rooms that are inaccessible to the music teacher handicaps adequate supervision.

Finally, the music unit should be located in consideration of the other departments. There is no question that the sounds coming from the music room are often painful to teachers of other subjects who do not have the same idealistic image of the final performance as the music teacher. If the music rooms are located so that rehearsing and practising disturbs other classes, the music department may be considered a nuisance. So the wise teacher will first consider a location of the music unit which will not disturb his associates.

The diagrams on pages 325 and 327 illustrate the location of the music unit in a separate building in both a large and a small city.

Physical Characteristics of Music Rooms

In describing the types of music rooms, some suggestions were made which would insure better functioning. First of all, they should have adequate lighting because reading music is a very exacting exercise for the eyes. Secondly, the physical nature of singing or playing music requires fresh air. So there must be sufficient ventilation. Finally, the rooms must be treated acoustically so that they

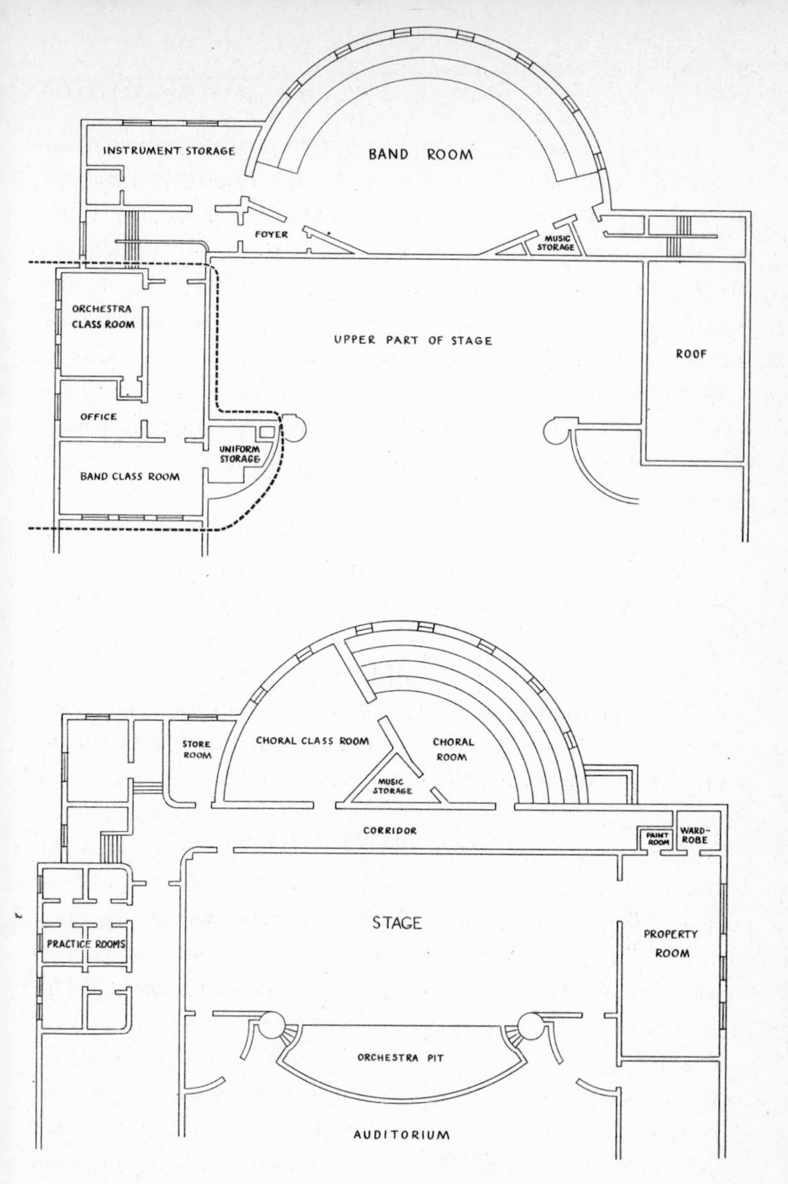

New Assembly Building, Sacramento Senior High School, showing first floor and second floor plans of music unit, with mezzanine indicated by dotted lines.

will not interfere with the studies being carried on in other classrooms and to reduce reverberation. The following cautions should be considered in sound-proofing rooms. These cautions are described in more detail in the bulletin of the Music Educators National Conference referred to earlier in this chapter. In this matter professional acousticians should be brought into consultation.

1. Music rooms should be located so that they are separated from other classrooms by corridors, courts, storage rooms, stairways, or by rooms where there is a minimum of rehearsing or practising.

2. Materials used in ceilings, walls, and floors should not serve as conductors of sound.

3. Absorbing materials may be used on the ceilings, walls, and floors.

4. Sound-proof doors should be provided.

5. Ventilating ducts to the music unit should be separate from those to other rooms to prevent transmission of sound from the music rooms through these ducts.

Equipment for Music Unit

Beautiful and spacious music rooms without the appropriate equipment in them is like a lovely swimming pool without water in it, nice to look at but not very useful. We have already made suggestions for permanent equipment such as floor risers and cabinets which seem to be a part of the room. Let us now turn our attention to other types of equipment which are necessary for the various types of activities suggested in preceding chapters. All music rooms should be equipped with teacher's desk, staff-lined blackboard, and attractive bulletin boards. The department can well consider the inclusion of self-recording equipment and sound-mirror as discussed in Chapter XI.

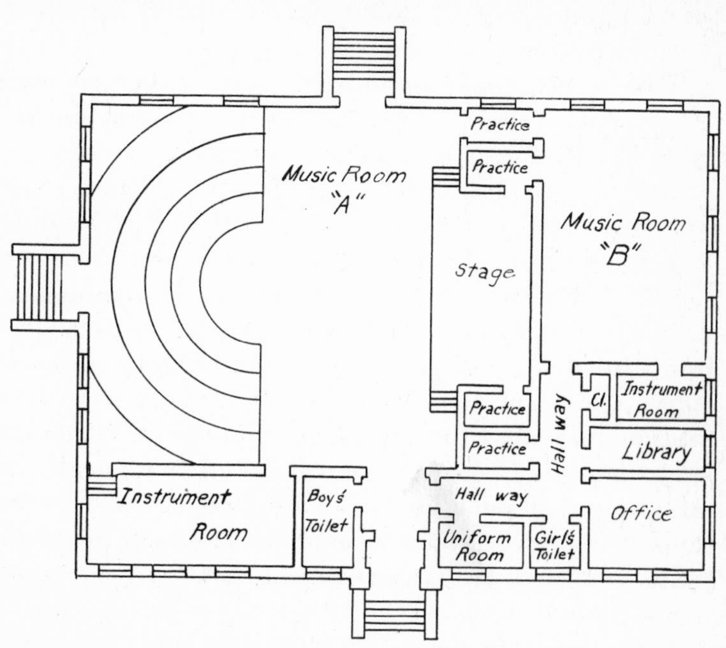

School Music Building, Salisbury, N.C. Exterior and floor plan.

For Singing

The correct sitting posture required for singing, which is an easy but erect position with the body leaning forward slightly to permit unrestricted action of the lower rib muscles in deep breathing, needs chairs which induce this posture. Therefore, a straight back chair is preferable in the chorus room. Since singers often stand while rehearsing, a chair with a desk arm on which they can place music that they are not singing is also preferable. The floor risers must be sufficiently wide for these chairs plus space for standing in front of them. The average folding chair is not desirable because it is not conducive to good sitting posture for singing. Manufacturers could well devote some effort toward constructing a folding chair suitable for use by singing groups.

Floor risers should not only be a part of the permanent equipment of the chorus room, but there should also be a sufficient number of collapsible risers for the cappella choir which can be transferred to other locations. Risers enable students of all organizations to see the conductor more easily and to hear each other better. A more musical performance results.

There should be a grand piano for singing activities tuned to A = 440. Pianos that are low in pitch, not only affect a brilliant musical performance, but over a period of time may affect the normal range of voices. Pianos that are continuously out of tune will definitely influence out-of-tune and off-pitch singing and in time may actually produce faulty ears. Pianos should be mounted on special roller frames to facilitate moving around without damaging the piano in any way.

An a cappella choir actually seems to sing better when dressed in robes or some type of uniform. The visual unity seems to give tonal unity. Since the choir is so often called upon to sing for the public, it is much more impressive when robed. The type of robe or uniform will depend somewhat upon the repertoire of the choir, but robes or uniforms are definitely a part of the equipment for such singing activities.

For Playing

A chair, similar to the one used in the chorus room, which induces correct sitting posture, should also be used in the orchestra and band room. However, this chair should not have an arm desk because it interferes with the arm movements of the players. In case one room must serve for the chorus, orchestra, and band, a number of chairs for the woodwind players may have arm desks and these, in turn, can be used by the singers. Floor risers in the instrumental room must be wide enough to accommodate a chair and a music stand with plenty of room between them so that the players will have freedom for arm movements.

Band and orchestra rooms should be equipped with as many strongly built, heavy base, all-metal music stands as is needed. Students playing two separate parts should not be asked to read from one stand. The practice of students' furnishing their own individual folding stands is not practicable. So much time is wasted in setting up the stands, not counting the times that the students forget them altogether, that the larger part of the rehearsal period is spent in preparing to play. Such a condition is not a saving. In fact, it is a waste of time and money. Neither should the school spend money on cheap folding stands as permanent equipment. The breakage and inconvenience make such expenditure inadvisable. Stands with workable set screws should be secured and students given direct instruction in adjusting them. There is now an excellent music stand on the market with no set screws which can be adjusted to any height and which has a steel desk that can be adjusted to any angle.

As in the chorus room, the orchestra room should have a grand piano, mounted on rollers, and tuned to A = 440. If the piano is not tuned to this pitch, many of the woodwind instruments will be unable to adjust their pitch sufficiently to play with the piano. If the orchestra and band rooms are separate, there need be no piano in the latter room. It has been mentioned that several uprights and one grand piano are needed in a room for piano classes, and these pianos should be tuned with each other. If possible, there should be one piano for every two students in high school piano classes. Students of this age lose interest when asked to use silent keyboards.

A tuning bar should be part of the equipment of the instrumental room. When school orchestras follow the practice of professional orchestras in tuning to the oboe, much rehearsal time is often wasted. The young oboeist usually cannot hold a steady true tone, and even when he can do this, many string players are too slow in tuning after the oboe "A" is sounded. Often the teacher needs to take time out to tune several violins. A far better procedure is for students to sound the tuning bar as soon as they have secured their instrument, and tune immediately. Then at the beginning of the rehearsal they may test their tuning with the oboe A. When the orchestra and band rooms are separate there should be an A tuning bar in the former and a B-flat tuning bar in the latter. There is now available a tuning bar that sounds A, B-flat, or E-flat which is recommended for combined instrumental rooms.

It has become the accepted practice, and rightly so, for high schools to own some of the large and more unusual instruments which are very expensive, cumbersome to carry, and cannot be used readily as solo instruments in the home and for social occasions. Many times students prefer these instruments, but it is often difficult to persuade the parents to purchase them because they are more expensive and less suitable for solo playing. The music department should budget its money allotment over a period of years while building up the orchestra and band. The following list of instruments which schools should own are listed not necessarily in order of importance. The order of purchase will be determined by the needs of an individual situation to secure balanced instrumental ensembles.

1. Percussion.
   a. *Bass drum*—for each band and for orchestras numbering more than twenty players.
   b. *Tympani* (kettle drums)—one pair for each orchestra or band numbering more than thirty players. Pedal tympani are superior to the ordinary type, but they are much more expensive. Only large high schools with a standard size orchestra and a player well schooled in their care and manipulation need pedal tympani.
   c. *Cymbals*—one pair (Turkish) for every band or orchestra.
   d. *Field drums*—necessary for marching bands and for bugle and drum corps.
   e. *Chimes*—one set for a band or orchestra of over sixty players.
   f. *Harp*—one or two for an orchestra of over seventy players.
   g. *Celeste*—one for an orchestra of ninety players.
2. Strings.
   a. *Double basses*—one for each ten members of the orchestra. String basses made of metal are better for school use.
   b. *'Cellos*—one for each four violinists in the orchestra, purchased as need arises.

c. *Violas*—one for each four violinists in the orchestra. A number of violas are needed to start beginners and to interest students in this instrument.
d. *Violins*—seldom necessary for schools to purchase violins because they are popular with students.

3. Brass.
   a. *Tubas*—one for each ten members of the band. The Sousaphone type is better for bands and the upright for orchestra.
   b. *French horn*—two for each orchestra of thirty players and four for each band of thirty players or more. A standard size orchestra can use six horns. Students will purchase French horns after they have learned to play them, but each school needs at least two for the purpose of starting beginners.
   c. *Baritone*—one for each band of twenty players. It is usually necessary for the school to own one baritone.
4. Woodwinds.
   a. *Oboe*—one for every orchestra of thirty players; two for orchestra of sixty players; schools should purchase only the conservatory system.
   b. *Bassoon*—one for every orchestra or band of 40 players. School should purchase only the Heckel system.
   c. *Contra-bassoon*—one for an orchestra of 90 players.
   d. *Alto clarinet*—one for each 8 B-flat clarinet players in the band.
   e. *Bass clarinet*—one for each 8 B-flat clarinet players in the band.
   f. *Bass saxophone*—one for a band of 60 players.

If bands are to win the complete approval of the public they should have attractive uniforms. Often some public spirited group will purchase uniforms for the band. Capes have certain advantages because the question of size is a minor difficulty. Sweaters and nifty overseas hats are economical and make the school band unique in contrast to the professional band. A drum major uniform and ferrule are rapidly becoming a prime necessity for every school band. Uniforms seem to cover many musical sins and the wise teacher will uniform his band.

For Listening and for Writing Music

It goes without saying that a *good phonograph* is needed in rooms where students devote time to listening. We have italicized *good phonograph* because we are convinced that poor phonographs, worn-out needles, and "scratchy" records have given students the wrong impression of fine music and curbed their love for it. Each school should own a good radio or a combined radio-phonograph. One or two practice rooms should contain phonographs in order that eager students may check out records from the library and listen to musical masterpieces to their heart's content.

A complete library of records should be the equipment of every school. These records should be available to students as well as teachers. A revolving fund should be established to replace broken and worn-out records.

Listening should not be confined to phonograph and radio. We cannot repeat this too often. Use the piano and other instruments. Students should attend school concerts and public recitals. The general music room should be attractive in appearance with a few lovely pictures on the wall. Special attention should be given to the bulletin board to make it neat and useful. It is more inspiring to listen to beautiful music in agreeable surroundings.

In the teaching of theory both a piano and phonograph are necessary equipment—a piano for playing student exercises and compositions, and both the piano and phonograph for ear-training and illustration.

Storage Rooms, Practice Rooms, Music Library

Equipment for these rooms was discussed separately in this chapter under the "Types of Music Rooms."

Upper left—*Lodi (Cal.) High School, Music rehearsal room.*
Upper right—*Teaneck (New Jersey), Instrumental class room.*
Bottom—*Charlotte (N.C.) High School, Music Room.*

Conclusion

The music unit and the equipment for it as presented in this chapter represent undoubtedly an ideal situation. Not many schools will reach this standard completely, but many schools are approaching this goal and most of them have the outstanding features proposed.

Superior teaching in music is dependent upon adequate rooms, equipment, and materials. However, if a teacher does not have rooms and equipment which meets with his ideal standard, there is no reason for him to become so discouraged that his work is seriously hampered. As necessary as these factors are for successful music teaching, nevertheless boundless energy, enthusiasm, and musicianship can overcome to a surprising degree the handicap of limited equipment.

Topics for General Discussion

1. Discuss the advantages and disadvantages of a separate building for a music department.

2. Do students feel as much responsibility for school-owned instruments as their own? What are some of the difficulties which arise from lending school-owned instruments to students?

3. Make a list of instruments you would purchase for a school if you had five hundred dollars to spend each year for a period of five years.

4. Organize a plan for card-indexing an octavo library; a band library; an orchestra library.

5. Suggest the re-organization of your own high school building to better house the music department.

LIFE AND SONG

If life were caught by a clarionet,
  And a wild heart, throbbing in the reed,
Should thrill its joy and trill its fret,
  And utter its heart in every deed,

Then would this breathing clarionet
  Type what the poet fain would be;
For none o' the singers ever yet
  Has wholly lived his minstrelsy,

Or clearly sung his true, true thought,
  Or utterly bodied forth his life,
Or out of life and song has wrought
  The perfect one of man and wife;

Or lived and sung, that Life and Song
  Might each express the other's all,
Careless if life or art were long
  Since both were one, to stand or fall:

So that the wonder struck the crowd,
  Who shouted it about the land:
His song was only living aloud,
  His work, a singing with his hand!

SIDNEY LANIER

Chapter 16

RELATIONS WITH THE COMMUNITY

Throughout this book we have pointed out the value of relating the music activities of school with various phases of community life. Much of the genuine social value of the music program is lost if this relationship is not stimulated and fostered. Let us now examine more closely the relationship between the music curriculum of the high school and the community, as well as the contributions the music teacher can make in establishing it.

The School and the Community

The American school today is considered a state institution, but it had its beginnings through the efforts of the community. As common needs, common interests, common religion, and common purposes developed among groups of people the common school was created. Although today the state may hold certain controls over the common school, it is to the community that the school owes its primary allegiance. The larger share of school funds is still provided by the community. The school board of education is composed of townspeople selected through a local election. The students and often many of the teachers are permanent members of the community. All these bonds between the school and community weld them together as units of society which are formed in order to be of mutual benefit to each other.

All-City High School Orchestra. Scene from "Song of the City", Detroit Schools presentation at North Central Music Educators Conference, 1939, Fowler Smith, Director.

Nature of the School

It has been pointed out in Chapter I that the school is a social institution. It is developed by society as an agency to transmit social and cultural values. The character of the school and the content of its curriculum are determined by the society it serves. Its influence upon society is reciprocal. The school not only attempts to re-live and continue the present patterns of society, but it also endeavors to use these patterns as a basis for creating improved modes of living. Most parents wish better returns from life for their children than those which they were privileged to enjoy.[1]

The school as a social institution should be aware of local problems and should contribute to community welfare and growth. The natural affinity between the school and community already mentioned through support, administration, and constituency places definite responsibilities on the school for active interest in community enterprises.

The public schools belong to the people of the community who support them. The high school should be the social as well as the intellectual center of the community. This is all the more important when we consider that a large per cent of our young people attend the high school. Within certain legal limitations and restrictions the use of the building by local groups brings the school and community closer together. The school building should not be used for private gain, for this is contrary to the purposes and spirit of public education. It belongs to the community and should be available for public functions. The music teacher should encourage the use of the music facilities of the school by community groups. He should be cogni-

[1] William A. Yeager, *Home-School-Community Relations*, 1939. University of Pittsburgh, Pittsburgh, Pennsylvania.

zant of the expanding opportunities in the field of adult education and plan and direct adult musical activities as part of his program.

The music teacher today can well ponder over the time when "many of the singing schools which were first established in New England and flourished in earlier years in numerous communities in other colonies and states were held in the school house. They extended over a period of one hundred years. Membership was not confined to any age or group, being attended by varying ages and both sexes. The primary purpose of the singing school was to improve the church music, although it was plain that the social life of the community found expression here. Without doubt it was the principal stimulus for the development of public school music, which came in at a later period. The singing schools contributed markedly to the development of a common interest in the public schools." [2]

Nature of the Community

Communities are formed as the varying interests of individuals and families merge for the common good of all. The school is one expression of this merging of interests. Since the community creates the school, it has certain responsibilities to the school. Furthermore, the high school, a community in itself, must be considered a part of a larger community and privileged to plan and grow according to its needs.

It should not be necessary to "sell" the school to the community. It is an expression of the community, and their interests are identical. It is the civic duty of the members of a community to support the school program. It may be necessary to convince the community of the value of certain activities in the high school, but after any subject has

[2] Ibid., p. 46.

been established in the curriculum, and is justifying itself, it should be maintained properly. This does not imply only moral and financial support, but also active co-operation. For music, it means not only adequate housing, equipment, and materials, but also attendance at school concerts and a supporting interest in musical projects. It is a part of the responsibility of the school administration and a school music director to make this clear to the community.

High School Music and the Community

Although it may be called the civic duty of the members of a community to support the school, it is a well-known observation that many of us do not perform all our civic duties. The surest way to gain support for the musical activities in the high school is to have outstanding organizations that are well disciplined. As parents and townspeople hear orchestras, bands, and choruses that are fine performing organizations, they become proud of the musical achievements of their school and their children. If the members of these same organizations behave as young ladies and gentlemen, both in performance and other public contacts, parents and townspeople realize that organized musical activities have educational values. The burden of proof rests with the teacher. If he is competent and understands young people, he will produce organizations which the community will be proud of and eager to support.

Stimulating Musical Activity

Probably the best way for the teacher to make the community musically aware is through the development of outstanding high school organizations. This method is indirect, but many times it produces better results than by stimulating musical activity through direct contact with local groups. The reason for this is found in the influence which high school students have on community life. If they are interested in good music, they will demand more and better music in the home and church, and even affect the music programs of clubs and civic organizations. However, the music teacher should make direct contact with various community institutions whenever possible and encourage his students to carry the musical gospel beyond the walls of the school building.[3]

In the Home

Throughout our discussion we have reiterated the idea that the true carry-over of high school music should be in the home. It will usually be the student that likes to make music by himself and for himself who continues his music after graduation. Many graduates "drop" their music after graduation except for desultory listening over the radio. However, music is a social art and these music-makers will enlist the interest of other members of the family. Happy is the home where all members can make music individually and together, even though it may be technically very simple. Through parent-teachers associations the music director can encourage parents to turn off the radio occasionally and listen to John or Mary play their latest piece. The music teacher should welcome not only "mother singers" and "father singers," but also should foster "family singers" through suggestion and encouragement to students, contact with parents, and direct aid in helping family groups "get the habit" of making music together. This refers to instrumental as well as vocal groups. Stimulating music in the home is one of the surest ways

[3] An unusual program of community music is described by Edwin M. Steckel, "Oglebay Park—Community Center of Wheeling," Music Educators National Conference, *Yearbook 1938*, p. 167.

for the teacher of music to reap educational rewards for his efforts to make a musical community.

In the Church

In recent years there has been a growing tendency on the part of music educators to look to the church as a natural means for relating high school music with one phase of community life. Since the beginnings of music, man has used it in his worship. In fact, in past centuries music, like painting, seemed almost inseparable from the church. There is a close affinity between music and worship. Music serves as an active means for keeping the spirit of worship alive in our young people.

One concrete result of the phenomenal growth of the musical activities in the high school has been the necessity for expanding the musical activities in the church. In many large churches there has been created a position which is titled "Minister of Music." He is considered an associate of the other ministers of the church. A person holding this office should be a qualified musician as well as someone who can conduct other church activities. His responsibilities include directing the adult choir as well as organizing and directing junior choirs for various age levels. He also coordinates other musical activities of the church so that music takes its rightful place in the religious life of the community.

Although few churches can afford the services of a "Minister of Music," they need music to permeate their entire program of activities. And so, more and more, the churches are turning to the high school for singers to fill in greatly needed voice-parts in the choir, for instrumentalists to play in the Sunday School orchestra, and for soloists and ensemble groups to perform at social functions. In this way young people are attracted to the church during their impressionable years and the high school music department makes itself a vital force in another phase of community life.

In Clubs and Civic Organizations

Wherever people gather in the spirit of fellowship, music is invariably present. A teacher who realizes the value of music for social purposes can not only create community-wide interest in his high school music program, but can also partly fulfill his responsibility as a useful citizen by stimulating more and better music in clubs and civic organizations. He may do this through his own participation by leading the singing, performing, or by giving short interesting talks on music in general. It can be done through the performance of high school students individually or in ensembles. (One director reports a most enthusiastic reception at a civic club of a demonstration of orchestral instruments by various members of the high school orchestra.) In time it can be accomplished by developing youthful musical leaders who will take their place in the social life of the community.

In all the teacher's associations with these civic and social organizations, he must enter into the spirit of their meetings. He may raise the level of the general music used in these clubs, but in his desire to educate them to use and enjoy better music he must not lose sight of the social function that music serves. The music teacher needs the support of these organizations and he must exercise the most tactful leadership in his relationship with them.

In Parent-Teacher Associations

The teacher of music should enlist the cooperation of the parent-teacher associations. Participation in the meetings by performance or by leading of general singing serves as an introduction which often blossoms into keener interest in the high school music program. (Another director reports unusual and helpful response from an association to a demonstration of teaching the various phases of music in the high school curriculum.)

Another method of developing interest on the part of the parent-teacher associations is through the organization of singing groups within the association. The idea seems to have originated with the formation of the "Mothersingers" in Cincinnati, about 1925 by Vera King Clark of that city. This Cincinnati group was presented on the convention program of The National Congress of Parents and Teachers in Washington, D. C., in 1929.[4] Their success was instantaneous and so popular that each year since that time a National Mothersingers Chorus has been featured on the national convention program. The idea has spread to Fathersingers, Teachersingers, and mixed groups of Parentsingers. Needless to say that these active participants in performing music directed by the music teacher become his most ardent supporters. They see the value in themselves of having an adequate program of musical activities for the high school student. The teacher, in turn, is spreading the message of music into the community and home.

Performing for Community Organizations

One of the first steps for a teacher of music is to make his department thoroughly respected by the community. In many ways the school world has become a world apart from the community. Performing for community organizations and meetings is probably the most immediate means of creating interest in the high school program of music.

It is a distinct asset if the teacher is a capable performer

[4] Mayme E. Irons, *Activities and Influences in Music Education Beyond the School-Room Door.* Music Educators National Conference, *Yearbook 1935,* Chicago, Ill. p. 127.

himself and can play or sing for community functions. This is especially true if the teacher is in a new situation. The initial respect gained by the teacher who is a competent performer is quickly transferred to the high school organizations that give creditable performances. We realize that many teachers have had outstanding success who make no claim as soloists, but the ability to perform in a new situation, especially in medium-size towns, is a great advantage.

We have already mentioned in this chapter the effect upon community interest of outstanding high school music organizations that are well disciplined. To gain and retain the respect of the community these organizations must give creditable performances. Ensembles that play or sing poorly are inexcusable in the first place and only cause the community to compare their work unfavorably with that done by high school groups in other communities. The townspeople are usually tolerant in the beginning when the music program is being developed, but continual performance by ensembles that are not prepared will only produce lack of interest, indifference, or antagonism.

Although performing for local functions is one of the surest ways of integrating high school music with the community it can be overdone. Competent high school ensembles will receive so many calls that there is a danger that the time and energies of these young people will unconsciously be imposed on to a degree that the educational values of such activities will be impaired. The services of such larger organizations as the orchestra, band, and choir should be reserved for functions which are of interest to the greater part of the community. They cannot be expected to accept calls to perform for clubs and groups which are limited in scope and do not have a total community outlook. The development of small vocal and instrumental ensembles provides the teacher of music with a point of contact with smaller clubs and organizations. Within reason these small ensembles may represent the school by performing for such groups and may be a tremendous influence in integrating high school music with community life.

Training Musical Leaders

An indirect method of relating the high school music with the community is through the training of young people who upon graduation will assume their place in its musical life. There are two groups of these young people. First of all, there are those, who, upon arriving at various positions of community leadership, will encourage music in both the school and the community because of their satisfying experiences with it in high school. Their contribution to music in the community can be of untold value. Secondly, there is a smaller group who will actually assume positions of leadership in the music life itself, such as soloists and directors of church choirs, conductors of Sunday School orchestras, leaders of singing in civic organizations, first chair members of community instrumental organizations, and active sponsors of civic concerts.

Training these two groups of musical leaders is part of the responsibility of the teacher. This may be done to a large degree by providing a rich and varied program of musical experiences as suggested throughout our book. However, there should be some direct training of these leaders through general suggestion of their civic responsibility, through proper guidance of talented students, and through the gradual induction of them into community musical life during their school days.

Earning Money

The emphasis in the program of high school music should be on cultural values rather than on professional training. However, there are always a number of students who are looking to music as a vocation. As these young musicians become more proficient, they may find opportunities to receive remuneration for their services at private clubs or societies and radio stations. Careful guidance for these students is needed so that they may not get the idea that they are "too good" to play without pay for a school or community function. In accepting engagements, members of dance bands who also play in the symphonic band or orchestra must realize that their first loyalty is to the school. When there is a conflict of dates, it is their duty to play with the larger school organizations. However, if students are made to realize their responsibilities and show professional possibilities, there is no reason why they should not receive a fee for outside work of a professional nature.

Most of the professional opportunities for the high school music student are in the field of the dance band. The school need not interfere with this activity unless it impairs their health and other work. In fact, since much of the professional music activity is in this field, many schools are giving training and guidance to students who wish to use the dance band as a means for making extra money, for paying their way through college, or for choosing it as a life vocation. The junior colleges in some of the large cities are turning their attention to this phase of music training.

If a jazz band is organized and trained in the high school, its chief function should be to play at all-school dances and social affairs. If these dances are few in number it does not seem an imposition to ask the band to play without remuneration, especially if the members use school-owned instruments. A difficult problem arises if the school dance band endeavors to secure professional engagements outside of the school. This difficulty is increased where such engagements mean competition with local professional musicians. It seems a very doubtful procedure for an educational institution to organize and train a dance band which would appear in professional engagements as a school organization. While the school may not undertake to restrict outside activities of individual pupils, it is the consensus of the opinion of music educators that a careful line should be drawn between school and professional activities.

Cooperating with the Musicians' Union

The question of playing for financial returns inevitably brings up the subject of relations with the musicians' union. Naturally the professional performer questions the propriety of the school training musicians at public expense and equipping them to become competitors in the field of his livelihood. There have been times and places where this issue has come to the front in quite disturbing ways.

To establish a common understanding as a basis for the sympathetic and cooperative relationship which should be maintained between musicians in the professional and educational fields, a statement of policy and practice was approved by the Executive Committee of the Music Educators National Conference and the Executive Council of the National School Band, Orchestra, and Vocal Associations. Other codes have since been adopted in various parts of the country by the educational and professional musicians, looking toward harmonious cooperation. The following Code was adopted in Ohio which in spirit and content is substantially the same as that mentioned above in the first sentence of this paragraph. A study of this document will clarify the issues and point to the principles upon which an equitable understanding may be reached.

The competition of school bands and orchestras has in the past years been a matter of great concern and hardship to the professional musicians.

The music educators and the professional musicians are

alike concerned with the general acceptance of music as a desirable factor in the social life and cultural growth of our country. The music educators contribute to this end by fostering the study of music among the children of the country and by developing a keen interest in better music among the masses. The professional musicians strive to improve musical taste by providing increasingly artistic performances of worthwhile musical works.

This unanimity of purpose is further exemplified by the fact that a great many professional musicians are music educators and a great many music educators are, or have been, actively engaged in the field of professional performance.

The members of high school orchestras and bands look to the professional organizations for inspiration and become active patrons of music in later life. They are not content to listen to twelve-piece ensembles, but demand adequate performances, resulting in an increased prestige on the part of professional musicians.

Since it is in the interest of the music educator to attract public attention to his attainments for the purpose of enhancing his prestige and subsequently his income, and it is in the interest of the professional musician to create more opportunities for employment at increased remuneration, it is only natural that upon certain occasions some incidents might occur in which the interests of the members of one or the other group might be infringed upon, either from lack of forethought or lack of ethical standards among individuals.

In order to establish a clear understanding as to the limitations of the fields of professional music and music education in the State of Ohio, the following statement of policy is adopted by the Ohio Music Education Association and Ohio Locals of the American Federation of Musicians, and is recommended to the membership of those serving in the respective fields:

I. MUSIC EDUCATION

The field of music education, including the teaching of music and such demonstrations of music education as do not directly conflict with the interests of the professional musician, is the province of the music educator. Under this heading should be included the following:

(1) School functions, initiated by the schools as a part of a school program, whether in a school building or other building.

(2) Community functions, organized in the interests of the schools strictly for educational purposes, such as those that might be originated by the parent-teacher association.

(3) School exhibits, prepared as a part of the school district's courtesies for educational organizations or educational conventions being entertained in the district.

(4) Educational broadcast demonstrations, such as "Music and American Youth," the "Ohio School of the Air," and the Ohio Education Association programs, when presented with the sole purpose of acquainting the public with the type of music instruction offered to the children of a community.

(5) Civic occasions, of local, state or national patriotic interest, of sufficient breadth to enlist the sympathies and cooperation of all persons, such as those held by the G. A. R., American Legion, and Veterans of Foreign Wars in connection with their Memorial Day services in the cemeteries. It is understood that affairs of this kind may be participated in only when such participation does not in the least usurp the rights and privileges of local professional musicians.

(6) Benefit performances, for local charity, such as the Welfare Federation, Red Cross, hospitals, etc., when and where professional musicians would likewise donate their services.

(7) Educational or civic services, that might beforehand be mutually agreed upon by the school authorities and official representatives of the local professional musicians.

II. ENTERTAINMENT

The field of entertainment is the province of the professional musician. Under this heading are the following:

(1) Civic parades, ceremonies, expositions, community concerts and community center activities (See I, paragraph 2 for further definition); regattas, non-scholastic contests, festivals, athletic games, activities or celebrations, and the like; state and county fairs (See I, paragraph 1, for further definition).

(2) Functions for the furtherance, directly or indirectly, of any public or private enterprise, functions by chambers of commerce, boards of trades, and commercial clubs or associations.

(3) Any occasion that is partisan or sectarian in character or purpose.

(4) Functions of clubs, societies, civic or fraternal organizations.

(5) Statements that funds are not available for the employment of professional musicians, or that if the talents of amateur musical organizations cannot be had, other musicians cannot, or will not be employed, or that the amateur musicians are to play without remuneration of any kind, are all immaterial.

(Signed) PUBLIC RELATIONS COMMITTEE

GROVER C. YAUS, *Chairman,* Supervisor of Music, Youngstown.
EDITH M. KELLER, *Secretary,* State Supervisor of Music, Columbus.
KARL H. BERNS, Assistant Secretary for Field Service of the Ohio Education Association, Columbus.
NELLIE L. GLOVER, Supervisor of Music, Akron.
EUGENE J. WEIGEL, President of the Ohio Music Education Association, Ohio State University, Columbus.
ARTHUR E. STRENG, President of the Columbus Local, American Federation of Musicians, Columbus.
L. O. TEAGLE, Secretary of the Akron Local, American Federation of Musicians, Akron.
HAL R. CARR, Secretary of the Toledo Local, American Federation of Musicians, Toledo.
DAN H. BROWN, President of the Greenville Local, American Federation of Musicians, Greenville.

DEVELOPING POST-GRADUATE ACTIVITIES

It is well for the teacher of music to seek at times the counsel of the administrator and educator to support his own opinions. On one occasion Guy Dickey, Superintendent of Schools, Hobart, Indiana, has expressed in a very helpful manner the problem of developing musical activities for post-graduates. We believe that it will be most convincing to quote his entire statement at this point.

Even when we have provided well for the students enrolled in the school, and taken care that the public has gained a

Upper left—*National Band Clinic, Urbana, Ill.*

Upper right—*Choral Clinic, Missouri Music Educators Association, George Howerton, conducting.*

Bottom—*Iowa Music Educators Association Orchestra, Oscar Anderson, Conductor.*

real understanding of our work, the major portion of the integration program is still ahead of us. Much of our work up to this time has been foundation work. The real question is—what about the students from our music departments after graduation? What can we do to give them an opportunity to use the talent the school has developed? An unused talent, you know, soon deteriorates. It is evident that we cannot stop with the school organizations. To complete our program we must go on to community bands and orchestras, choruses, and all the various groups that we have developed in the school program.

In our own city, we have realized the need of such organizations for some time. Each year we send out a group of young people who have spent several years participating in our musical organizations. A number of them go on to higher institutions of learning and there find their opportunity in musical organizations of their choice. We have been especially fortunate in getting scholarships for many of these people. This group, then, is taken care of for the next few years at least. However, in time, they will complete the work of the school, and leaving the college world behind, return to some community for a permanent home. Will that community then, offer them the organizations in which their diverse talents may find an outlet? So you see their problem is not really solved. It is only deferred, and finally reverts to the same status as existed on their graduation from high school. So these persons too, remain our problems.

Another small group of the graduates take up music as a vocation in professional organizations or in the teaching field. If this is really a life work for them, they are no longer an element in this problem.

But the larger part of the group goes out into our own community or other communities in search of employment. Some find it, many in the past have not. For a little time you hear of them playing a solo here or there or taking part in some volunteer group of players. But all too soon, even such activities cease and when you question them they admit the instrument has been put away and other interests (many of them unworthy) have crowded out the musical one. Is it not possible that if a community will provide the organizations, musical interest can be kept alive and active? If so, we certainly have not completed our job until we have made such provisions.

As I say, we have been conscious of this problem in our own community for some time and have made a few feeble attempts at beginning a solution. We have made tentative plans for a community band, but the truth of the matter is that one man cannot do the work of the school and the community too. We added an assistant one year hoping to branch out into this additional work; but with depression retrenchment he had to go and so the plans still remain tentative. Frankly, I do not see how school funds in our community can be stretched to include this activity. Nor am I sure they should be. If conditions continue to improve, and recovery is really on the way, which now appears likely, it is possible that the financing can be done by community effort. However it is accomplished in my community or any other, *the initiative will have to come from the people in the music department itself*. You furnish the aggressive leadership and we administrators will come to your assistance. Together, then, we can get the general public interested in the movement, and with the cooperation of all groups, the goal is in sight. Of course, we cannot do all this in a day. But a step in that direction is a step forward, and enough steps forward and we will soon be there.[5]

Sponsoring Music Ensembles

Mention was made in the preceding section of the organization of community music ensembles which would absorb the high school graduate and lead him to continue his active interest in music. These ensembles may take many forms, such as post-graduate glee clubs, community orchestras and bands, civic choirs, musical dramatic clubs, oratorio societies, and music appreciation groups in the adult education field.

One widespread movement should be pointed out,

[5] Guy Dickey, *Integrating Public School Music in the Community Life*, Music Educators National Conference, *Yearbook 1935*. Chicago, Illinois, pp. 122-123.

namely, the development of junior male glee clubs. This is a nation-wide project to continue high school male chorus activities into adult life and it has been inaugurated by a combination of three national organizations: Kiwanis International, Associated Glee Clubs of America, and the Music Educators National Conference. Any person interested in organizing a junior male glee club should get in touch with the representatives of one of these organizations and cooperate with them in working out the most practicable plan for forming a club. The Associated Glee Clubs prepare lists of materials which are especially adapted for the use of Junior Clubs.

We have used the word "sponsoring" in the title of this section rather than "directing" for a specific reason. As a rule, the teacher of music works under a very heavy schedule during school hours and it is a question how much can be expected of him to make his music program function in the community. It is out of the question for him to become the conductor of the numerous ensemble groups which may call upon him. We are not referring to professional positions, such as choir director, church organist, conductor of the chorus or orchestra of some particular organization for which he receives remuneration in addition to the salary that he receives for his services to the school. Within limits these private arrangements are his own individual privilege unless they interfere with his work at the school. Nevertheless, he can encourage any group that wishes to organize a music ensemble, he can give them the benefit of his greater experience, and he can help them secure a director who will be free to consult him when problems arise.

In the organization of a civic orchestra, band, or chorus it seems natural that the director of music should take an active interest. In fact the impetus for such organizations usually comes from him or from some member of the high school music staff. The school music director is the logical leader for such organizations. It is assumed that he has the education, personality, judgment, tact, and musicianship to organize and develop such ensembles composed of adults. When any music organization is the project of the entire community and its membership is open to everyone, then it is the duty of the music director of the school to be willing to assume the responsibility for conducting it. If there is more than one type of community music organization, he will probably conduct the one for which he is best prepared. Members of the music teaching staff can usually be found who are qualified to assume the directorship of other community music organizations.

Such activity in the community will make the music director and his department indispensable to the community and the school administration. It is the best kind of job security. But even more important than job security are the gains made in warm friendships, community respect, support of other music projects, personal growth, and widespread interest and appreciation of better music.

Conducting Community Sings

Nearly everyone loves to sing if he is made to feel that he is not spoiling a musical effect. Most people do not think that they have the musical ability to participate in a selected choral group or even a general chorus where standard music is sung. However, these same people like to sing the old songs and participate with others in lending their voices to the rolling surge of mass singing.

The wise and enthusiastic school music director will conduct a series of community sings. In the series will be a Christmas carol sing in the town square. There will be at least one more community sing during Music Week in conjunction with other festivals. Music is indispensable at a patriotic mass meeting. If the community enjoys these occasions there may be more. If the director can "put it over," there is nothing like a general sing to make the community realize the value of a little music in their lives and the need for music in the lives of their children.

Coordinating Community Musical Activities

It was suggested in the preceding section that the director of music in the high school should sponsor the development of many types of music ensembles throughout the community and probably conduct one all-community organization. As these ensembles and activities develop, they must be in some way articulated with the work done in the school. The school music director is in a position to be the coordinator of all of the musical activities in the school and community. In some cities they provide for proper coordination by making the school music director also head of the community music association.[6]

The problem of articulation will be solved by building a consistent program from the elementary to the adult level. The teacher must first concentrate on the school, for the all-round musical development of the child and the high school student is the best preparation for community music. By establishing high standards of musical performance in the schools the community will expect the same from adult organizations. By using a fine quality of music in the schools the community will be dissatisfied with inferior music.

The school music director must remember, however, that every leader must have followers. He must take care not to get so far out in front of his followers that they lose sight of him entirely. As he leads the school and commu-

[6] William W. Norton, "Community Music in Flint, Michigan." Music Educators Nat'l Conference, *Yearbook, 1938*. Chicago, Illinois, p. 159.

nity to a love for better music he must be patient. In his effort to raise tastes he may occasionally need to cater to public tastes. Advancement will necessarily be slow. His reward will be in seeing real growth that is lasting.

Coordinating the musical activities of a community can be influenced by bringing the music leaders together to discuss their common problems. The In-and-About Music Educators Club movement is a step in this direction, and all music teachers should endeavor to be members of one of these clubs. The development of a city library of music records and scores which circulate from the public library is a worthy project for the schools to initiate. Civic concert series can be supported if a public is developed that likes its music first hand. If the school music director displays qualities of leadership and has the initiative to organize and coordinate community musical activities, he will have little trouble in securing the support of the school administration, the city fathers, and the public.

Music Week

It is during our National Music Week [7] that the leadership of the school music director must be most strongly felt in the community. He should be instrumental in organizing a committee which will coordinate the activities in the school and community for the entire week. It was a happy thought on the part of the originators of this idea to make this week the first full week in May because it gives a chance to demonstrate the culmination of the music work for the year in both school and community.

Music Week activities may include school concerts and festivals, church choir festivals, a festival of children's

[7] Information and materials for organizing Music Week in your community may be secured from the Bureau for the Advancement of Music, 45 West 45th Street, New York, and National Recreation Association, 315 Fourth Avenue, New York City.

choruses from recreational centers, folk song and dance festivals, a day of home-music, music in industries, artist recitals, community concerts, and community "sings." To arrange an entire week of music in a community requires careful planning. To finance it requires executive ability of the first order. But Music Week should climax the relation of school music with the community. It can become like the Christmas season, a joyful time to make music together and foster the spirit of fellowship and good will.

Conclusion

There is no question that the relation of the high school music program with the community largely depends upon the director of music and his corps of teachers. Of all teachers the music teacher seems to have the heaviest schedules. Besides the regular classroom teaching and daily rehearsals there are concerts, operettas, and sundry other activities to occupy his time. Is it physically possible for him to devote time and energy to outside activities?

First of all, the rôle of the teacher is that of a public servant. His life and his teaching cannot be confined to the four walls of the school. Moreover, the success of the music teacher in the school so often depends upon his success in the community. On the other hand, the teacher is an individual and deserves some time to pursue his own personal desires for self-improvement and recreation. It is not only his right but his duty also to continue to search for ways that he may make himself a more cultured person. However, as the musical leader of the community he has a civic responsibility that cannot be denied. There is no doubt that the teacher of music needs unbounded enthusiasm, energy, and a brand of missionary zeal. Only then will he seize upon all opportunities to make his sacred trust a golden privilege.

Topics for General Discussion

1. Outline the musical activities that you would introduce in your community for a program of adult education. In what ways do they differ from a music program of studies in the high school?

2. Review the section in this chapter devoted to stimulating community musical activities. How should the music teacher allocate his time and energy to stimulating music in the home, the church, civic clubs and organizations, and parent-teacher associations?

3. Have you had any experience with the local musicians' union regarding permission for the high school band to play at a holiday celebration in the community? What were the final arrangements? If this situation ever confronted you, how would you meet it?

4. To what extent should the music teacher guide high school students in their professional contacts?

5. If several of the boys in your high school have a dance band and they contracted for an engagement on the same night that the high school orchestra and band, in which they play, were giving their annual concert, how would you solve the problem?

6. Outline a program of activities during Music Week for your school and community.

A TEACHER SPEAKS

I must not interfere with any child, I have been told,
To bend his will to mine, or try to shape him through
some mold
Of thought. Naturally as a flower he must unfold.
Yet flowers have the discipline of wind and rain,
And though I know it gives the gardener much pain,
I've seen him use his pruning shears to gain
More strength and beauty for some blossoms bright.
And he would do whatever he thought right
To save his flowers from a deadening blight.
I do not know—yet it does seem to me
That only weeds unfold just naturally.

ALICE GAY JUDD

Chapter 17

THE TEACHER OF MUSIC

With the phenomenal growth of music in the public schools of today there has arisen an insistent demand that the teacher of music be better prepared to meet his responsibilities. New criteria have been set up for evaluating his qualifications. No longer can he be a person of meager cultural background and limited musicianship. No longer may he be recruited from the ranks of disappointed professional musicians. The field of music and the public expect from him a high type of attainment in his profession. What then, should be the personal and professional equipment of the music teacher of today, as determined by his needs in service?

Personal Equipment

First of all, it seems advisable to consider the kind of person who should be selected as a teacher of music. Will such a person be similar to teachers of other subjects? Is there need for emphasis on certain personality traits? What will he need to know besides music? These and other questions should be carefully considered in determining the requirements of the teacher of music.

The general testimony of school administrators and supervisors, as reflected in criteria used in selecting teachers and in the emphasis placed upon personality traits on rating scales, indicates that a "good teaching personality" is considered an outstanding element in the teacher's equipment. Increasing attention must be given to personality traits in the teacher of music. A pleasing personality is desirable in all teachers, but it is especially so in the school music teacher because of the aesthetic and social qualities inherent in his field.

Personal Appearance

There is no doubt that an attractive personal appearance is desirable for all teachers; there seems to be adequate basis for the opinion that it is particularly desirable for the teacher of music. The subject itself calls for a sensitivity to the beautiful. Can the spirit inherent in the music be conveyed to the student except by a personality which gives a physical demonstration of these qualities through a neat and attractive appearance?

Moreover, the success of the teacher of music in his relation with the community depends to a great extent upon an attractive personal appearance. Few teachers are called upon to appear before the public as frequently as is the teacher of music. It is only natural that the community should expect musical performances by the teacher and the organizations which he has trained. For this reason, he is often the center of attraction, and regardless of how competent he may be musically, much of his success depends upon appearance and his ability to get along with people.

Enthusiasm

Above all, the music teacher must have an infectious enthusiasm for music. He must live music, act it, breathe it. He must arouse enthusiasm in the students by the tone of his voice and by his manner. He must keep young with his pupils.

From early years throughout the school life, music should

be less a subject to be taught and more a spark to be caught. A love of music and a sensitivity to its beauties are acquired only by contagion. By exhibiting a keen zest for music the teacher can transform the music period for a group of children or adults from one of mere routine into one of inspired interest. A group of children usually have a zest and enthusiasm for music, unless it has been killed by some teacher with a lesson-learning complex. This initial enthusiasm for music should be nurtured. It must be aroused if lacking. The unique values in music are the emotional qualities. Only the teacher with a genuine enthusiasm for his art will develop in the children the desire to be musical.

Human Understanding

The person who does not have a sympathetic nature should not go into the field of teaching music. He must be interested in young people, realize their limitations, and be sincerely happy over their progress. He is using music to educate boys and girls, and the human factor in his relations with them is his first consideration. The musician who is not tolerant of mediocre musical ability does not belong in the school. He must not devote his attention only to the talented, but all students must know and experience the value of music in their lives. Only the sympathetic person who loves to teach will make the most of his opportunity.

Leadership

A final attribute which is indispensable for the teacher of music is leadership. Leadership does not mean domination; it is the result of a sincere understanding between teacher and pupil and of mutual participation in group activity. Leadership develops in the individual pupil a sense of responsibility, and in the group as a whole, a spirit of harmony and happiness.

Leadership is a quality which is universally acknowledged as desirable for all teachers. With the teacher of music, leadership must express itself to a large extent in three situations: first, in class, which provides the natural setting for effective leadership; second, in the school, where the teacher of music should be one of the most important integrating nuclei in the school as a whole; and, finally, in the community, where social leadership is primary.[1]

Musical activities demand a high quality of group leadership. The music teacher is primarily associated with coöperative musical projects. He is constantly placed in such situations as the developing of large choral and orchestral organizations and social musical functions, which test his ability to direct, guide, and lead. The teacher of music must be able, after only one group rehearsal, to direct choruses composed of several hundred, or even one or two thousand children. Few teachers of other subjects are confronted with similar situations. Only the music teacher who can function as a group leader will be effective.

Summary

In addition to possessing certain personality traits, the teacher of music must be an integrated and well-adjusted individual. He must have the emotional stability and character necessary to lead children in the coöperative effort which is requisite for successful musical organizations. Personality in the teacher may be described as personal adequacy. It includes proper attitudes in regard to work, students, fellow teachers, administrators, and the community as a whole. Such attitudes are dependent upon sincerity of

[1] James L. Mursell, *Human Values in Music Education*. New York: Silver Burdett Company, 1934, p. 286.

National Music Supervisors Chorus, Hollis Dann, Conductor, Chicago Conference, 1934, assisted by the Lane Technical High School orchestra.

purpose. Only such a person is qualified to be a teacher of music in the public schools.

Professional Equipment

In the discussion of the personal equipment of the teacher of music, the importance of personality and character was emphasized. Although it is recognized that personal equipment for the teacher is also professional equipment, and that the latter in turn becomes a part of the teacher's personal equipment, it has seemed desirable to discuss the two types of equipment separately.

One of the earliest attempts to standardize the education necessary for a teacher of music was made in 1921, when the Research Council of the Music Educators National Conference presented a course for the training of supervisors of music. The Research Council was composed of fifteen outstanding music educators of schools and colleges. A four-year course with a total of 120 semester hours was organized with this distribution:

General Academic Courses	30 hours
Education (including Music Education).	30 hours
Music (Theoretical and Applied) . .	60 hours

This recommendation by the Conference was widely accepted by the leading schools and colleges, and it tended to raise the standards to such an extent that nothing less than a four-year degree course is now considered acceptable in the professional training of music teachers. In 1930, the Music Teachers National Association recommended another course, which placed more emphasis upon applied music.

Recent studies indicate that, for the most part, the training of the music teacher for the schools should include the three phases of preparation recommended by the Conference in 1921. The proportions may vary somewhat in practice but all the programs of studies recommended by recent surveys indicate a belief that the teacher of music in the schools needs to be a well-rounded individual with a good general education, an understanding of pedagogical principles, and a thorough training in music. The programs suggest several areas which should be included in the preparation of those who are to be music educators.

An Educational Philosophy

One's philosophy of music education is determined by one's philosophy of all education. It is in reality one's philosophy of life.[2] Only through a well-defined philosophy of education will the teacher be able to understand the place of music in normal living. Such a philosophy should conceive the part that the arts and music play in enriching life; it should identify the educative process with actual life and experience; and it should embrace an understanding of the relation of music to this process.

Education primarily is not something that adults do to students. It is primarily something that students do for themselves. And yet the teacher has a share in contributing to student growth, for both the teacher and student have a definite place in the educational process. The success of the teacher's part in this process can be measured by the degree to which the student becomes better of his own accord. Such change is brought about through living. The school must find a way to make music a manner of living, so that the group may live more joyously together. Through such harmonious living together each individual will enrich his own personal life, as well as relationship with the community. Such a philosophy implies this specific goal.

[2] Hazel B. Nohavec, "The Education of Music Teachers for the Modern School," Music Educators National Conference, *Yearbook 1937*, pp. 182-186.

The Resolutions adopted by the Music Educators National Conference at its Biennial meeting held in Los Angeles in 1940 may well be taken as an initial credo.

Throughout the ages, man has found music to be essential in voicing his own innate sense of beauty. Music is not a thing apart from man; it is the spiritualized expression of his finest and best inner self.

There is no one wholly unresponsive to the elevating appeal of music. If only the right contacts and experiences are provided, every life can find in music some answer to its fundamental need for aesthetic and emotional outlet. Education fails of its cultural objectives unless it brings to every child the consciousness that his own spirit may find satisfying expression through the arts.

The responsibility of offering every child a rich and varied experience in music rests upon the music teacher. It becomes his duty to see that music contributes its significant part in leading mankind to a higher plane of existence.

The Music Educators National Conference, in full acceptance of its responsibilities as the representative and champion of progressive thought and practice in music education, pledges its united efforts in behalf of a broad and constructive program which shall include:

(1) Provision in all the schools of our country, both urban and rural, for musical experience and training for every child, in accordance with his interests and capacities.

(2) Continued effort to improve music teaching and to provide adequate equipment.

(3) Carry-over of school music training into the musical, social, and home life of the community, as a vital part of its cultural, recreational, and leisure-time activities.

(4) Increased opportunities for adult education in music.

(5) Improvement of choir and congregational singing in the churches and Sunday schools; increased use of instrumental ensemble playing in connection with church activities.

(6) Encouragement and support of all worth-while musical enterprises as desirable factors in making our country a better place in which to live.[3]

[3] From *Music Educators National Conference,* Volume 30, *Yearbook 1939-1940,* page 8.

If this goal is comprehended and accepted, music education will reach into all phases and levels of life, instead of remaining a separate compartment. Such a goal will determine steps toward a broad and constructive program in the attainment of aims. Teaching will be effective only if there is a constructive philosophy and a goal to direct it. Only with such a goal will the teacher of music be able to adapt materials and procedures to the realization of the human values in music education.

A Functioning Psychology

Following closely an educational philosophy and goal is a psychology which will function in the interpretation of the relation between aims and procedures. A theoretical understanding of psychology alone will not suffice. This functioning psychology can best be developed through a practical understanding of the various systems of modern psychology, such as the mechanistic, and the newer and emerging psychology variously called purposive psychology, organismic psychology, or the psychology of Gestalt. It is not within the scope of this chapter to describe the conflicting theories of these schools of thought or the pertinent implications for the teaching of music. It can be pointed out, however, that music, with its emphasis on feeling, emotional development, and awakening of the imagination and creative power, is nurtured best by the purposive psychology.

Too many music educators betray a complete ignorance of the changes that have taken place in the development of scientific psychological thought. Psychology can help the teacher to understand better the needs and interests of all students. Only through a conception of psychology in its functional application can the music teacher successfully fulfill his responsibility as an educator.

A Scientific Attitude

Two considerations should be pointed out in discussing the contribution of science to the education of teachers of music. First, the teacher should understand the physical basis of music and the contribution that science has made to the development of music as an art. Scientific aids and demonstrations can increase our sensitivity to music by making us more conscious of what we hear. The music educator should make himself aware of the possibilities for the use of modern science in the field of music education. Science is willing to be a handmaiden of art. The music educator should enlist the services of the scientist.

Even more important is the truly scientific attitude—the attitude of inquiry and evaluation. In contrast to purely empirical thinking, the scientific method employs analysis and synthesis, utilizes experimentation, lessens the liability of error, is able to manage the new or novel, and stimulates an interest in the future.[4] This method does not employ statistics and facts for the purpose of upholding established opinion. It is based upon a sincere desire to know and be guided toward truth by impersonal and unbiased findings.

An Understanding of the Social Values of Music

There is no doubt of the importance of sociology for the music teacher, if the amount of space devoted to it in the literature of music education is a criterion. What is the true sociological significance of music?

Two essential characteristics make music a social art. First of all, as pointed out in Chapter II, both the performance of music and the listening to music normally are social acts. The listener plays an important role in the communication from the creator, the expression of which is in-

[4] John Dewey, *How We Think*. New York: D. C. Heath and Company. 1933.

terpreted by the performer. This expression is conveyed through the medium of music, which is often called the universal language. Secondly, one of the most characteristic types of musical performance is the ensemble. Such performance depends upon group participation and coöperative effort.

From these characteristics it can be understood that the true significance of music sociologically is to be found not in its economic elements, but rather in its human and psychological elements. Although this true significance cannot always be analyzed, it is unmistakably present. In all ages music has been a handmaiden to man. It has accompanied him in his work, worship, and war. It has pervaded the home, church, school, theatre, and community. It has comforted man in his sorrows, enriched his memories, and through his own participation has brought him joy. Thus music is important for the social development of the participating individual and, as a result, for its effect upon society.

It is often pointed out that the coöperative performance in music is a demonstration of the democratic spirit. In such a performance the individual must contribute not only some skill, however elementary, but must be able to participate with others in achieving a common end. These musical organizations are often called "laboratories" for developing the desirable traits toward coöperative spirit and democratic understanding.

Technological advances continue to affect our lives by an increased emphasis on mechanization and materialism at the sacrifice of spiritual values. It provides more leisure time but it does not prepare man to use this gift to the fullest advantage. It is like giving an expensive present to a child who has no idea what to do with it. Life has become increasingly complex and we seem to have lost our faith in simple things. When a premium is made on material values, human and social values seem to be lost. Educational leaders are turning to music and the arts to provide experiences which will offset the present-day emphasis on a materialistic philosophy. They are utilizing music and the arts as a means toward social betterment. Only the teacher of music who is aware of the social significance of his art will be ready to serve the community and to fulfill the true functions of a music educator.

Musicianship

On all sides there is a plea for genuine musicianship in those who hope to lead others in the joy of singing, playing, and creating music. This musicianship must be broad and cultural. It must be one of service. The essentials of musicianship are the ability to feel and the ability to understand the aesthetic intentions of the composer as he attempts to express himself through the medium of tone; and as a corollary, it includes the ability to interpret this expression, and to some degree express one's own musical thoughts through this same medium. Briefly, musicianship means the power to appreciate, to interpret, and to create music to varying degrees. It certainly demands musical literacy and a wide acquaintance with the literature of good music.

In this area of preparation all the colleges that are training teachers of music have a genuine responsibility. The worst thing that any training school can do is to send out teachers who are well equipped in every way except musicianship. Schools and colleges must hold to high musical standards, for only then will the teachers they send into the field be able to meet their responsibilities. The opportunities for creative expression, emotional development, and personal satisfaction inherent in the study of music will be nurtured only if the student comes in contact with a teacher who is a sensitive musician.

The teacher, first of all, must have a keen appreciation of music and a genuine love for it. Only such a person will develop a love for music in the student—a love that is made deeper through understanding. Such appreciation is enhanced by knowledge and participation.

A phase of musicianship which should be given added emphasis for the teacher of music is performance proficiency. It is through participation that one increases his understanding of the highest aesthetic qualities of an art and his sensitivity to these qualities. The scope of the program of music education today demands more than a balance between teaching ability and performance ability; it calls for the highest possible attainment in both.

Professional Attitudes

The music educator, first of all, must see himself as a member of the great body of professional educators. He cannot fulfill his obligations and duties to his pupils, his school, and to society unless he plans his work and his conduct along the finest plane of professional attitudes, ethics, and practices.

It is not enough that the music instructor occupies his school time with energetic efforts to achieve musical results with his performing student groups. Of course this is an essential part of his duties. But he must also see beyond to the effect of his work on the individual students and on the community. He must see himself as a part of the community and with obligations just as compelling even if different from those of the doctor or the minister.

For one thing, his business ethics must be above question, as discussed elsewhere in this chapter. His personal conduct must be an inspiration and example to his pupils. Music must mean more to them because of their admiration, regard, and respect for their instructor.

Moreover, he must be in close contact with all the individuals, groups, and forces that are concerned with the advancement of music as an educational constructive force in our national and civic life. There are many ways in which this may be done; a few of the essential ways may be mentioned.

Every music instructor in the public schools should be an active member of the Music Educators National Conference and of his state and other organizations of music educators. He should attend every possible meeting, and take part in discussions, committee activities, and other duties as far as practicable. This should not be merely in the spirit of the "joiner," but in the inquiring spirit of one who would serve and would learn by associating and coöperating with those who are leaders.

The music instructor should keep abreast of the times by subscribing to the professional magazines in his field, by reading the proceedings of the Music Educators National Conference, the Music Teachers National Association, and other professional organizations.

The music instructor must realize that leadership does not come from one's official position alone, nor from one's personality either. The spirit of leadership is largely a result of the right kind of professional attitude, a thing really sensed by the student body. Therefore the instructor must not allow his own performance skills to deteriorate. He must be an example through his own enthusiasm in singing and playing, and his own joy in using these skills to give pleasure to others. The music instructor in high schools of small or remote districts must feel an especial obligation to supply the cultural atmosphere of the community through his own musical activities as well as those of his school organizations. The town may quite properly look to him for such leadership in its musical life.

Finally, the music instructor should keep himself abreast of the times in all fields of current affairs. This, of course, includes music matters in general, but it also means a comprehensive familiarity with every matter of moment—world, national, local. He should be a man among men or a woman among women, a citizen among citizens, a teacher among teachers, a musician among musicians, a personality among people.

Business Attitude

"Today's successful music educator is business-like and efficient in the planning of his work.

"He is necessarily more than a musician and teacher.

"His greatly enlarged program of music education activities demands efficient organization and administration." [5]

There seems to be a general notion that musicians are not reliable or business-like. Perhaps this has been all too true in some phases of the music profession. This notion has even permeated the field of music education. It is not uncommon to hear that the music instructor has upset the administrative routine of a school.

The modern school system is conducted in a business-like manner with carefully planned budgets. It is the duty of the music teacher to acquaint himself with the financial routine of such items as budgets, requisitions, and accounts. If he can prove himself to be an efficient business person rather than one who keeps haphazard accounts, and is dilatory with budgets, he will accomplish something of

[5] These quotations are from a bulletin designed to assist the music educator in some of his daily business problems as they relate to the materials and services of music education supplied by the firms who are members of the Music Education Exhibitors Association. Copies may be secured free of charge by writing to the Music Educators National Conference, 64 East Jackson Boulevard, Chicago, Illinois.

real value for both the music program and himself. If he is not familiar with the financial routine established for the entire school system, he should sit down with his principal or superintendent and have it explained carefully to him.

After the teacher understands the routine, he must be diligent in observing it. The teacher that knows his business will keep acquainted with available materials and sources of supply. He will have his name placed on the mailing list of a number of publishers. In examining new books and music, he should adhere to the ethical practice of sending for music on approval, rather than requesting complimentary copies. He should see to it that, if not purchased, the material is returned in saleable condition. He will anticipate his needs at least a year in advance in order that he can accurately make out his budget the preceding spring. He will properly fill out requisitions and order blanks, and take the pains to present valid reasons for his requests. He will keep his personal accounts separate from school accounts in order that there will be no misunderstanding or confusion of payments.

As a matter of professional ethics the teacher of music will refuse commissions on materials or instruments purchased by the school or by parents. This practice inevitably makes the teacher responsible to the persons or firm that gives the commission. He is not getting something for nothing. Through higher prices the money that he receives eventually comes from the school budget. Making purchases for the school or students is part of his job as a teacher. It is not extra work. Accepting commissions can only in the end hamper his teaching results and cause unfortunate misunderstandings.

Elsewhere in this book we have referred to the habitual practice of teachers infringing upon the copyright law.

Publishers are most coöperative in the requests of teachers but they have a right to the protection of their copyrighted works. It is unlawful to print on the blackboard, typewrite, or mimeograph music or other materials from a published book without permission from the publisher. Arrangements cannot be made of copyrighted music without permission unless it is in public domain. The same is true for song slides. Performances of musical or dramatic productions cannot be given without permission from the publishers, which usually involves a royalty fee or the purchase of a certain number of copies of the work. Permission should be obtained to perform published music on the radio. It is very important that every teacher of music acquaint himself with the copyright law and observe it.

It is true that few colleges preparing teachers stress the importance of these practical phases of the teacher's responsibility. It is one of their failings which should be corrected. Besides the handbook referred to above, teachers can receive valuable aid in these matters, as well as others, from a recent book entitled "More Than a Pitchpipe." [6]

Conclusion

From the discussion in this chapter the reader may feel that the music teacher in the high school must be a "superman" with a lifetime devoted to preparation for his work. The authors only hope to point out the personal qualities and professional areas that need special consideration in his training. No teacher will attain perfection in any one phase, let alone all of them. But the zest that he receives from his work will depend upon his reaching out into areas that will make his life more interesting and his teaching more fruitful. There is no doubt that due to the rigid de-

[6] Ennis Davis, *More Than a Pitchpipe*, C. C. Birchard, Boston, Mass., 1941.

mands of his art, the teacher of music must be a teacher plus. In short, the music educator of today and of the future must be a broad-gauged person of wide, general education, including a good command of English both in speaking and in writing. He must possess musicality and be well-educated musically. He must have such desirable personal traits as sympathy, tact, judgment, humor, forcefulness, enthusiasm, and leadership. He must be genuinely interested in music, in boys and girls, and in life generally. He must see his service in the classroom as one that is primarily social, and he must bring to that service a teaching power.

There is a real challenge to those institutions which are preparing teachers of music for the public schools of today. The field calls for talented, capable, intelligent and cultured teachers of music. The field needs teachers of music who will utilize sociological, psychological, and scientific interpretations and aids; teachers with an educational philosophy which will carry them through to the realization of their ultimate goal; teachers who are filled with the spirit of music and the will to strive for the technical perfection necessary for the development and fulfillment of their own musical possibilities.

Self-Survey for Teachers of Music

It is almost impossible to evaluate oneself objectively. Many of us fail to realize our own powers or to pay heed to our limitations. The stamp of approval by a college preparing teachers does not necessarily mean that one is qualified to take his rightful place in the field of teaching music. The superior teacher is one who is constantly endeavoring to improve his professional qualifications. It is well to make a check on ourselves occasionally. Readers of this book who are teachers or expect to become so may find it interesting to check their qualifications against a short self-survey to better understand their shortcomings and strengths.

This brief self-survey is based upon the five areas of professional equipment discussed in the chapter. Each area is divided into five specific questions. A horizontal rating scale is used from one to five representing five degrees of ability. Each number on the scale is also divided into five points. Indicate by a small x on the scale your rating of yourself on each question. Then draw straight lines connecting these points. The resulting profile will give you an idea of your general qualifications. Two hypothetical profiles are indicated on the rating scale in solid and dotted lines. Which teacher do you think has the better professional qualifications on the whole? The scale makes no attempt to rate oneself on personal qualifications because of the difficulty of evaluating them with any degree of objectivity. Occasional self-scrutiny can be valuable. See what your own teaching profile looks like! (By making a line in dashes or a line with color pencil, the reader can compare himself with those profiles drawn.)

RATING SCALE

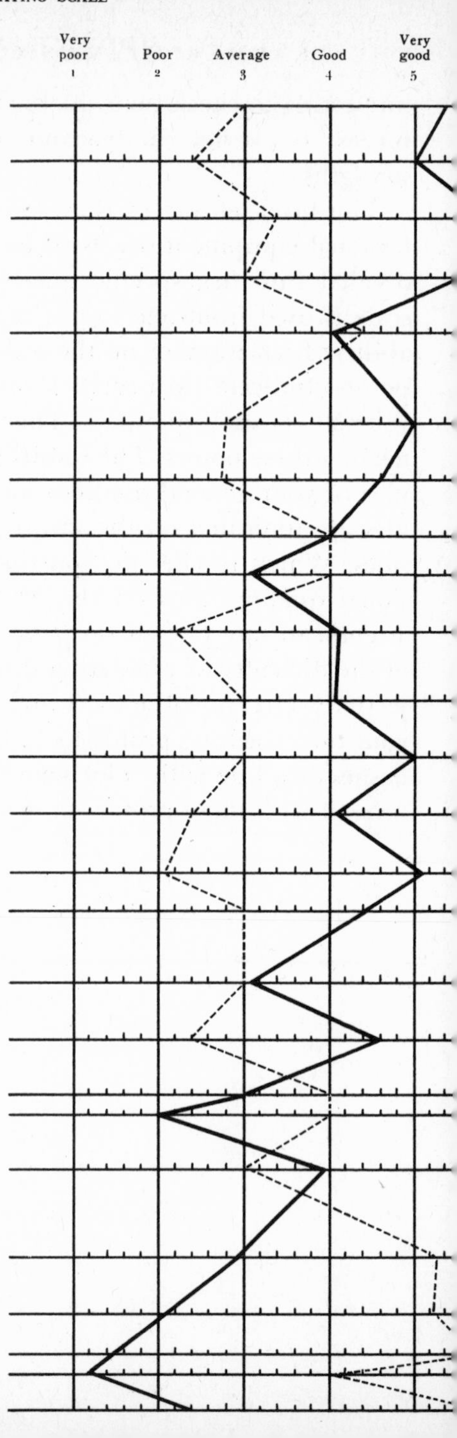

I. *An educational philosophy*

1. Is your own educational background of such nature that you have a broad-gauged view of life?
2. Are you acquainted with the whole field of general arts and realize their place in normal living?
3. Can you discuss intelligently the views and controversial issues in music education?
4. Do you support professional organizations and make yourself conversant with new professional literature?
5. Are you widely acquainted with music materials for teaching which coincide with your educational philosophy?

II. *A functioning psychology*

1. Do you have an adequate understanding of the learning process and its relation to music?
2. Do you have sufficient understanding of music education to do your part in the guidance program?
3. Can you create an attitude of interest and enjoyment in a group during the music hour?
4. Are you able to adapt musical activities to take care of individual differences?
5. Can you use approved psychological procedures in teaching the various phases of the music program?

III. *A scientific attitude*

1. Are you guided by the "spirit of inquiry" in your work?
2. Are you acquainted with the outstanding contributions science has made to the development of music?
3. Do you keep abreast of the new scientific aids for teaching music which are being made available?
4. Can you administer and interpret the scores of the better-known standardized tests?
5. Can you cope with problems of rooms, equipment, budget, and organization?

IV. *An understanding of the social values of music*

1. Can you capitalize on the inherent social qualities of music in your teaching?
2. Do you understand the part music can play in the life of the community?
3. Are you qualified to assume leadership in organizing music activities in the community?
4. Can you conduct a community sing?
5. Are you acquainted with music materials which will emphasize wholesome social values?

V. *Musicianship*

1. Are you acquainted with a wide range of music literature and are you continually trying to broaden it?
2. Are your skills in vocal and instrumental performance adequate for your teaching assignment?
3. How do you rate in sight-reading and ear-training?
4. How well do you arrange or compose?
5. Can you perform as a soloist when called upon?

APPENDIX A

It is not the object of the authors to make the appendixes an appendage to the main body of this book. Rather, it is our hope that the material included in them will serve as very practical suggestions which will be of decided help to teachers in problems of organization and in selection of music materials. Appendix A contains forms, letters, diagrams, and other materials which will enable readers to make comparisons with their own teaching situations.

1. Schedules of Music Classes

The first schedule is that of the vocal and instrumental teachers in the Junior and Senior High School of Red Wing, Minnesota. There are approximately 600 students in the six-year high school. All classes

Red Wing, Minnesota, Population 9962

Red Wing High School

Periods	Vocal Instructor	Instrumental Instructor
8:15 A.M.	Seventh and Eighth Grade General Music (9 sections)	Beginning Band
9:15		Advanced Band
10:15	Junior Girls' Chorus—3 days Junior Boys' Chorus—2 days	Small Instrumental Ensembles
10:45	High School A Cappella Choir	Band Sectional Rehearsals
11:45	Lunch	Lunch
1:00 P.M.	Supervise Elementary School Music	Rudiments of Music
2:00		Free
3:00	Small Vocal Ensembles	Bugle and Drum Corps (3 days)
4:00	High School Girls' Glee Club 2 days High School Boys' Glee Club 2 days	Instrumental Lessons

Lewiston, Ohio

Washington School

Periods	Monday	Tuesday	Wednesday	Thursday	Friday
9:00 A.M.	Grade I	Grade VI	Grade I	Grade VI	Grade I
9:20	Grade II	Elementary Chorus	Grade II		Elementary Chorus
9:40	Grade V	Grade III	Grade V	Grade III	Advanced Cornets
10:10	'Cello Class	Grade IV	'Cello Class	Grade IV	" "
10:30	Combined Band	Beginning Brass	Beginning Cornets	Advanced Violins	Beginning Clarinets
11:15	Beginning Cornets	Beginning Violins	Beginning Clarinets	Beginning Violins	Beginning Brass
12:00	Lunch	(Reserved for spec	ial rehearsals —	—	—)
1:00 P.M.	H. S. Girls' Glee Club	H. S. Boys' Glee Club	H. S. Girls' Glee Club	H. S. Boys' Glee Club	H. S. General Chorus
1:45	Intermediate Clarinet	Grade VIII	Heavy Brass Class	Grade VIII	Drums
2:30	Advanced Violin	Grade VII	Advanced Clarinet	Combined Band	Grade VII
3:15	Study Hall	Study Hall	Study Hall	Study Hall	Study Hall

meet every day except those indicated. There are 80 boys in the Junior Boys' Chorus.

The second schedule is that of the director of music, Washington School, Lewiston, Ohio. It gives an idea of the music teacher's load in a small school of twelve grades, built on the 8-4 plan. There are 110 pupils in the upper four grades, the high school. Fifty-six of these students are in the general chorus—twenty-six boys and thirty girls. The director reports that he began an Honor Award System in 1940 with very satisfactory results.

The following schedule is that of the Harry P. Harding High School, Charlotte, North Carolina. It is a junior-senior high school with grades from 7 through 12 and with an enrollment of 1080 pupils. There are two teachers. The vocal instructor teaches full time and has charge of the general and choral music classes. The instrumental instructor teaches half time and has charge of the instrumental organizations.

All classes meet every day for a 45 minute period, with the exception of Seventh Grade Music Classes, which meet every other day, alternating each week, so that one week a class meets three times and the next week only twice. Music is a required subject of seventh grade students.

The Junior High Girls' and Boys' Glee Clubs are open to all students of the eighth and ninth grades who can meet the requirements of having a pleasant singing voice and ability to read simple three-part music. Membership in the Senior High School General Chorus is restricted to students in the tenth, eleventh, and twelfth grades who have been members of the Junior High School Glee Clubs for two years, and have shown marked ability in their work in that group. There are exceptions in the case of transfers if they can meet requirements.

Charlotte, North Carolina, Population 100,899

Harry P. Harding High School

Period	
1	Junior High Girls' Glee Club
2	Seventh Grade Music
3	Junior High Boys' Glee Club
4	Seventh Grade Music
5	Senior High General Chrous
Lunch	
6	Beginning Band
7	Orchestra
8	Advanced Band

The orchestra is a junior-senior organization, open to all students in the entire school. Membership in this group depends upon the ability to play an orchestral instrument satisfactorily, and the willingness to practice one hour each day. The Beginning Band requires no previous experience for admission, but each student must own his own instrument. The advanced band is composed of senior high school students with previous membership in the Beginning Band required.

The schedule of Frederick High School, Frederick, Maryland, indicates an emphasis of a General Music Class during the entire four years. The school system is organized on the 8-4 plan. The following material is taken from a letter of one of the music instructors in the school.

1. Number of students: 1300
2. Type of school: four-year high school
3. Type of enrollment: city and rural (about half of the students come in buses)
4. Schedules for classes and rehearsals:
   General Music: Required of all students in grades 9 and 10. Classes meet twice each week. Boys and girls are in the same class. The average enrollment for each section is 40.
   General Music: Elective for students in grades 11 and 12. Class meets five times each week. Only one section.
   Beginning Band: Once each week
   Advanced Band: Twice each week
   Orchestra: Twice each week
   Glee clubs: Mixed—twice each week
   Girls—once each week
   Boys—once each week
5. Number of members on staff and teaching load:
   Staff: two music instructors
   Teaching load:
   Teacher A: 23 out of 30 periods per week. This includes one elective general music class (5 periods a week), four 9th grade sections (2 periods a week), three 10th grade sections (2 periods a week). All glee clubs
   Teacher B: 22 out of 30 periods per week. This includes five 9th grade sections (2 periods a week), four 10th grade sections (two periods a week). All instrumental organizations.

The next schedule is that of the director of music, Technical High School, Springfield, Massachusetts. It is one of the three senior high schools of this city whose system is organized on the 6-3-3 plan. The enrollment in the school is 2,193 students. Each period is 42 minutes in length. The teaching load of the music instructor is 285 students per day.

The schedule indicates a balance between choral and instrumental activities.

Springfield, Massachusetts, Population 148,989
Technical High School

Period	Monday	Tuesday	Wednesday	Thursday	Friday
8:30–9:00 Home room free for special rehearsals, preparation, office hours					
I	Advanced Girls Chorus	Advanced Girls Chorus	Advanced Girls Chorus	Advanced Girls Chorus	Advanced Girls Chorus
II	Mixed Choir	Mixed Choir	Mixed Choir	Mixed Choir	Mixed Choir
III	Orchestra	Orchestra	Orchestra	Orchestra	Orchestra
IV	Band	Band	Band	Band	Band
V	Freshman Boys Chorus	Advanced Boys Chorus	Freshman Boys Chorus	Advanced Boys Chorus	Freshman Boys Chorus
VI	Freshman Boys Chorus				
VII	Training Mixed Choir	Training Girls Chorus	Training Girls Chorus	Training Girls Chorus	Training Girls Chorus
2:30–3:00 Reserved for special projects					

Cleveland, Ohio, Population 878,385
Curriculum in Music for Senior High Schools

Applied Music

I. *Vocal*

1. Choral Club
   This is the advanced chorus; and if two levels are used, indicate the higher level by CHORAL CLUB ADVANCED, and the lower level by CHORAL CLUB INTERMEDIATE. Meeting five days a week. 5 points each semester.
2. Chorus
   The beginning level of choral activity. Three to five days a week, with the corresponding number of points each semester.

3. Voice Culture Classes
Development of the individual voice through the study of song literature. This course may be extended through a maximum of four semesters. It is recommended that the class meet five days a week, for 5 points each semester; but there may be need for some flexibility in this, due to teacher load and other factors.
4. Vocal Ensembles
Various forms of vocal ensembles to be organized and coached by the music teacher. To receive no credit.

II. *Instrumental*

1. Band
If there are two group levels of instruction, the terms to be used are BAND ADVANCED for the upper level, and for the lower level, BAND INTERMEDIATE. These should meet five days a week, with 5 points each semester.
2. Orchestra
If there are two group levels of instruction, the terms to be used are ORCHESTRA ADVANCED for the upper level, and for the lower level, ORCHESTRA INTERMEDIATE. These should meet five days a week, with 5 points each semester.
3. Instrumental Classes
There is need of flexibility in scheduling instrumental classes, because of teacher time, class enrollment, and other factors. The number of points credit should equal the number of days the class meets.

II. *Instrumental*

4. Instrumental Ensembles
Various forms of instrumental ensembles to be organized and coached by the music teacher. To receive no credit.

Theory

1. Fundamentals of Music (Grade 10)
This is a course in elementary theory, rhythm, ear training, and sight singing, that should be considered a foundation for all music students. Two semesters, 5 points each semester.
2. Harmony (Grade 11)
This second year course in theory has to do with organizing the harmonic materials of music, together with a continuation of sight reading, ear training, and instrumentation. Two semesters, 10 points each semester.

History of Music (Grade 12)

A course open to 12th grade students; required of all music majors and recommended to others having sufficient musical experience. The purpose of this course is to trace the development of the art of music, its forms and trends, as shown in the works of the outstanding composers of every period. Two semesters. 10 points each semester.

Music Appreciation

A one semester course open to all 10th, 11th and 12th grade students. Various types of music will be presented through group singing, listening and background reading. This course is designed for those who wish to increase their enjoyment of music by knowing more about it. 5 points credit.

The Music Major

80 points credit assigned to a music major, to be distributed as follows:

Theory —30 points
History of Music—20 points
Applied Music —30 points (9th grade not included)

The Music Minor

40 points credit assigned to a music minor, to be distributed as follows:

Theory —10 points (Fundamentals of Music)
Applied Music —30 points (9th grade not included)

NOTE: Those who make a minor of music education are urged to consider the election of an additional course, MUSIC APPRECIATION, for 5 points, unless their background is sufficient to be acceptable in the HISTORY OF MUSIC course, which they could substitute for the first-mentioned course.

Reference has been made several times to the stagger plan of scheduling instrumental classes. The following schedule is one worked out for the classes in the high school of Katonah, New York. The schedule is for Mondays only; there is a similar schedule worked out for Wednesdays and Fridays. The original schedule gave the names of the students. We have included only the number of students in each group.

IMPORTANT NOTICE TO STUDENTS:

While you will be excused from one period of English, History, etc. every seven weeks for music lesson, you will not be excused from handing in any homework which may be due during your music lesson.

Students who will be absent from French, Geometry, Band, etc. because of their music lesson will please notify their teacher in advance so that the teacher may give you your new homework assignment.

Mondays KATONAH PUBLIC SCHOOL

Temporary Instrumental music schedule

	Date	10/28/40 1/13/41	11/18/40 1/20/41	11/25/40 1/27/41	12/2/40 2/3/41	12/9/40 2/10/41	12/16/40 2/17/41	1/6/41 2/24/41
	Period	*Group*						
1	9:00	3	2	1	7	6	5	4
2	9:46	4	3	2	1	7	6	5
3	10:32	5	4	3	2	1	7	6
4	11:18	6	5	4	3	2	1	7
5	1:15	7	6	5	4	3	2	1
6	2:01	1	7	6	5	4	3	2
7	2:48	2	1	7	6	5	4	3

Group I	*Group II*	*Group III*	*Group IV*
Four students	Six students	Three students	Two students
Group V	*Group VI*	*Group VII*	
Three students	Five students	One student	

2. Letters and Forms in Instrumental and Vocal Teaching

In carrying on a program of instrumental and vocal activities it is helpful to have several mimeographed or printed letters and forms to aid in organization, management, and the keeping of records. We are including a few of the forms used in the high schools of East Orange, New Jersey, to aid young teachers in the formulation of such material.

It is usually necessary to write a letter to parents to announce the introduction of instrumental teaching in a high school or to hold the interest after an instrumental program has been started, explaining in detail the plan, procedure, and costs.

As soon as a high school owns its own band and orchestra instruments the teacher is confronted with the problem of lending them to students. Many misunderstandings arise if this is not done in a business-like manner. Very often students do not feel the proper responsibility for school-owned instruments. It is part of their education to learn to accept responsibility. To avoid misunderstandings and to impress upon the students their responsibility, it is better to have both parents and students sign such typical forms as the one at the top of the next page.

EAST ORANGE PUBLIC SCHOOLS

Instrument.................... School............

RECEIPT FOR LOANED INSTRUMENT

East Orange......................194

Received today in .... condition a ....

from .... acting for the Board of Education of East Orange. I agree to take proper care of this instrument and to return it uninjured whenever so requested.

Signature.........................Address...................

PARENT'S OR GUARDIAN'S GUARANTEE.

I hereby assume full responsibility for the above mentioned instrument and guarantee its return uninjured. In case of loss of, or damage to, the instrument, ordinary wear excepted, I guarantee to replace, or to repair such loss or damage.

Signature..............................

The instrument is loaned for home practice, and is to be played in a school organization only.

The privilege of using this instrument may be revoked at any time for failure on the part of the pupil to live to the condition specified above, or for his lack of satisfactory progress.

Each year many schools lose music unless a record is kept of loans to students. If the teacher will take the trouble to check out music on some simple form like the one below, the continual loss of music can be prevented.

EAST ORANGE PUBLIC SCHOOLS

Receipt for music loaned to pupil

Selection...................................

Date..

Student.......................

It is understood that the student shall pay for any lost or damaged music.

When class lessons are taken by students and a small fee is charged, some record is needed to account for payments. Students are charged a fee of 25¢ each for lessons in groups of four. Payments are made to the school and a record is kept on the following form.

EAST ORANGE PUBLIC SCHOOLS

Department of Instrumental Music

Name.............................School..................

Address...........................Grade..................

Telephone.........................Instrument.............

Lesson	Date Paid	Rec'd by	Lesson	Date Paid	Rec'd by
1			5		
2			6		
3			7		
4			8		

(See reverse side)

Note: The East Orange form provides space for record of 28 lessons.

Pupils who cannot devote a minimum total of five hours a week in concentrated practice will be requested to discontinue lessons. Instruments demand faithful care. Keep from smaller children. Be careful of extreme heat or cold. Repairs are sometimes costly. Much valuable time is lost in not having on hand such small things as extra strings or extra reeds for quick replacement. Lessons are payable four in advance. Owing to the very low rate charged it is necessary that missed lessons be paid for except in case of long illness. Pupils will show this card for admission to class.

Do not lose this card. It is your record.
Keep it in your instrument case. Finder please return.

In all music teaching one of the instructor's chief problems is to get the student to practice regularly. If students of the high school age keep a record of their practice, it often serves as excellent training in teaching students to budget their time. Also a practice record enables a teacher to check whether the student's failure to progress is due to lack of work or other limitations. The following record is for voice classes. A similar form could be used for piano and other instruments.

East Orange High School **Vocal Music Department**

Name........................Home Room........Date........

Voice................Piano in the Home........Age of Pupil.....

To the Parent or Guardian: Regular practice in voice is essential if progress is to be made by the pupil, and credit is given with the understanding that this practice is carried on from day to day, the same as home-work in other subjects. Your assistance in finding a regular time in which to practice, and your moral support will be appreciated by both student and teacher.

This card will be presented for inspection at the close of each quarter.

Amount of practice per day recommended..................

Voice I, 15 Minutes *Voice II, 30 Minutes* *Voice III, 45 Minutes*
Voice IV, 45 Minutes

Parent or Guardian Sign Below: ....Vocal Instructor

1st Quarter...................3rd Quarter...................

2nd Quarter...................4th Quarter...................

Note: The reverse side of East Orange form provides space for student to indicate in minutes the time he practices each week from September through June.

If classes are numerous and large, a written record of students' progress is very helpful in teaching and guidance. The form on p. 394 is for voice classes and provides for evaluation of three different individual performances of the same composition.

VOICE CLASS ACCOMPLISHMENT RECORD

Student's Name..Home Room.................

Date..Final Grade...............

Song Title.........................Composer...............................

Source...

Memory–Words	Music	Rhythm	Enunciation & Pronunciation
1.	1.	1.	1. ....
2.	2.	2.	2. ....
3.	3.	3.	3. ....

Phrasing and Interpretation	Vocal Technique & Tone	Total Effectiveness
1.	1.	1. ....
2.	2.	2. ....
3.	3.	3. ....

REMARKS:

3. Instrumentation and Formation of Bands and Orchestras

Although many high schools are striving for bands and orchestras of symphonic proportions, we recognize that this is impossible in many situations. The enclosed diagrams of various size orchestras and bands include the instrumentation as well as the seating plan.[1]

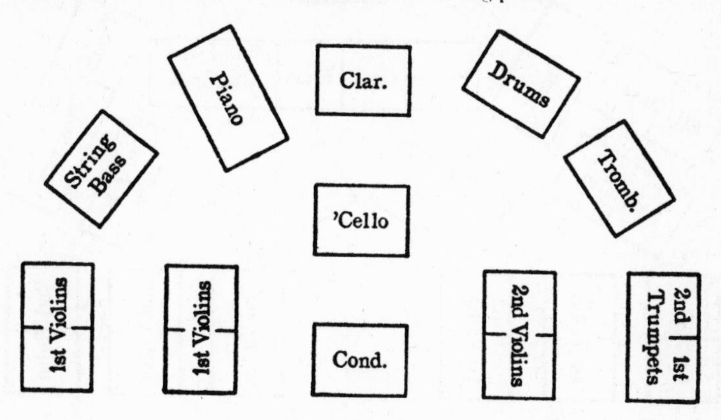

No. 1. Orchestra of 13 Players and Piano

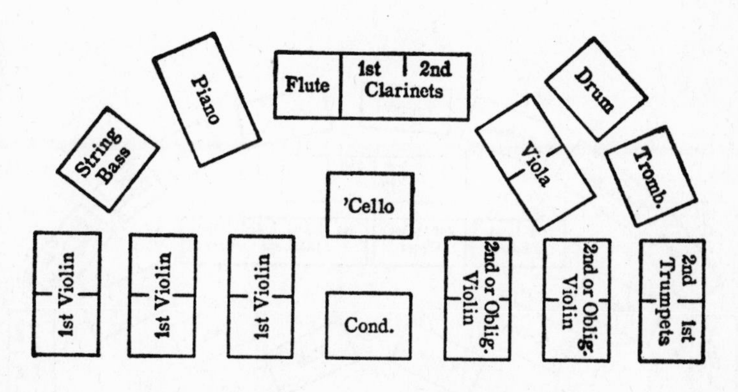

No. 2. Orchestra of 21 Players and Piano

[1] John W. Beattie, Osbourne McConathy, Russell V. Morgan, *Music in the Junior High School;* New York: Silver Burdett Company, 1938.

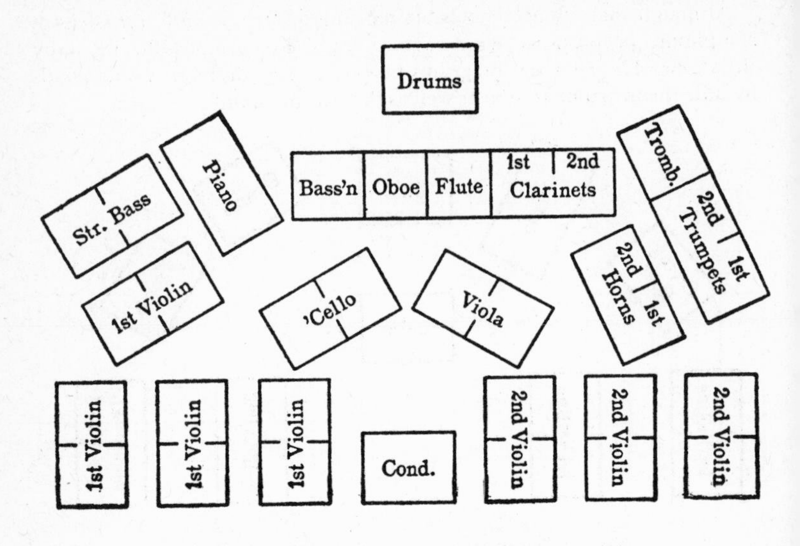

No. 3. Orchestra of 31 Players and Piano

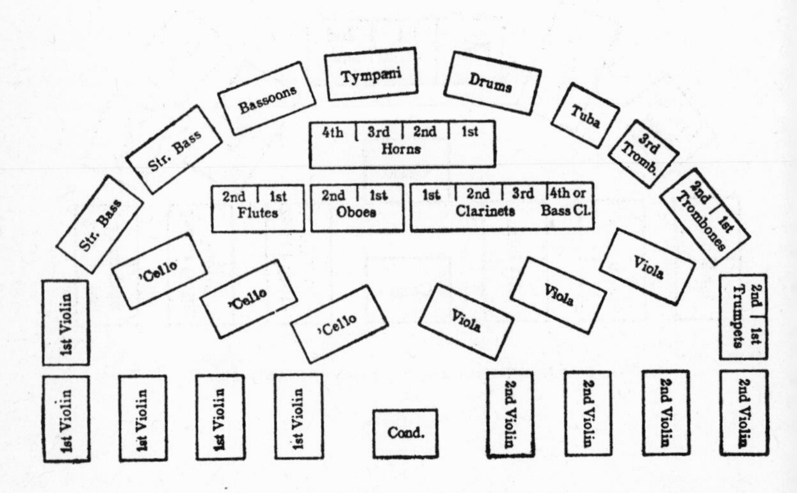

No. 4. Orchestra of 58 Players

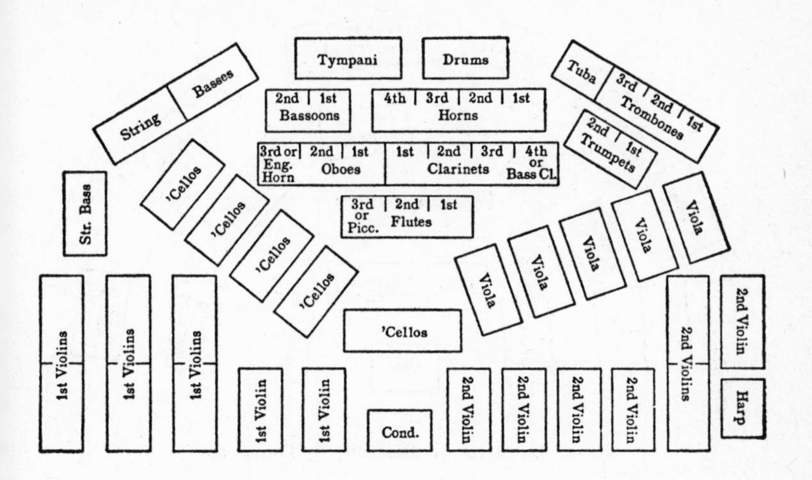

No. 5. Orchestra of 80 Players (Symphony)

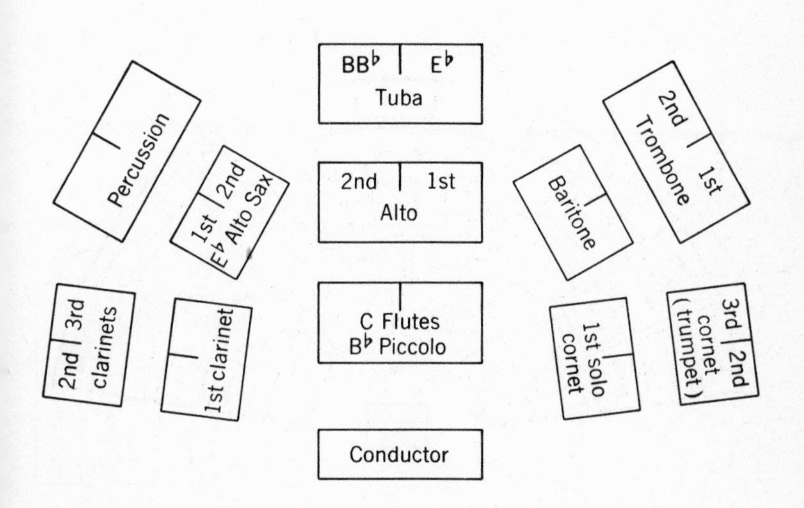

No. 1. Band of 21 Players (2 Drummers)

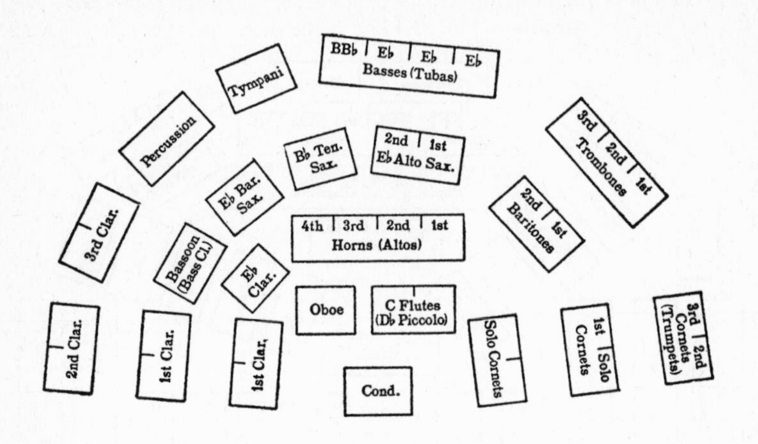

No. 2. Band of 40 Players (3 Drummers)

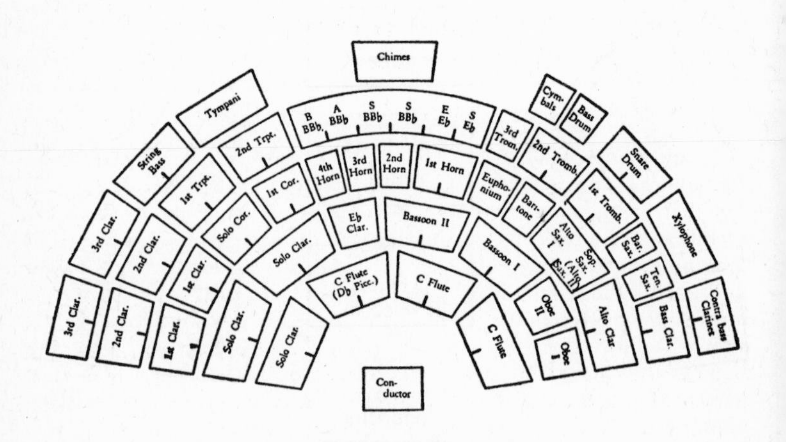

No. 3. Seating Arrangement for a 75 Piece Symphonic Band

Formations for the marching band will vary according to the instrumentation of the individual school bands. The following diagrams give some idea for variation. The first one is the usual formation for a small military band. It has been adopted by many schools.

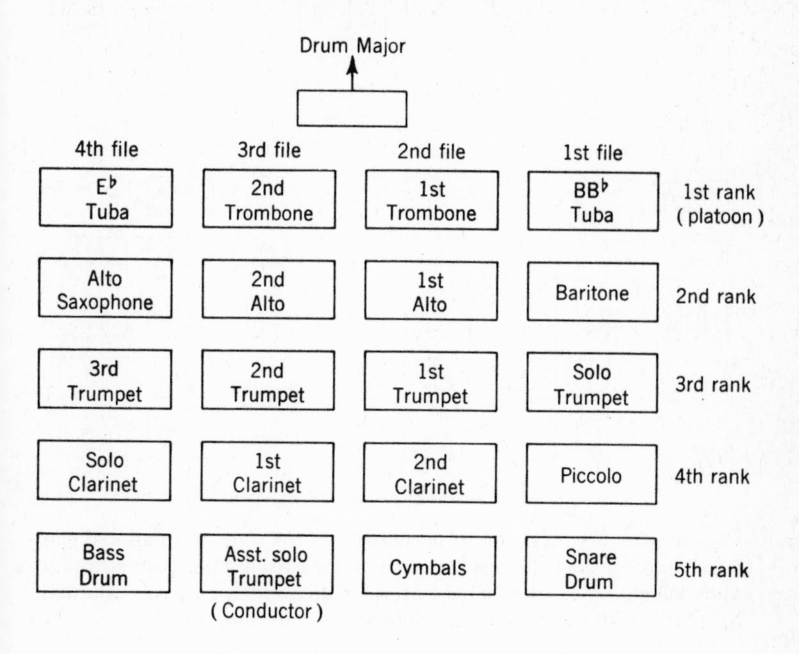

1. Marching Band of 20 Players

Many school conductors have been experimenting with different formations from the preceding one, especially for large bands. They point out that, in the older formation, the melody is often lost to the other members of the band by placing the solo instruments toward the front and in the outside files. Also, they point out that the fundamental bass is not heard by the band when the tubas are placed in the front ranks. In large bands many conductors place the drums in the center to provide a strong beat for young players. Some conductors compare the marching band to the chorus and arrange the instruments according to the voice parts, as far as possible. In the following formation of a marching symphonic band, most of these suggestions are followed. Undoubtedly, this arrangement gives a more cohesive musical quality to the playing of a large band. If fewer drums are desired than indicated in the diagram, these files may remain open.

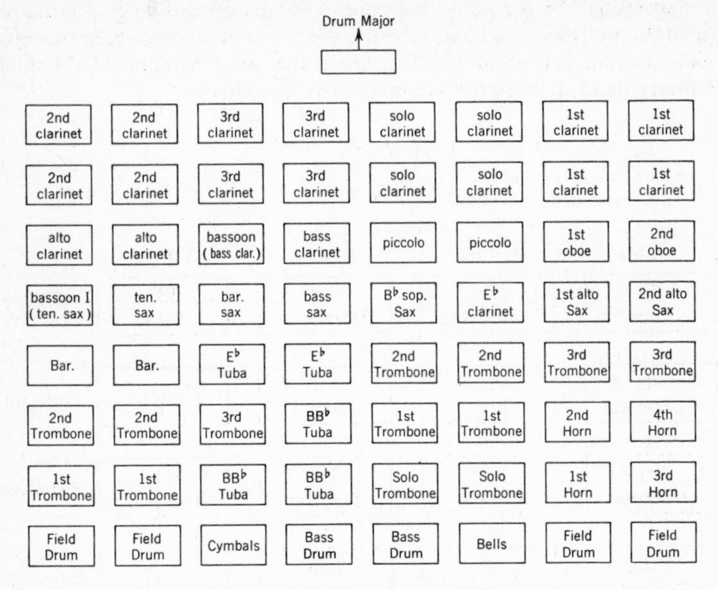

2. Marching Band of 64 Players

Those schools who desire to participate in the state and national contests should consider the instrumentation for various class orchestras and bands suggested in the School-Music Competition-Festivals Manual, 1941, Music Educators National Conference, Chicago, Illinois.

4. Credit for Outside Study

(*See* Chapter XIV.)

Twelve States Accrediting Teachers of Private Music (As summarized by Marjorie Dwyer, Oklahoma College for Women, Chickasha, Oklahoma)

1. Alabama

   Certification by examination through State Department of Education. Permanent and temporary certificates, credit granted to high school students for private study with accredited teachers. (one unit)

2. Arkansas
   Accrediting teachers based entirely upon college credits. No examination conducted. Credit granted to high school students for private study with an accredited teacher.
3. Idaho
   Applied teachers of music in piano, voice, instruments accredited by State Department of Education if holding a degree (music) from accredited institution.
4. Kansas
   Certification by State Department of Education.
5. Louisiana
   Issues certificate only upon degree completion. No life certificate issued. Issued directly through Department of Education.
6. Montana
   Certification of music teachers administered by examinations given to their students.
7. Missouri
   Certification by examination through an applied music board consisting of State Music Teachers Association, University of Missouri, and State Department of Education.
8. Nevada
   Does not credit private music teachers.
9. North Dakota
   Applied teachers of piano, voice, violin certified through examination by board from State Department of Education or equivalent of 94 credits toward music degree.
10. Oklahoma
    A person is eligible for a music certificate of accredited private teaching if he has earned a certain number of hours' credit in music subjects and academic subjects combined, from an institution of higher learning which is recognized by the State Department of Education; to be exact, 90 hours for a one-year certificate; 120 hours, carrying a degree, for a life certificate.
11. South Carolina
    Accrediting of teachers by examination of their students. Certificates issued to students through South Carolina Music Teachers' Association.
12. Texas
    Accrediting of teachers by examination of their students. Certificates issued by State Department of Education.

Credits for Private Music Study, Wichita, Kansas

Application for Outside Music Credit

Wichita Public Schools

Wichita High School ....

Student's Signature .... Parent's Signature ....

Address .... Telephone ....

Grade in school .... Average school grade past semester .... Voice .... Instrumental .... No. of years previously studied .... Name of past teachers ....

Name of present teacher ....

Address .... Name of any music class in school this semester ....

No. of years in Glee Club or Chorus .... Band or Orchestra .... Credit received for previous outside music .... Lessons per week .... Length of each lesson .... Any ensemble training during the lesson or at other times in connection with the lesson ....

Do you intend to specialize in music at college ....

Date filed ....

....

Head of Music Department

....

Registrar of High School

Outside Music Credit Requirements

No credit will be given for less than one full year of lessons or for more than three years.

All students desiring credit must file application with the Head of the Music Department within one week after the opening of the semester.

One-year of lessons within the past three years and previous to the date of enrollment for school credit.

Not less than 18 lessons per semester.

No credit given for lessons taken previous to the date of enrollment.

Nine (9) hours per week practice required.

Piano students must take one (1) semester of harmony, history, appreciation of theory to each semester of outside music for credit.

Vocal and instrumental students must take glee club, chorus, band or orchestra for each semester of outside credit.

All lessons must be made up before the semester ends, or not later than three weeks after the semester ends. This pertains to first (1) semester only. All second semester lessons must be finished one week before commencement. No one excused from final examinations for this credit.

No student may take more than one (1) outside music credit lesson per week, unless given permission by the Registrar and the Head of the Music Department.

No credit will be given where more than two (2) lessons have been missed in one term of six weeks, unless excused by the Registrar and the Head of the Music Department.

The Head of the Music Department has the privilege of denying credit to any one at the end of any semester for not fulfilling the above requirements.

5. Financing Trips

In Chapter XIV, there is a brief statement about trips taken by school music organizations to perform at festivals, contests, etc. One of the problems incidental to such trips is that of expense. A letter was sent to several music instructors in various parts of the country, asking what methods of financing were found most practicable. Brief quotations from their replies are given here.

Gerald R. Prescott, Director of Bands, University of Minnesota, Minneapolis, Minnesota:

(1) At Ida Grove, Iowa, we raised money by concerts, benefits, and local contributions by business men and others.
(2) At Mason City, Iowa, every instrumental music student (grades and high school) pays 25¢ a week for the instruction received in the schools. This is paid quarterly at $3.00 per payment.
(3) At Iowa City, Iowa, *Superintendent Iver A. Opstead* believed in having the Band Parents Club sponsor various benefits far enough in advance so that the school year started with the funds raised.
(4) Activity Tickets for all activities of the school which set aside cash for music trips.
(5) Some schools in this territory have the students pay a part of the transportation cost even though other money is raised as a group.
(6) At Mason City before the Tuition fund was used for travel, the President of the Board used to take it upon himself to secure donations for trips to the National. It was his personal opinion that the high school should make the effort to raise the money for all district and state contests, and the obligation of the city to send the band to the nationals after winning the state.
(7) A few schools report that their Board of Education vote the necessary funds for trips.

W. Gibson Walters, Texas State College for Women, Denton, Texas:

(1) All expenses paid by school board (in wealthy school districts where there is a great deal of oil money. There are only a few of these.)
(2) Students themselves paying for all the expenses (but in some cases where a student is financially unable to take care of his expenses, they are taken care of by the school when a note is written from home, saying that the parents are unable to make the expenditure.)
(3) Raising the money through concerts given by the organization and other projects such as the selling of doughnuts and generally accepted food stuffs, carnivals, wind shield stickers, band organization plates to be attached to automobile licenses, movie tickets

on a commission basis, skating parties, dances, concessions at various high school athletic activities (some high school athletic associations grant the band a stipulated sum for their performance at football games, basketball games, etc.)

(4) Donations from merchants and private cars donated.

Lois J. Scott, Seattle Public Schools, Seattle, Washington:

"Our boys have done a great deal of singing at Civic Clubs throughout the city which has necessitated our taking special buses to and from performances. When there have been several during the year, our principal has helped pay for the transportation, the boys paying half and the school the other half.

"We have met with no opposition so far from either parents or children in regard to their paying all or part of the cash.

"Before the Civic Clubs were hit with so many welfare activities, they paid in full for the transportation of all the groups and in addition a 'lollypop,' ice cream cone, or such, at the end of the program."

David Hughes, Director of Instrumental Music, Elkhart, Indiana:

"In the fall of 1939 we were invited to Detroit to appear on one of the programs of the Music Educators Conference.

"I was anxious to have the students go and in taking it up with the Board of Education, they said we could go if we did not have to go out and beg for the money and if we could do enough playing on the program to warrant the expense. Our part of the program was 30 minutes. We also played at noon for a 30-minute program. It cost around $500.00 to make the trip.

"We have a rule established in our school that any small ensemble such as a string quartet, should pay their own expenses if they are going to appear before any conference or festival program."

Frederic Fay Swift, Chairman, Region 4, National School Band Association:

"In Ilion we finance our trips entirely through the receipts of our music programs and personal assessments levied on individual students. For example, a student may sell tickets for our various programs and the balance which we have in our treasury at the end of the year is apportioned so that a certain percentage of the tickets which a student has sold is credited toward his costs. This year we are allowing 40% of the total amount which the students have sold. In this way some students may earn all of their expenses."

Marcia E. Lampert, Supervisor of Music, Public Schools, Lexington, Kentucky:

"There were approximately 125 girls and boys in the group; I visited the local Greyhound Bus Terminal Office and found that it would take two large buses and one small one to accommodate the group. They quoted me a price which we pro-rated. The round trip amounted to about $1.80 per person. They returned to Lexington the same day. The three chaperones' fares were accounted for in the amount charged."

W. P. Twaddell, Supervisor of Music, Public Schools, Durham, North Carolina:

"Some twelve years ago we were invited to carry our 'Children's Choir' (elementary school age) to Boston—(the Federation of Music Clubs Convention). The Monarch's Club of Durham sponsored this project—collected from the community the necessary funds—planned the whole trip and took the group from Durham to Boston with no responsibility thrown upon our organization save that of chaperonage.

"Since then our major 'trips' have been to sectional music educators conferences. The most costly to Louisville in 1939. One of the mothers of our children undertook the leadership in this project. She was instrumental in collecting about ⅓ the necessary total cost ($2900). The children themselves provided the balance."

Paul Van Bodegraven, Assoc. Prof. of Music Ed., University of Missouri, Columbia, Missouri:

"Our trip to the Eastern Music Educators Conference in 1939 was financed by giving two public concerts and by having the students pay part of their own expenses. We have attended contest festivals since 1934 at points as far distant as Cleveland and Columbus, Ohio. In the main, the following methods have been used to raise money:

(1) Two public concerts a year, one by the band and one by the orchestra and choral groups.
(2) One benefit movie a year. We have had an arrangement with the local movie house whereby we received approximately 40% of all ticket sales made before the night of the movie. The band would usually appear on the program.
(3) One benefit bridge sponsored by parents of band and orchestra members.
(4) When we have needed additional money that could not be raised by the above methods, some of the students who had a dance band of their own would give a dance and donate their services, the returns of which would go into our fund.

(5) On two occasions we found it necessary to ask for individual contributions by private citizens and civic organizations. This, however, was handled by the local newspaper. It took the responsibility of raising sufficient funds to send our groups to the National Competitions at Cleveland and Columbus. We do not like this method since it implies obligations. Normally we propose to raise money through methods which will give the patron a return for his money which would be great enough so as not to leave any organization obligated to any particular individual or group.

In addition to the above methods, the students would be expected to save a certain amount each and accumulate enough by contest time to pay for either their meals or their lodging."

Chester Hayden, Supervisor of Music, Public Schools, Dinuba, California:

"From 1932-1940 I was connected with the small school system (Dinuba High School) and during this time we took about sixteen long-distance trips—200 miles or more—and following are some of the things we did in order to accomplish our goals.

I. Invitation
II. Secure consent of Principal and Board of Trustees
III. Secure consent of Parent; explaining all details; giving plan; a return slip was to be signed by parent and student.
IV. Extensive advertising
 1. About honor of receiving invitation. 2. Need help of school and community in order to go. 3. Purpose. 4. Worthwhileness.
V. Financing campaign
 A. Transportation
  1. School furnished one bus, driver, gas
  2. School furnished one luggage car, driver, gas
  3. Interested parents furnished extra cars if needed
   a. Parents drove, also acted as chaperones
   b. Gas furnished by school
   c. Lodging for all parents, chaperones, and bus driver paid from funds raised for trip
 B. Food
  1. Each person was left responsible for providing for his own meals.
  (Note) In some cases where financial embarrassment seemed to exist all expenses were taken from the fund. This was strictly private between director and student.

In many cases parents who were able to take care of all expenses did so. All this was handled through the questionnaire sent to the parents as in Part III. It was often found that as many as one-third of the parents were willing to take care of all expenses.

C. Housing

1. Hotel
2. Private Homes

(Note) On nearly all occasions we stayed in hotels. Girls and boys on different floors. Two or more in a room. All group expenses were paid by the director. (Checks used). Director was repaid upon return. Many times the money was deposited to the director's checking account before leaving. When we stayed in private homes we usually worked through a church or churches giving concerts to help pay our way.

D. Methods used for raising funds

1. Solicit donations from well-to-do people.
2. Benefit concerts
3. Concerts
4. Selling season tickets at beginning of year
5. Donations from Chamber of Commerce; Service clubs; P.T.A., Churches (we would give a series of sacred concerts and keep the collection)
6. Secure help from student body
7. Secure help from Board of Trustees"

Dean E. Douglass, Supervisor of Fine Arts, Department of Public Schools, Jefferson, Missouri:

"In our area there are three methods of financing trips: First, expenses paid by the Board of Education; second, expenses paid from some activity fund, either belonging to the school or supported by P.T.A. or parent group activities; third, expenses paid by parents of participating students.

"There is an element connected with transportation which is poorly considered by many people; namely: the element of risk. It is never wise for any school, individual, or group to be transported in any conveyance not properly covered by insurance. The element of risk is far more important than the element of expenses in dollars and cents. Probably the fastest and most convenient method is by chartered bus, particularly inasmuch as it remains usable and convenient at the point of destination. Such is not true of trains nor is it usually true of private cars."

Ruth Hill, Director of Music, Public Schools, Anderson, Indiana:

"(1) We have never received any amount of money from the school board. They gave us the use of buildings for benefits, of course.
(2) I, as the director, always paid my own way.
(3) I took 4 girls to the National Chorus in Los Angeles last year, and their parents paid all expenses.

Of course, the backbone of a campaign was our parents organization. This was a working unit the year through so that money was always being raised. The newspapers were splendid to cooperate, and always served as a depository for citizens who wished to aid.

However, the bulk of our budget was raised by benefits. I list some of the most successful.

1. Lecturers
2. Sponsoring Movies
3. Cafeteria suppers
4. Tag day
5. After-school dances
6. Civic clubs (women) gave parties in their homes"

6. Diagrams of Rooms and Equipment

The following drawings and diagrams show practical music rooms and equipment that has been used with success in actual school situations. Sufficient details are given in the drawings to enable any competent workman to build much of the equipment:[1]

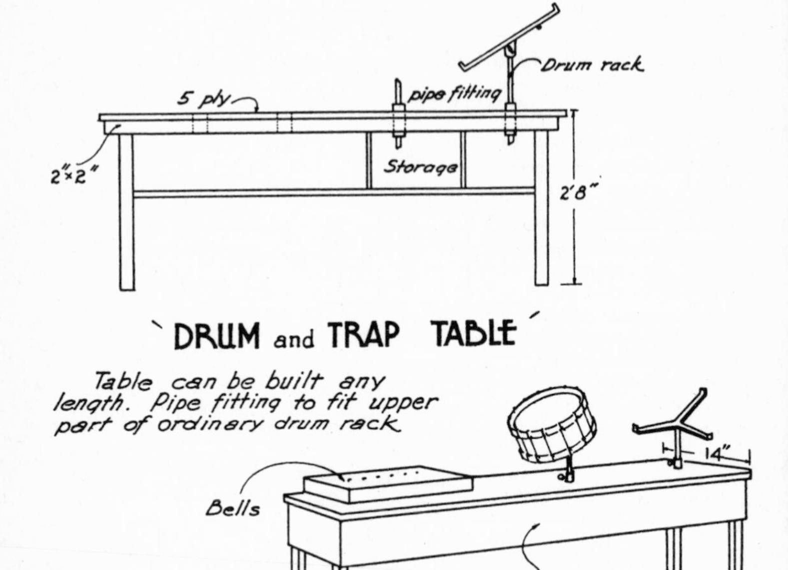

[1] Course of Study, State of Oregon High Schools, *Music*. Issued by Rex Putnam, Superintendent of Public Instruction, Oregon State Printing Department, 1940. Used by permission.

PORTABLE RISER

Submitted by Chester Duncan, Music Supervisor
Portland Schools

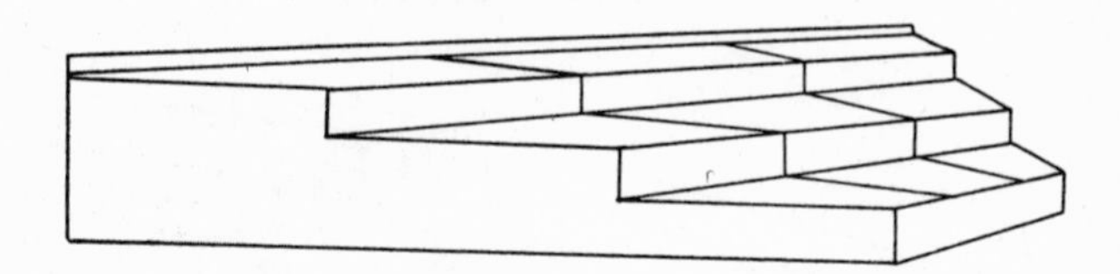

To make complete assembly 8 of each unit should be used. Risers can be combined in any combination. 5-ply wood for floor, 3-ply wood for exposed sides and back. Added features: drawers in rear of units for instruments, sockets and removable casters on sides for ease in moving.

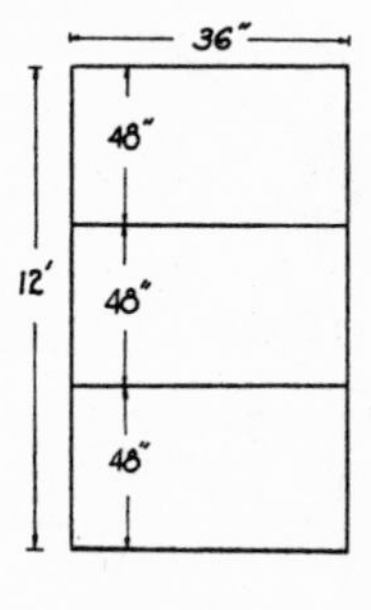

UNIT # 1.

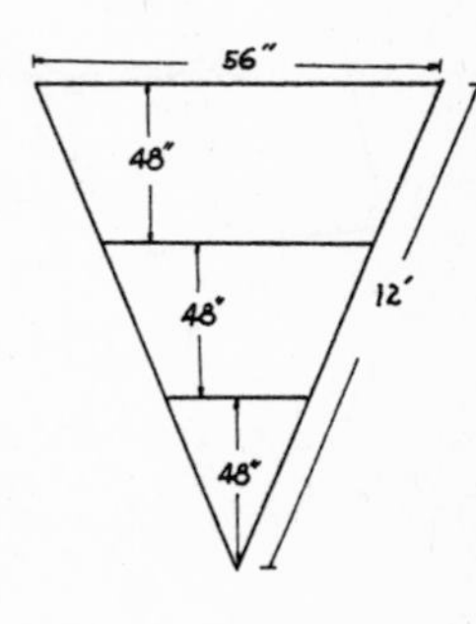

UNIT # 2

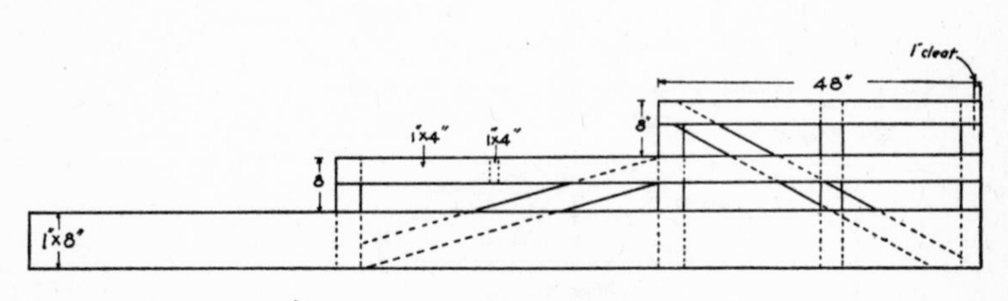

Side view showing braces

KNOCK DOWN RISER FOR CHORUS

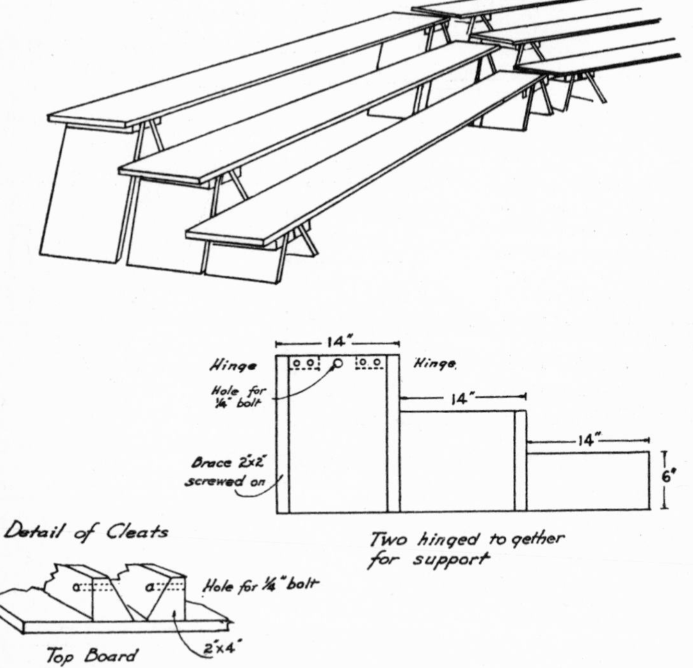

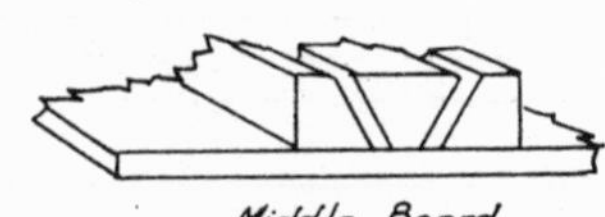

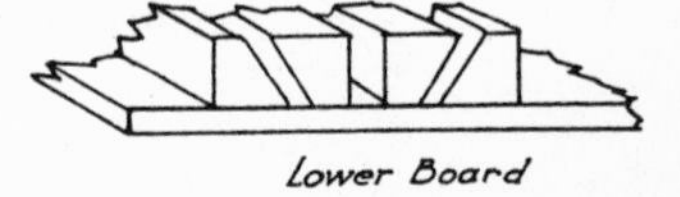

BASS DRUM RACKS

Submitted by Chester Duncan Music Supervisor
Portland Schools

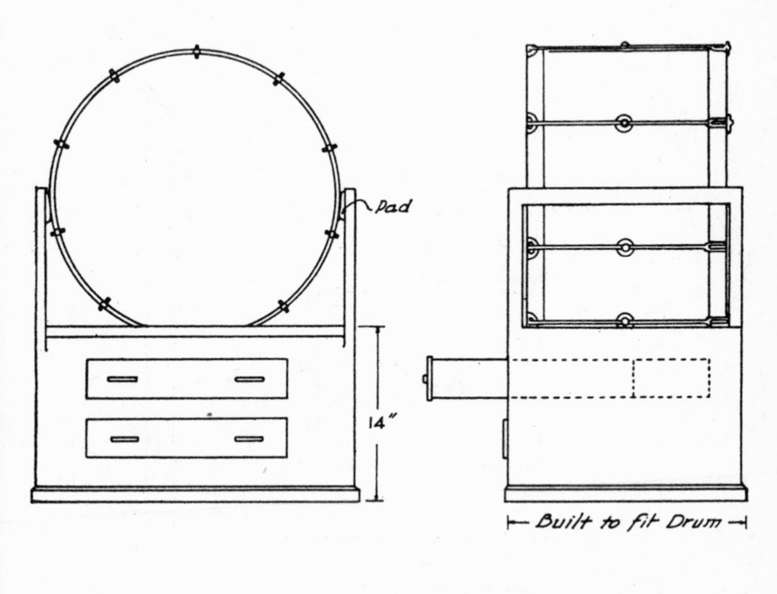

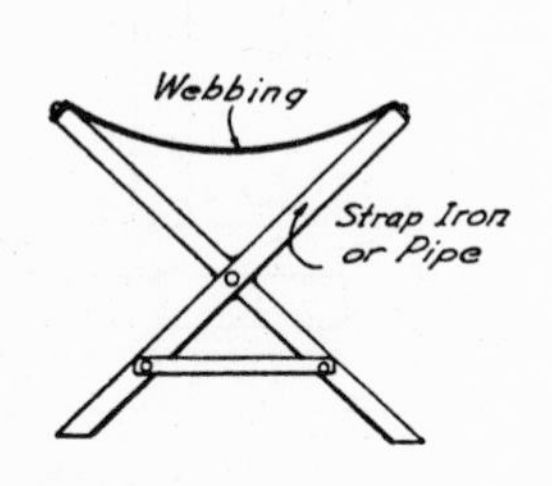

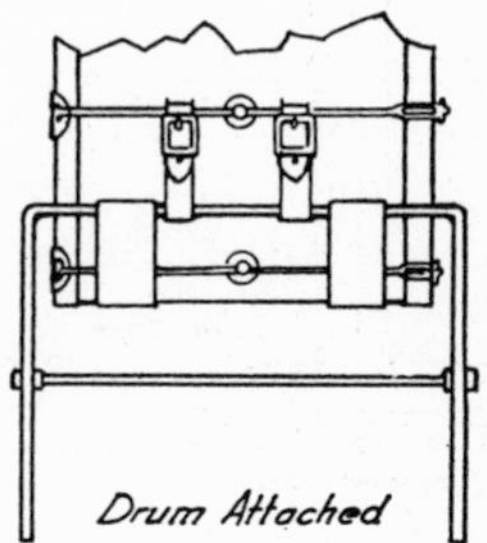

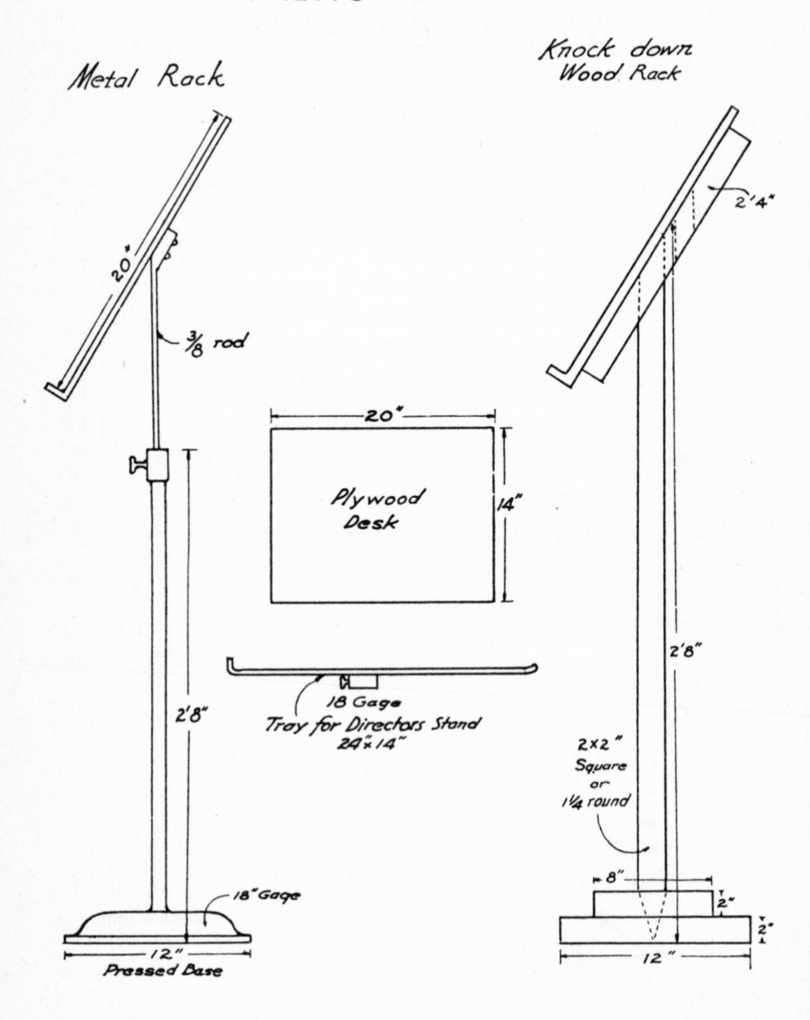
MUSIC RACKS
Metal Rack
20"
3/8 rod
2'8"
18" Gage
12"
Pressed Base
20"
Plywood
Desk
14"
18 Gage
Tray for Directors Stand
24" x 14"
Knock down
Wood Rack
2'4"
2'8"
2x2"
Square
or
1¼ round
8"
2"
2"
12"

APPENDIX B

Materials

A good teacher is ever on the search for better materials. In fact, a music program can almost be evaluated by the kind of materials used. We believe that the final service to our readers can be rendered in no better way than by suggesting materials that have proved successful in teaching situations. This list of materials is by no means complete. In fact, in this book it is definitely limited. However, it does represent material which has demonstrated its worth and which will warrant careful examination. Few classic composers are represented in the individual numbers for their compositions are usually found in the collections. The small list of individual numbers suggests a few titles which have been used by the author.

A list of materials of this kind is especially designed to help the young teacher during his first years of teaching. After he has gained experience he undoubtedly will be acquainted with many sources to which he can turn. At first, however, a young teacher is often confused with the long lists which he may receive from publishers. The materials found in this appendix may be ordered with a certain degree of assurance. It is usually best to order collections at first until a fairly complete library is obtained.

For a longer and more complete list of materials we recommend to all teachers the *School Music Competition-Festivals Manual*, published by the Music Educators National Conference. This manual is published every year for the state and national contests. It represents the selection made by special committees and includes instrumental and choral music for both small and large ensembles.

As a final word, we caution every teacher of music to be searching constantly for more interesting material. Do not rely entirely upon hackneyed numbers. Experiment with novelties occasionally. Dull selections can hamper musical activities as much as any one factor. The time spent on seeking new materials will be remunerated by more satisfying classes and rehearsals. *Let music itself do much of your work.*

General Reading

The books suggested for general reading should be *owned* and *studied* by every teacher of music in the high school. They will prove invaluable in gaining a general background in the arts as well as a broader and deeper point of view of music education. The number included has been limited to a "must" list.

1. *Secondary Education.* Briggs, Thomas H. The Macmillan Publishing Co. Price: $2.75.[1]

   A comprehensive treatment of secondary education, including an historical summary and the current controversial issues.

2. *Curriculum Development.* Caswell, H. and Campbell, D. S. The American Book Co. Price: $2.50.

   An enlightened discussion of the trends in curriculum development.

3. *Art As Experience.* Dewey, John. Minton, Balch & Co. Price: $4.00.

   One of the most searching studies in the field of aesthetics.

4. *The Arts.* Van Loon, Hendrik. Simon and Schuster. Price: $3.95.

   A survey of all the arts written in a conversational style. Delightful reading, very informative, but not always factually authoritative. Illustrations not to be taken too seriously.

5. *Yearbooks.* Music Educators National Conference, 64 East Jackson Boulevard, Chicago, Illinois. Price: $2.50.

   The Reports of the Annual Proceedings of the Music Educators National Conference. Invaluable professional guides for all music teachers.

6. *Psychology of School Music Teaching.* Mursell, James L. and Glenn, Mabelle. Silver Burdett Co. Price: $2.40.

   A book that has had far-reaching effect upon the procedures of teaching music in recent years.

7. *The New School Music Handbook.* Dykema, Peter W. C. C. Birchard and Co. Price: $3.50.

   One of the most useful books published on music education. Literally, an encyclopedia of theory, practice, and material in the field of school music.

8. *Music in History.* McKinney, Howard D., and Anderson, W. R. American Book Co. Price: $5.00.

   A readable discussion of the place that music and the other arts have played in the history of mankind.

9. *Music Educators Journal.* Music Educators National Conference, 64 East Jackson Boulevard, Chicago, Illinois. Price: $1.00 per year.

   The official organ of the national and sectional music conferences. Every music teacher in the schools should be a member of the Conference and a subscriber to this journal. Articles are helpful and, what is more important, they enable the teacher to be professionally informed.

Music Appreciation and History Textbooks

1. *A Short History of Music.* Einstein, Alfred. Alfred A. Knopf. Price: $3.00.

[1] All prices of materials quoted are list prices at the time of writing. Publishers may make some changes in these quotations.

The high spots of music history written in an interesting manner. A large number of music examples.

2. *Discovering Music*. McKinney, Howard D., and Anderson, W. R. American Book Co. Price: $3.25.
   An informal approach to the study of music appreciation. Correlates material with the other arts.
3. *Listening to Music*. Moore, Douglas. W. W. Norton. Price: $3.00.
   An approach to music as a tonal language through a study of its elements.
4. *Making Friends With Music*. Hartshorn, William C., and Leavitt, Helen S. Ginn and Co. Price: student books, $.60 each.

Teacher's Manuals	Pupils' Books	
1. The Pilot, $2.00	1. Prelude	2. Progress
2. The Mentor, $2.40	3. At Home and Abroad	4. New Horizons

   A new and complete series of books for the study of music appreciation at various levels in the school. Well organized for both student and teacher.
5. *Music Appreciation for the Junior High School*. Glenn, Mabelle, and Lowry, Margaret. Silver Burdett Co. Price: Teacher's Manual, $.80; Music Notes, Book Four, $.32; Music Notes, Book Five, $.40
   A standard series of books for music appreciation used widely in high schools.

Music Theory Textbooks

1. *An Approach to Harmony*. McConathy, Embs, Howes, Fouser. Silver Burdett Co. Price: $1.76.
   An interesting approach to the study of harmony which draws its materials from actual music and emphasizes creative work.
2. *Applied Harmony*. Alchin, Carolyn A. L. R. Jones. Price: $2.00.
   A text that has proved popular because it takes a musical approach to the study of harmony.
3. *Harmony for Ear, Eye, and Keyboard*. Heacox, A. E. Oliver Ditson Co. Price: $1.50.
   A simple and concise approach to harmony which combines written work with ear-training and keyboard harmony.

Choral Collections

Community and Assembly Song Books

1. *Favorite Songs* (The Blue Book). Hall and McCreary. Prices: $.75 each, postpaid; two or more, $.60 each, postpaid; $.48 each, transportation extra.

Includes all the songs in the Golden and Gray books. Provides a wide variety of songs for school and community use. Printed on heavier paper than the lower-priced, separate editions. Covers made of strong and attractive textbook cloth.

2. *Keep on Singing*. Paull-Pioneer Music Corp. Price: $.25 each.

   A melodious collection of folk songs, art songs, part-songs, and other material suitable for unison or choral singing. A wide variety of composers represented.

3. *Singing America*. C. C. Birchard Co. Price: $.25 each.

   Here in 120 songs and choruses is a comprehensive variety of fresh, lastingly lovable music for informal singing in homes, schools, recreation centers, clubs, and camps.

4. *Songs We Sing*. Hall and McCreary. Price: $.25 each; 100 or more, $.20 each.

   A new and excellent collection of songs suited to every singing occasion. The book includes complete piano accompaniments.

5. *Twice 55 Plus Community Songs* (The Brown Book). C. C. Birchard & Co. Prices: vocal edition, $.15 (paper cover); $.45 (cloth cover); complete edition (cloth cover), $1.50. Orchestration is available, each instrumental part, $.75.

   A fine collection of 175 of the world's best loved songs. Most harmonizations for mixed voices. Few numbers arranged for treble and male voices. One section devoted to responsive readings.

6. *Twice 55 Plus Community Songs* (The Green Book). C. C. Birchard & Co. Prices: vocal edition, $.25 (paper cover); $.55 (cloth cover); complete edition (cloth cover), $2.00.

   The second book in the "Twice 55" series. Contains special program numbers, selections from the famous operas and oratorios, distinctive choruses from the great composers, representative folk songs from many nations, and songs for special occasions. Suitable for assembly singing and various choral groups.

General Chorus

1. *Master Choruses*. Smallman-Matthews. Oliver Ditson Co. Prices: choral edition, $1.00; complete edition, $3.00.

   Outstanding anthems and varied choruses of the master composers, 49 in all. Especially suitable for large choruses in high school, college, church, or community.

2. *Music of Many Lands and Peoples*. McConathy, Beattie, Morgan. Silver Burdett Co. Price: $1.52.

   A complete and an easy collection of choral numbers designed for both the classroom and the program.

3. *Music, the Universal Language*. McConathy, Lindsay, Morgan. Silver Burdett Co. Price: $1.92.

A new collection of song and choral material, beautifully illustrated. Has a direct and realistic appeal to the interests of young people from its choice of music representative of all eras of recorded history, especially the modern American unit. Suitable for classwork, assembly, general chorus, selected ensembles, and concert programs in high schools and colleges.

4. *Program Choruses* (The Red Book). Hall and McCreary. Prices: 1-3 (paper cover), $.40 each; 4-49, $.36 each, postpaid; 50 or more, $.30 each, transportation extra; (cloth cover), $.80 each, postpaid; 2 or more, $.72 each, postpaid, or $.60 each, transportation extra.

   A variety of delightful program numbers, 79 in all. Includes numbers for mixed voices, both accompanied and a cappella, girls' voices, boys' voices, and a few in unison.

5. *Program Choruses* (The Green Book). Hall and McCreary. Prices: Same as "Red Book" above.

   Organization similar to that of the "Red Book." Choruses somewhat more difficult. Suitable for the high school or even college groups.

6. *Senior Laurel Songs*. Armitage, Teresa M. C. C. Birchard & Co. Price: student's edition, $1.68; teacher's edition, $4.00.

   A standard collection of songs and choruses used in many high schools for assemblies and the general chorus.

A Cappella Choir

1. *A Cappella Chorus, The*. Jones-Krone. M. Witmark and Sons. Published in five volumes. Price: $.60 each.

   Very fine selection of material with musical value. The following volumes suitable for high school: Volume III—S. A. B.—16 numbers—medium to difficult; Volume IV—S. A. T. B.—12 numbers—easy to medium; Volume V—S. A. T. B.—10 numbers—medium to moderately difficult.

2. *A Cappella Primer, The*. Horton. Willis Music Company. Price: $.60 each.

   First introduction to a cappella singing. 20 numbers in all, offering wide variety.

3. *A Cappella Chorus Book, The*. Christiansen-Cain. Oliver Ditson Co. Price: $1.00 each.

   A standard collection of a cappella numbers, 27 in all, well chosen and edited.

4. *Art of A Cappella Singing, The*. Smallman and Wilcox. Oliver Ditson Co. Price: $2.00 each.

   A guide to a cappella singing as well as a collection of 14 standard numbers.

5. *Junior A Cappella Chorus, The.* Christiansen-Pitts. Oliver Ditson Co. Price: $1.00 each.
   38 numbers in all. Designed to fit the needs of the beginning choir.
6. *Select A Cappella Choruses.* Cain. Hall and McCreary. Prices: 1-11 copies, $.20 each; 12 or more, $2.16 a dozen, transportation extra.
   14 carefully selected numbers at a very reasonable price.
7. *Singing Through the Ages.* Harris-Evanson. American Book Co. Price: vol. I, $1.60. vol. II, $1.95.
   Volume I—Melodic and Harmonic Songs
   Volume II—Contrapuntal Songs
   New collections of challenging numbers for organizations interested in the best in music literature.

Treble Voices

1. *Concert Songs.* Armitage. C. C. Birchard & Co. Prices: student edition, $1.25; teacher edition, $3.00.
   An unusually wide variety of numbers, 106 in all, arranged for two-, three-, and four-part treble voices. A few numbers are in unison.
2. *Favorite Choruses.* G. Schirmer. Price: $.60 each.
   Arranged for S.S.A. 13 numbers from Schirmer catalogue, numbers also published separately.
3. *Glenn Glee Club, The.* Glenn and French. Oliver Ditson Co. Price: $1.00 each.
   A collection of 43 folk songs, sacred songs, and art songs arranged for girls of high school age. All arrangements in three parts; a few a cappella.
4. *Repertoire: Songs for Women's Voices.* Bridgman, William C. American Book Co. Price: accompaniment edition, $2.20; student edition, $1.20
   Two volumes of standard repertoire for treble voices.
5. *Seventeen Three-Part Choruses.* Boston Music Company. Price: $.60 each.
   Good selections and arrangements.
6. *Three-Part Choruses for Treble Voices.* Wilson. Hall and McCreary. Prices: 1-11 copies, $.20 each; 12 or more, $2.16 a dozen, transportation extra.
   A collection of unusual arrangements and original numbers with many modern effects.

Male Voices

1. *Basic Songs for Male Voices.* Bridgman. American Book Co. Prices: A cappella edition, $1.56; complete edition, $3.00.

A fine collection with good arrangements, 230 in all. Fills the needs of most high school glee clubs.

2. *Choral Collection*. Harold Flammer. Price: $.60.
   Three-part choruses for boys' voices. Numbers with appeal.
3. *Eighteen Easy Choruses*. Boston Music Co. Price: $.60 each.
   All numbers arranged in three parts. Possible to sing some in unison and two-part.
4. *Glee and Chorus Book for Male Voices*. Towner and Hesser. Silver Burdett Co. Price: $1.28.
   Book of standard selections, many in three-part with which all glee clubs should be familiar.
5. *Three-Part Choruses for Male Voices*. Wilson. Hall and McCreary. Prices: 1-11 copies, $.20 each; 12 or more, $2.16 a dozen, transportation extra.
   Modern and novel effects in these arrangements. Tenors do not go above top line *f* or basses below first line *g*. Arranged for tenor, baritone, and bass. Each part interesting to sing and fun to rehearse.

Voice Class

1. *Art Songs for School and Studio*. Glenn and Spouse. Oliver Ditson. Price: $1.00 each.
   A collection of very good songs published in two volumes. Both volumes issued for medium-high and medium-low voices.
2. *Class Lessons in Singing*. Pierce-Liebling. Silver Burdett Co. Price: $2.00.
   One of the finest books on class lessons; includes excellent songs.
3. *Class Method of Voice Culture*. Clippinger, D. A. Oliver Ditson Co. Price: $1.25.
   A systematic approach to the study of voice. Includes fine songs.
4. *Pathways of Song*. La Forge and Earhart. G. Schirmer, Inc. Price: $1.00.
   A large collection of songs published in two volumes. Each volume published for high and low voices.
5. *The Singing Road*. Ward, Arthur E. Carl Fischer, Inc. Price: $1.00.
   21 selected classical and modern songs. Supplemented with 11 Vaccaj exercises. For medium-high and medium-low voices.
6. *Solo Singer, The*. Wilson. Carl Fischer, Inc. Price: $.60 each.
   A new collection of songs and exercises, reasonably priced. Songs designed to illustrate various principles of singing.
7. *Universal Song*. Haywood, Frederick H. G. Schirmer, Inc. Price: $.75 each volume.
   A voice-culture course in three volumes for the studio and the classroom. Includes some of F. Sieber's eight-measure vocalises.

Individual Choral Numbers

General Chorus

Title	Composer and Arranger	Publisher	P *	D **	Description
By Babylon's Wave	Gounod	Birchard	$.15	5	Stirring
Come to the Fair	Martin-Brower	Boosey	.15	3	A lively favorite
Dedication (Widmung)	Franz	Flammer	.15	2	May be sung a cappella
Festival Prelude, A	Bach-Stoessel	Birchard	.25	2	Based on three chorales and one choral-prelude
God Bless America	Berlin	Berlin	.35	1	Wide popular appeal
Lift Every Voice and Sing	Johnson	Marks	.15	1	Negro national hymn
Morning	Speaks	G. Schirmer	.15	2	Two contrasting moods
Old King Cole	Forsyth	J. Fischer	.15	2	Humorous
Onward, Ye People	Sibelius	Galaxy	.15	3	Festival number
Prologue	Schumann, W.	G. Schirmer	.20	3	Modern. Orchestra accompaniment available
Psalm CL—Praise Ye the Lord	Franck	Ditson	.20	3	Standard anthem
Romany Life	Liszt-Reibold	Rubank	.30	4	Second Hungarian Rhapsody (May be dramatized)
Sing a While Longer	O'Hara	C. Fischer	.15	2	Incidental soprano or tenor solo
Sleigh, The	Kountz	G. Schirmer	.12	3	Exciting—also a cappella
Star Dust	Carmichael	Mills	.15	2	A popular classic
Take It as It Comes	Sullivan	Boston	.12	2	From "The Gondoliers"
Tales from the Vienna Woods	Strauss	Boosey	.60	4	Popular choral waltz
Ten Miles Away from Home	Holmes	Hoffman	.15	3	Old Oklahoma song
Wassail Song	Davis	E. C. Schirmer	.19	2	Gloucestershire song
Waters Ripple and Flow	Taylor, arr.	J. Fischer	.15	3	Haunting melody
Ye Watchers and Ye Holy Ones	D.T.D.	E. C. Schirmer	.16	2	17th century German-melody

* P—list price
**D—difficulty which is based on a rating scale of 1 to 5

A Cappella Choir—Sacred

Title	Composer and Arranger	Publisher	P	D	Description
Chillun' Come on Home	Cain, arr.	Hoffman	$.15	4	Unusually effective
Emmitte Spiritum Tuum	Schuetky	Birchard	.11	4	S.A.T.T.B.
Holy Child, The	Wilson	Hall & McCreary	.12	2	Easy Christmas number
How Blest Are They	Tschaikowsky	Gamble	.15	5	Worth the effort
Hozanna to the Son of David	Gibbons	Birchard	.25	5	One of the finest numbers from the English Church
Little David, Play on Your Harp	Wilson, arr.	Hall & McCreary	.18	4	Eight-part, rhythmical
Listen to the Lambs	Dett	G. Schirmer	.16	3	Suitable for any program
Lo, a Voice to Heaven Sounding	Bortniansky	E. C. Schirmer	.12	3	Cherubic hymn
Lo, God is Here	Mueller	G. Schirmer	.15	4	Eight-part
Lord Bless You and Keep You, The	Lutkin	Summy	.10	2	Farewell anthem and sevenfold amen
Passion Trilogy, The	Koshetz	Witmark		4	Songs of the Ukraine
(1) Trial before Pilate			.15		
(2) Crucifixion			.12		
(3) Resurrection			.15		
Rise Up, My Love, My Fair One	Willard	Oxford	.15	3	Easter
Shepherd's Story, The	Dickinson	H. W. Gray	.15	5	Incidental solos
Were You There	Burleigh	Ricordi	.15	4	A favorite spiritual
A Cappella Choir—Secular					
As Torrents In Summer	Elgar	Novello	.12	2	Has become a classic
Beautiful Dreamer	Foster-Riegger	Flammer	.15	1	Foster's last song
Carol of the Bells	Leontovich-Wilhousky	C. Fischer	.12	2	Ukrainian carol
Christmas Pie, The	Loomis	Birchard	.10	2	Old English melody
Fire, Fire My Heart	Morley	G. Schirmer	.12	5	Five-part madrigal

A Cappella Choir—Secular (continued)

Title	Composer and Arranger	Publisher	P	D	Description
Fireflies	Arranged	E. C. Schirmer	$.12	1	Russian
Goodnight	Wilson	Hall & McCreary	.15	3	A good closing number
Kye Song of the Saint Bride	Clokey	Birchard	.08	1	Delightful
Pretty Little Miss	Horton	Hoffman	.15	4	Kentucky Mountain Tune
Red River Valley	Horton	Hoffman	.12	1	Tennessee Mountain Tune
Scandalize My Name	Pitcher	Birchard	.12	2	Negro folk song
Summer Is A-Comin' In	Fornsete	Novello	.12	3	Significant historically
Voix Celestes	Alcock	Chappell-Harms	.15	3	A humming chorus
Welcome Yule	Parry	Novello	.15	3	Christmas program
Which is the Properest Day to Sing	Arne	Hall & McCreary	.12	2	Sure-fire glee
Treble Voices					
Alleluja	Mozart	Sprague-Coleman	.16	5	Optional second alto
Alphabet	Mozart	H. W. Gray	.10	1	A musical joke
Dance a Cachucha	Sullivan	Boston	.12	2	From "The Gondoliers"
Death of Trenar, The	Brahms	Novello	.16	4	Dramatic; accompaniment includes 2 horns, harp or piano
Father Most Merciful (Panis Angelicus)	Franck-Dies	G. Schirmer	.09	2	Violin or 'cello obbligato
Fly Singing Bird	Elgar	Novello	.25	4	Accompaniment with two violins
God's Blacksmith	Kodaly	Oxford	.12	2	Hungarian Song
Loon, The	Strom	Hall & McCreary	.15	3	Modern harmonies—flute or violin obbligato
Though Philomela Lost Her Love	Morley	Galaxy	.15	2	S.S.A or S.A.T.

Treble Voices (continued)

Title	Composer and Arranger	Publisher	P	D	Description
To A Wild Rose	MacDowell	Schmidt	$.12	1	A favorite
Tulips	Wilson	C. Fischer	.15	2	Encore number
Male Voices					
Band, The	Fishburn	Hall & McCreary	.18	2	A snappy marching song
Broken Melody	Sibelius-Spaeth	G. Schirmer		4	Selection in 5/4 meter
Drums	De Leone	G. Schirmer	.12	1	Two-part
Eight Bells	Bartholomew	G. Schirmer	.20	2	Sea chantey
Good Bye Ol' Paint	Wilson, arr.	Hall & McCreary	.12	1	Cowboy song, three-part
Give a Man a Horse He Can Ride	O'Hara	G. Schirmer	.15	2	A man's song
Heigh-ho	Churchill	Berlin	.12	.1	From the picture "Snow-White"
John Peel	Andrews	H. W. Gray	.15	3	A man's song
Sea Dreams	Wilson	Hall & McCreary	.15	2	On looking into "Treasure Island"
Shadow March	Protheroe	Boston Music	.15	2	Standard number
Singers March, The	From the German	Presser	.12	4	Unusual
Tinker Chorus	De Koven	G. Schirmer	.12	1	Unison chorus from "Robin Hood"
Winter Song	Bullard	Ditson	.15	3	Every club should sing this one
Operetta					
Around the World	Christopher	Hoffman	1.00	1	Pageant-operetta of the nations
Belle of Barcelona	Chaney	Willis ·	1.25	2	Spanish color
Chimes of Normandy	Planquette	Ditson	1.25	3	Perennial favorite

Operetta (continued)

Title	Composer and Arranger	Publisher	P	D	Description
Frantic Physician	Gounod	Silver Burdett	$1.50	5	Comedy by Molière
Gilbert-Sullivan Operettas (1) Iolanthe (2) Mikado, The (3) Patience (4) Pinafore (5) Pirates of Penzance	Gilbert-Sullivan	Birchard (Standard editions by other publishers)	(1.00 (Voice (parts, (30 cts.	2	Editions abridged and simplified. Also standard editions are practicable in large high schools.
In Old Vienna (Pickles)	Benedict	FitzSimons	1.50	4	Became popular as "Pickles"
Jerry of Jericho Road	Clark	Hoffman	1.50	3	American scene—light comedy
Rosamunde	Schubert	Silver Burdett	1.50	3	A pastorale melodrama
Trial by Jury	Gilbert-Sullivan	Birchard	(.60 (Voice (parts, (20 cts.	3	One Act, forty-five minutes
Red Mill, The	Victor Herbert	Tams-Witmark	.35	5	Comedy favorite
Tulip Time	Johnson	FitzSimons	1.50	2	Dutch scene
Yuletide at the Court of King Arthur	Hoppin	Birchard	.50	1	Christmas music drama of the sixth century
Cantata					
Before the Paling of the Stars	Dale	Novello	.25	4	A Christmas hymn
Choral Fantasies from the Operas (1) Faust (2) Carmen (3) Trovatore (4) Tannhäuser (5) Pinafore	 Gounod Bizet Verdi Wagner Sullivan	Fox	.50	5	Not too demanding on the voices. Can be used to acquaint students with the music of the operas.

Cantata (continued)

Title	Composer and Arranger	Publisher	P	D	Description
Gallia	Gounod	Novello	$ .40	3	Soprano solo
Hear My Prayer	Mendelssohn	G. Schirmer	.25	2	With soprano solo
Hiawatha's Wedding Feast	Coleridge-Taylor	G. Schirmer	1.50	4	Good tenor soloist needed
Highwayman, The	Andrews	Ditson	1.00	4	Baritone solo
Jesu, Priceless Treasure	Bach	G. Schirmer	.40	5	Motet for five voices. Excellent with strings.
Lochinvar	Hammond	Presser	.40	4	For male voices
Peasant Cantata	Bach-Diack	Paterson Publication	Score 1.20 Chorus .60	3	Secular text
Spring Cometh	Kountz	Witmark	.60	1	Seasonal
Robin Hood and Alan-a-Dale	Dykema	C. Fischer	.60	2	Two-parts. S. A.
When the Christ Child Came	Clokey	Birchard	.75	3	Four incidental soloists
Land of Our Hearts	Chadwick	Boston Music	.75	4	Thrillingly patriotic
A Ballad for Americans	Robinson	Big 3	1.00	4	Made popular over the radio

Instrumental Collections

Orchestra

1. *Educational Orchestral Album*. Lindsay, Spangler, Roberts. Carl Fischer, Inc. Prices: conductor $1.00, parts 50¢ each.
   A successful collection of interesting music of medium difficulty.
2. *Follow Through Orchestra Folio*. Cheyette, Roberts. Carl Fischer, Inc. Prices: piano conductor $1.00, parts 50¢ each.
   A complete program for intermediate orchestras.
3. *Golden Key Orchestra Series*. Reibold and Dykema. Theodore Presser Co. Prices: piano, $1.00; other parts, 50¢.
   For advanced high school and professional orchestras.
4. *Master Series for Young Orchestras*. Rebmann and Clark. G. Schirmer. Prices: full score $2.00; full orchestra with piano conductor $2.25; small orchestra $1.50.
   In twelve suites: Schumann, Bach, Grieg, Classic Dances, Weber, Handel, Mendelssohn, Beethoven, Schubert, Haydn, Mozart, Tschaikowsky.
5. *Modern Orchestra Training Series*. Church and Dykema. C. C. Birchard. Prices: each instrument 50¢; two-hand piano $1.00; four-hand piano conductor $1.50.
   Designed to enable players with different degrees of ability to play together. Two volumes. Better for strings than winds.
6. *String Orchestra Album #1*. Lehnhoff, Sheppard. Clayton F. Summy. Prices: conductor $1.00; each part 50¢.
   Fine collection of the classics, 10 in all.
7. *Symphony Series*. Stock, Dasch, McConathy. Silver Burdett Co. Prices: 75¢ to $1.00 each part, depending on volume. Conductor's score for each number varies from $1.00 to $2.00.
   Five volumes organized as programs progressing from easy to difficult. A rich library of orchestral music. Recently an All-Wagner Program has been added to this series.
8. *Philharmonic Orchestra Folio*. Oliver Ditson Co. Prices: full score $5.00; piano part $1.00; parts 50¢ each.
   An excellent collection of standard numbers of moderate difficulty for high school orchestras.
9. *Tune A Day, A*. Herfurth. Boston Music Co. Prices: violin 60¢; teacher's manual $1.00.
   In three volumes. Title gives clue to the organization. There are also a 'cello volume and orchestra folio.
10. *World of Music, The.—Orchestra Course*. Righter, Rebmann, Revelli, Schmidt. Ginn & Co. Prices: 85¢ each part; conductor's score $4.00.
    Very complete. Sections for individual instruments, different choirs of the orchestra, and finally, numbers for entire orchestra.

Band

1. *American Band Book.* Mayhew Lake. American Book Co. Prices: 40¢ each part; conductor's score $1.00.
In two volumes. Fourteen numbers in each volume consisting of several marches and other types of pieces.
2. *Bach Chorales.* Ditson. Prices: conductor's book, 75¢; each part 50¢.
Excellent material for developing sustained tones.
3. *Bennett Band Book.* Fillmore Music Co. Prices: 30¢ per book; small conductor's score 50¢.
Three volumes. Good collection of medium easy pieces that sound well with a small band. Marches especially good.
4. *Bridging the Gap.* Cheyette and Roberts. C. Fischer. Prices: 30¢ each part; manual 60¢.
Four line conductor's score. Very good for first year bands.
5. *Foundation to Band Playing.* Griffen, Jenkins Music Co. Price: 75¢ each part.
A good method to develop young bands from the beginning to a public program in a short time.
6. *Junior Band Course.* McConathy, Morgan, Clark. Ditson Music Co. Price: each part $.75.
A course of instruction where beginners and more advanced players can play together each at his own level.
7. *Modern Band Training Series.* Church and Dykema. C. C. Birchard. Price: 50¢ each part.
Graded material for simultaneous performance by players of various degrees of advancement.
Full score, piano part.
8. *Music Educators Basic Method, The.* Carl Fischer. Price: 75¢ each.
Separate books for class or individual instruction for all the instruments of the orchestra and band. No pieces for entire band.
9. *School and Community Band Course.* McConathy, Morgan, Clark. Ditson Music Co. Price: teacher's manual, $1.50; each part 75¢.
A combination of instruction on the individual instruments and band ensemble.
10. *Victor Method, The.* Victor, John F. Victor Publishing Co. Price: $1.00 each part.
A comprehensive ensemble text for all instruments. Books for class lessons on different instruments supplemented with pieces for the entire band.
11. *World of Music, The—Band Course.* Righter, Rebmann, Revelli, Schmidt. Prices: 85¢ each part; conductor score $4.00.
Very complete. Sections for beginning individual instruments, various groups of instruments, and finally, excellent numbers for the entire band.

Drum Corps

1. *Drum and Bugle Corps Music.* Ludwig and Ludwig. Price: $1.00 each.
   An adequate collection for most needs.
2. *Modern Bugle Method.* Latham. Boston Music Co. Price: 60¢ each.
   Sections devoted to producing a free tone, reading music, bugle calls, and pieces with drums.

Piano Class

1. *Adult Explorer at the Piano.* Ahearn, Blake, and Burrows. Willis Music Co. Price: $1.00.
   Keyboard harmony, ear-training, and easy repertoire.
2. *Beginners Book for Older Pupils.* Schelling, Haake, C. Haake, McConathy. Oxford Piano Course, Carl Fischer. Price: $1.00.
   Standard book for adult beginners.
3. *First Book for the Adult Beginner.* Williams, John M. Price: $1.00.
   Based upon the well-known Williams' approach.
4. *Music Study for Adults.* McConathy, Scarborough, Hold, Eckstein. Carl Fischer. Price: $1.00.
   A new approach from the keyboard harmony standpoint.

Orchestra

Title	Composer and Arranger	Publisher	P	D	Description
Air de Ballet (Alceste)	Gluck	C. Fischer	Small $ .85 Full 1.25	2	Classic melody
Concerto in A minor	Vivaldi-Franko	G. Schirmer	Score 2.50 Parts	4	Early concerto grosso
Cossack Dance	Moussorgsky	C. Fischer	Small .85 Full 1.25	2	Exciting
Country Dance in C	Beethoven	Ditson	Score 1.50 Parts 1.00	3	Rhythmical
Sarabanda	Handel	Witmark	1.00	1	Theme and variations for strings and harp—(piano)
Suite in the Olden Style	Lubin	Gorston	Score 1.50 Parts 1.50	3	Good music for high school string orchestra
Two Preludes (C minor—A major)	Chopin	Witmark	1.00	1	For young string orchestras
Band					
Attilla	Käroly	C. Fischer	Small .75 Full 1.15 Grand 2.35	2	Hungarian Overture
Cabins	Gilette	Witmark	Score 1.50 Small B. 2.00 Sym. B. 4.50	2	An American Rhapsody
Picture at an Exhibition (Suite three parts)	Moussorgsky	C. Fischer	Each part: S. B. 3.50 C. B. 5.00 S. B. 6.50	5	A fine transcription
Sunday Morning at Glion	Bendel	Witmark	Complete with score	3	Contrasting moods
Jesu, Joy of Man's Desiring	Bach-Leidzer	C. Fischer	Score .50 St. B. 3.00 C. B. 4.50 Sym. B. 5.75	2	Famous chorale

Directory of Publishers and Dealers

(A complete, annotated list appears in the Business Handbook, prepared by the Music Education Exhibitors Association, 64 East Jackson Blvd., Chicago.)

American Book Company, 88 Lexington Ave., New York City.
General textbooks, music textbooks, and song books.

Emil Ascher, Inc., 315 Fourth Ave., New York City.
Instrumental collections and sheet music.

Associated Music Publishers, 25 West 45th St., New York City.
Sheet music and octavo.

Augsburg Publishing Company, 425 South 4th St., Minneapolis.
Textbooks and sheet music.

C. L. Barnhouse Music Publisher, Oskaloosa, Iowa.
Octavo.

Irving Berlin, Inc., 799 Seventh Ave., New York City.
Sheet music, instrumental and choral music.

The Big 3 Music Corporation, 152 West 52nd St., New York City.
Popular music, octavo.

C. C. Birchard and Company, 221 Columbus Ave., Boston, Mass.
Textbooks, song books, instrumental music, octavo, operettas.

Boosey-Hawkes-Belwin, Inc., 43 W. 23rd St., New York City.
Songs and octavo.

Boston Music Company, 116 Boylston Ave., Boston, Mass.
Textbooks, instrumental music, octavo.

Buescher Band Instrument Company, Elkhart, Ind.
Instruments.

Chappell and Company, Inc., RKO Building, New York
Sheet music, octavo, operettas

John Church Company, 1712 Chestnut Street, Philadelphia, Pa.
Songs, octavo.

M. M. Cole Publishing Company, 2611 Indiana Ave., Chicago.
Textbooks, octavo.

C. G. Conn, Ltd., Elkhart, Ind.
Instruments.

Craddock Uniforms, Kansas City, Mo.
Band and choir uniforms.

F. S. Crofts and Company, 41 Union Sq. W., New York City.
General books, music books.

T. S. Denison Company, 623 S. Wabash Ave., Chicago.
Plays, novelties, minstrel shows.

Oliver Ditson Company, 1712 Chestnut St., Philadelphia.
Textbooks, instrumental and choral music, songs.

Educational Music Bureau, Inc., 30 E. Adams St., Chicago.
Instrumental and choral music.

Eldridge Entertainment House, Franklin, Ohio.
Plays, novelties, minstrel shows.

Elkan-Vogel Company, 1716 Sansom St., Philadelphia, Pa.
Sheet music, instrumental and choral music.

Fillmore Music House, 528 Elm St., Cincinnati, Ohio.
Band and orchestra music.

Carl Fischer, Inc., 62 Cooper Sq., New York City.
Publisher and dealer in all kinds of music publications.

J. Fischer and Brother, 119 W. 40th St., New York City.
Instrumental and choral music.

H. T. FitzSimons Company, 23 E. Jackson Boulevard, Chicago.
Instrumental and choral music, operettas.

Harold Flammer, Inc., 10 E. 43rd St., New York City.
Songs, instrumental and choral music, operettas and cantatas.

Sam Fox Publishing Company, 1250 Sixth Ave., New York City.
Songs, instrumental and choral music, abridged operas.

Samuel French, Inc., 25 W. 45th St., New York City.
Plays, entertainments.

Galaxy Music Corp., 17 W. 46th St., New York City.
Songs, octavo.

Gamble Hinged Music Company, 228 S. Wabash Ave., Chicago.
Instrumental and choral music.

Ginn and Company, 70 Fifth Ave., New York City.
Textbooks, song books, instrumental music.

Fred Gretsch Manufacturing Company, 529 S. Wabash Ave., Chicago.
Instruments.

Harcourt, Brace and Company, 383 Madison Ave., New York City.
Textbooks.

Hall and McCreary Company, 434 S. Wabash Ave., Chicago.
Song books, choral collections, octavo.

Wm. S. Haynes Company, 108 Massachusetts Ave., Boston.
Instruments.

Hinds, Hayden and Eldredge, Inc., 5 Union Square, New York City.
Textbooks, song books.

Raymond A. Hoffman Company, 509 S. Wabash Ave., Chicago.
Octavo, operettas and cantatas.

M. Hohner, Inc., 351 Fourth Ave., New York City.
Instruments.

Jenkins Music Company, 1217-23 Walnut St., Kansas City, Mo.
Songs, instrumental and choral music, instruments.

Neil A. Kjos Music Company, 14 W. Lake St., Chicago.
Textbooks, choral music.

Lorenz Publishing Company, 501 E. 3rd St., Dayton, Ohio.
Songs, choral music.

Ludwig and Ludwig, Inc., 1611 N. Wolcott Ave., Chicago, Ill.
Instruments.

Lyon and Healy, Inc., Wabash Ave. and Jackson Blvd., Chicago.
Sheet music, instrumental and choral music, instruments.

Lyons Band Instrument Company, Chicago.
Instruments.

The Macmillan Company, 60 Fifth Ave., New York City.
General textbooks.

Martin Band Instrument Company, Elkhart, Ind.
Instruments.

Miessner Institute of Music, 1222 Kimball Bldg., Chicago.
Sheet music, instruments..

Minton, Balch and Company, New York City.
General textbooks.

Music Publishers Holding Corporation. (Witmark-Harms-Remick) 1250 Sixth Ave., New York City.

Music Educators National Conference, 64 E. Jackson Blvd., Chicago.
Conference books and professional bulletins.

Music Service, 1166 Sixth Ave., New York City.
Sheet music, octavo, miscellaneous.

Myers and Carrington, 19 Fulton St., Redwood City, California.
Operettas.

New York Band Instrument Company, 111 E. 14th St., New York City.
Instruments, sheet music.

Pan-American Band Instrument Company, Elkhart, Ind.
Instruments.

Paull-Pioneer Music Company, 1657 Broadway, New York City.
Sheet music, song books.

Paysen Manufacturing Company, Hebron, Nebraska.
Chorus platforms.

Pioneer Music Press, Salt Lake City, Utah.
Sheet music.

Theodore Presser Company, 1712 Chestnut St., Philadelphia.
Publisher and dealer in all kinds of music publications.

R.C.A. Manufacturing Company, Camden, N. J.
Textbooks, victrolas, sound recording instruments.

G. Ricordi and Company, Inc., 12 W. 45th St., New York City.
Sheet music, octavo, operas.

E. T. Root and Son, 1501 E. 55th St., Chicago.
Sheet music, miscellaneous.

Rubank, Inc., Campbell Ave. and Lexington Street, Chicago.
Sheet music, choral and instrumental music.

Saxette Company, Delaware, Ohio.
Instruments.

E. C. Schirmer Music Company, 221 Columbus Ave., Boston, Mass.
Sheet music, choral collections, octavo, song books.

G. Schirmer, Inc., 3 E. 43rd St., New York City.
Publisher and dealer in all kinds of music publications.

Arthur P. Schmidt Company, 120 Boylston St., Boston.
Sheet music, choral and instrumental music.

Paul A. Schmitt Music Company, 86 S. 10th St., Minneapolis.
Sheet music, miscellaneous.

H. and A. Selmer, Inc., Elkhart, Ind.
Instruments.

Silver Burdett Company, 45 E. 17th St., New York City.
Textbooks, song books, instrumental music, operettas.

Simon and Schuster, 386 Fourth Ave., New York City.
Music books, unusual song books.

Sims Visual Music Company, Quincy, Ill.
Song slides.

Clayton F. Summy Company, 321 S. Wabash Ave., Chicago.
Sheet music, choral and instrumental music.

Tracy Music Library, Inc., 1 Beacon St., Boston.
Sheet music, operas and operettas, miscellaneous.

"Uniforms by Ostwald," Inc., 18 E. 16th St., New York City.
Band and choir uniforms.

Victor Publishing Company, 309 Santa Fe Bldg., Dallas, Texas.
Instrumental books.

H. N. White Company, 5225 Superior Ave., Cleveland, Ohio.
Instruments.

White-Smith Publishing Company, 40 Winchester St., Boston.
Sheet music, octavo.

Willis Music Company, 127 E. 4th St., Cincinnati, Ohio.
Publishers and dealers in all kinds of music publications.

B. F. Wood Music Company, 88 St. Stephen Street, Boston.
Sheet music, octavo.

Rudolph Wurlitzer Company, De-Kalb, Ill.
Instruments.

York Band Instrument Company, 1600 S. Division Ave., Grand Rapids, Mich.
Instruments.

INDEX